CW01647853

The Official History of
THE
BRIGHTON FOOTBALL CLUB
(R.F.U.)

150 years of Rugby Football

Best Wishes

John Honeysett

John Honeysett

The Official History of
THE
BRIGHTON FOOTBALL CLUB
(R.F.U.)

150 years of Rugby Football

Published by
John Honeysett
Brighton BN1 7ES

Registered With
UK Copyright Service
Reg. No.: 284723280
UKCCS

©John Honeysett 2018
All rights reserved

This book is sold subject to the condition that
it shall not, by way of trade or otherwise, be lent,
re-sold, hired out, or otherwise circulated without
the publisher's prior consent in any form
of binding or cover other than that in which it is
published and without a similar condition
being imposed on the subsequent purchaser.

A catalogue record of this book
is available from the British Library

ISBN 978-1-5272-2616-6

Editorial consultant Barry Hughes
Format and jacket cover artwork by StewART
Typesetting in 12pt Times New Roman
Printed and bound by CPI Group (UK) Ltd,
Croydon, CR0 4YY

The Official History of
THE
BRIGHTON FOOTBALL CLUB
(R.F.U.)

150 years of Rugby Football

CONTENTS

Page

Acknowledgements 12

Foreword 13
Steve Morris, Chairman

Preface 14
John Honeysett

Introduction 16
Phil McGowan
(Curator "World of Rugby" Museum)

Chapter I
The Early Years of Rugby Football 18

Chapter II
The first 'Rugby Football Union' 22

Chapter III
‘1866 and all that’ 24

Chapter IV
The Brighton Club 43

Chapter V
The 'Shoo-Flies' (Brighton Football Club) 49
1880-1900 76

Chapter VI
The Brighton Football Club 'Barbarians' 94

Chapter VII
1900 -1910 107

Chapter VIII
A Poignant Decade. 1910-1919 126
1920-1925 131

Chapter IX
The Golden Years' 1926-1929 142
1930-1939 155

Chapter X
World War II and subsequent years. 1939-1949 174

Chapter XI
1950-1959 185

Chapter XII
"A Bitter Sweet Decade" 1960-1969 201
1970 - 1978 218

Chapter XIII
The "Brighton Boot" 1979-1989 236

Chapter XIV
Horsdean - the end of an era 253

Chapter XV
Waterhall 263

Chapter XVI
The Twickenham Years 309

Chapter XVII
The Modern Era 332

Brighton Football Club Presidents 344
Vice Presidents 345
Honorary Life Members 347
Captains 348
Honours Caps 350
International Honours 353

"Never Let the Truth Spoil a Good Story" 355

Plates

1. Rugby College Students c1830, page 18
2. William IV 'Kings Birthday' Advertisement, c 1833, page 19
3. Painting 'Foot -Ball' Thomas Webster, c 1839, page 20
4. Painting 'The Roses Match' page 21
5. The Wick School, Hove, page 23
6. Map of Brighton showing Queens Park Cricket Ground. (1880) page 28
7. 'Sussex County Football Matches', c 1865 page 38
8. 'Royal Cricket Ground' challenge, c1792, page 45
9. 'Royal Cricket Ground' & 'Irelands Pleasure Gardens' c1832 page 48
10. 'Royal Cricket Ground' c1821, page 48
11. 'Charles Gervais Boxall' co-founder of Brighton Football Club, page 49
12. First Armoured Train designed by Charles Boxhall, page 50
13. Boxalls funeral cortege, Church Street, page 51
14. Boxalls funeral cortege, Grand Parade, page 51
15. 'Drill Hall' Gloucester Road page 52
16. 'Shoo-Fly' music sheet, page 53
17. 'Brighton Wasps' Extract from Alcock's football Annual 1870, page 58
18. 'Rugby Football Union' plaque, page 60
19. England v Scotland (Painting) 1871, page 61
20. J.A. Body, Invitation letter to play for England, c1873, page 64
21. England Team 1873, James Body, page 65
22. Brighton (Shoeflies) "Alcocks" Football Annual 1975, page 71
23. Brighton College, "Alcocks" Football Annual 1976, page 72
24. Advertisement from "Alcocks" Football Annual 1879, page 75
25. "Smoking Concert" programme, Oct 2nd, 1886, page 81
26. "Smoking Concert" programme, Oct 30th, 1886, page 82
27. Brighton Football Club 1888-9, page 83

28. Brighton Football Club 1889-90, page 84
29. The earliest fixture card known 1899 - 90, page 85
30. "Barbarians" and R.D. Budworth, page 95
31. Barbarian 'Cyril Wells' page 95
32. Eustace Herbert Guest North. 1889 Oxford Varsity Team, page 96
33. England Team photo with W. Falcon, page 96
34. Cambridge University Rugby Football Team 1894 - 95, page 97
35. 'Frank Mitchell' 1896, page 98.
36. Bernard Charles Hartley, 'Barbarians', 1904, page 100
37. Bernard Charles Hartley, British Lions, 1938, page 100
38. Reginald Birket, England team 1871, page 102
39. J.G.G. Burkett, Barbarians Team 1915, page 104
40. Ernest Dye Galbraith Hammett, Barbarians Team 1922, page 105.
41. Ernest Dye Galbraith Hammett, British Isles cover photo, page 106
42. Gary Halpin, page 106
43. Fixture Card, 1900 - 01, page 107
44. 'Smoking Concert' ticket 1903, page 110
45. 'Crown & Anchor' advertisement 1901, page 112
46. Brighton team photograph, Crown & Anchor 1905, page 113
47. 'Charles William Alcock' page 116
48. Brighton v Stade Francais, team photograph 1903, page 119
49. Letter from "Racing Club" (Paris) in Brighton, page 121
50. Dinner Menu Card, Brighton v Rugby Club Compiegnois, 1909, page 125
51. Fixture Card 1912-13, page 126
52. 'Great Rugby Match' Shoreham Camp v 'Barbarians' service team 1914, page 127
53. 'Edgar Mobbs', page 128
54. British War Poster, page 130
55. V.C.W. Jupp, newspaper clip, 1920, page 133
56. Jubilee Dinner Menu and ticket 1920, page 133
57. Brighton v Blackheath poster 1920s, page 134
58. Annual Dinner Card 1922, page 134
59. Annual Dinner Card 1922, page 135

60. Littlehampton v Brighton Poster 1924, page 136
61. Fixture Card, Rule Book and Enclosure Ticket 1920 -21, page 139
62. The 1921-1922 Honour cap belonged to G.W.H. Bentley page 141
63. Fixture Handbook Brighton F.C. & Brighton College RFU 1922-23, page 144
64. Brighton Team photograph v Saracens 1927, page 144
65. Brighton Team photograph 1927, 'Crown & Anchor' page 147
66. Fixture Card 1926-27, page 147
67. Brighton v Neath Poster, 1928, page 149
68. Neath Honours Cap (J. Owens) 1931-32, page 151
69. Spectators at Preston Park 1928, page 154
70. Members Season ticket 1929-30 'Hove Stadium', page 154
71. Brighton v Neath Programme 1931, page 155
72. Brighton v Neath match photograph 1931, page 156
73. Brighton & Neath combined photograph before match, page 156
74. Luncheon Card, South Africa at the Royal Pavilion, 1931, page 157
75. Brighton v Harlequins, Preston Park, photograph 1936, page162
76. Brighton v Harlequins, Preston Park, photograph 1936, page163
77. 70th Dinner & Dance Card 1939, page 165
78. The President receiving guests at the Royal Pavilion, 70th Dinner 1939, page 166
79. Guests at the 70th Dinner in the Royal Pavilion 1939, page 167
80. Brighton Team photograph, 70th ceremonial match, Preston Park, 1939, page 169
81. "70th Anniversary, 8th March 1939, Brighton v Rosslyn Park" page 170
82. Fixture Cards 1930s, page 170
83. Brighton v Rosslyn Park, match photograph 1939, page 172
84. 'Harlequins' telegram 1939, page 173
85. Brighton v Rosslyn Park poster, 1939 page 173
86. Brighton Football Club, 'Roll of Honour' Plaque, page 175

87. The Mayor of Brighton & Sir Winston Churchill 1947, page 177
88. Brighton Team photograph 1947, page 178
89. Annual Dinner Card 1948, page 179
90. Annual Dinner Card 1948, page 180
91. David Benjamin photograph, page 183
92. 'Gibbys' cartoon 1949, page 184
93. Fixture Poster 1953, page 186
94. 'De bagging incident' 1951, page 187
95. Brighton programme 1950s, page 190
96. Brighton fixture 1952, (partial) page 192
97. 'All Blacks' v Southern Counties, Hove, programme 1953, page 193
98. Brighton v Storrington College, half-time refreshments 'Oranges' page 194
99. Brighton Team photograph Preston Park, page 195
100. Official Programme of the opening of Withdean Sports Arena 1955, page 1977
101. W.A. Gibb "taking a kick off" at Withdean Stadium 1954, page 194
102. Fixture Card 1953-54, page 198
103. The 'Sportsman' at Withdean Stadium 1954, page 199
104. Brighton & Commonwealth v US Marines XV programme 1959, page 200
105. "The Brighton Belles" 1961, page 201
106. Lille v Brighton poster 1961, page 203
107. "Gibbs" memorial match programme 1962, page 204
108. W.A. Gibbs, Brighton College Honours cap, page 208
109. Appeal Leaflet for funding of Horsdean Clubhouse, 1967, page 211
110. 'Dinner at the Arches' 1969, page 222
111. Laying of Foundation Stone at Horsdean 1970, page 222
112. Brighton Team photograph 1971, page 223
113. Sussex Knock Out Final programme 1971, page 224
114. Sussex Champions Team photograph 1971, page 226
115. Brighton v Lille Cup 1972, page 227
116. Lille team photograph, Horsdean, 1973, page 227
117. "Bums", page 228

118. Unveiling of Honours Board 1973, page 229
119. Fixture Cards 1970s, page 232
120. Brighton team photograph, Withdean 1974-75, page 232
121. R. Lowrie, match photograph Withdean, 1977, page 234
122. William Webb Ellis Morris Men, page 235
123. Steve Russell, William Webb Ellis, page 235
124. "Brighton Boot" newsletter 1979, page 236
125. Brighton v Lewes match photograph 1981, page 238
126. 'Jane Warner' in Brighton changing room 1981, page 238
127. Brighton Carnival 'Bill Holt' page 240
128. Brighton Carnival 'Bill Holt' page 241
129. Brighton Carnival 'Bill Holt' page 242
130. Dover Harbour Board Invoice page 243
131. 'Linda Lusardi' page 244
132. "The Stiletto" 1989, page 250
133. Mixed Rugby Match, 1989 page 251
134. A27 on the Downs, page 254
135. Demolition of Horsdean Clubhouse, page 254
136. A27 'Mill Hill', page 255
137. Brighton match photograph Horsdean 1990, page 256
138. "Goodbye" Horsdean, page 257
139. Brighton Team photograph 1988, page 261
140. Brighton Team photograph 1989, page 264
141. Building of the Clubhouse Waterhall, 1990, page 269
142. Building of the Clubhouse Waterhall, 1990, page 270
143. Building of the Clubhouse Waterhall 1991, page 271
144. Brighton Team photograph 1992-93, page 271
145. League Merit Table 1992, page 272
146. 'Opening of the Clubhouse' 1992, page 272
147. 'Opening of the Clubhouse' programme 1992, page 273
148. "Boys" at the Opening of the Clubhouse 1992, page 274
149. 'Mark Appleton', page 276
150. 'Mark Appleton' medal, page 277
151. Veterans team photograph , Charlies Bar, 1990s, page 278
152. Fred Eloy photograph, page 279
153. Veterans in Dieppe, team photograph, page 279
154. 'Pat Ward-Lee' team photograph at Horsdean page 282
155. Pat and Sally Ward-Lee, page 284

156. 'Handbook' 1996-97, page 287
157. 'Mike Brownhill', page 288
158. A. McCarthy, N. Thomas and Matin Johnson photograph, 1997, page 291
159. Katie Price, aka "Jordan" photograph, page 292
160. 'Alex Pincus', page 293
161. London 3 South East league table 2000-01, page 302
162. 'Andy Rice' match photograph, page 302
163. 'Gary Halpin' 2002, page 303
164. 'Handbook' 2002-03, page 304
165. Opening of ATP, Sir Clive Goodward, page 307
166. C.Salter, M.Buckingham & J. Taylor, ATP Opening, page 308
167. Opening of ATP Sir Clive Woodward, page 308
168. A. Salvage & M.Gibb Twickenham, page 314
169. Twickenham Celebrations 2009, page 315
170. M. Gibb, T.Ellis, M Jenkins, Twickenham 2010, page 318
171. Twickenham Celebrations 2010, page 319
172. Twickenham intermediate Cup Winners, page 320
173. M.Jenkins & M,Gibb, 2016 Annual Ball. page 320
174. 'Old Farts' in Blazers, page 321
175. 'Roll of Honour' plaque, page 321
176. 'Roll of Honour' unveiling, page 322
177. Memorial Wreath laying, page 323
178. The young 'Blazer Boys', page 324
179. Fixture Cards and handbooks, page 324
180. Brighton F.C. programmes, page 325
181. Marcus Smith and Jon Searle 325
182. S. Morley, match photograph, page 326
183. N. McGovern, page 327
184. 'Old Farts Luncheon' 2018, page 328
185. 'Old Farts Luncheon' 2018, page 329
186. 'Old Farts Luncheon' 2018, page 330
187. 'Girls behind bars' page 331
188. 'Frank Taggart' page 332
189. 'Frank Taggart' page 334
190. 'Joel Forward' page 340
191. 'Brighton Crest' page 342

Acknowledgements

The research into the 19th century history of the Club would not have been possible without "The Keep" Falmer, Brighton (The Keep is a world-class centre for archives that opens up access to all the collections of the East Sussex Record Office (ESRO), the Royal Pavilion & Museums Local History Collections and the internationally significant University of Sussex Special Collections.) Andrew Bennett and his team have been extremely helpful and their enthusiasm has been untiring.

Roger Lowrie who in the early years waded through numerous newspapers looking for the odd gem. The "World of Rugby" Museum at Twickenham, curators Rex King, Michael Rowe and Phil McGowan, each have been invaluable. Frederic Humbert my "French connection", Mike Price (Neath), Mandy Allen & Peter Brown (Blackheath). Ivor Body (James Body) Roy Grant, Carol Homewood and Anna Antoniou (Brighton Historians), Peter Shortell for his article on William Webb Ellis. Jon Orrell for his help and advice. Tim Carder, (Historian with Brighton & Hove Albion) who supplied snippets of information that were invaluable. Dick Tyson, author of "London's Oldest Rugby Clubs", David Barber, the "Football Association", Peter Sealey and Dewi Vaughan "Sussex R.F.U." Nigel Trueman, www.rugbyfootballhistory.com. Members of Brighton Football Club (RFU) to numerous to name, however, I must mention Sally and Pat Ward-Lee for their help in numerous aspects of this history. Mark Gibb and his contribution on "Twickenham Finals", Mark Jenkins, Steve Morris, Andy Rice, Gary Henderson, Justin Burt, Neil Thomas, Joel Forward, Frank Taggart, Derek Pickering, David Benjamin, Ivor O'Mahony, Ann Holt, Alex Pincus, David Malby, John Wallace, Peter Harbidge, Mick Morley, Jamie Mitchell and Ray Dunk. Lastly thank you to my daughter Sarah and my wife Valerie Dowley who has been a rock, nurse, secretary and typist.

Foreword

Brighton Football Club (RFU) Ltd. has a long history that very few rugby clubs can match. We know we were founded in 1868 but from then on the history trail is sketchy at best.

In the 1930's William Gibb admitted "It is with regret our early history has been lost or forgotten". Snippets of information exist in the odd minute book and our more recent history, including our Twickenham exploits, have been well documented but the history outside living memory it is rather scarce.

John Honeysett has spent countless hours trying to rediscover this lost history and has uncovered a raft of exciting and unknown pieces of information that will be of interest to the members of Brighton Football Club as well as enlightening the rugby fraternity in general. I'm sure even the local Brighton historians will find certain aspects of this history intriguing.

This new insight into the journey of Brighton Football Club (RFU), from its foundation through the ages to the current day, will form an important part of the Club's celebrations in this our sesquicentennial anniversary year giving the forthcoming season an air of excitement, alongside the first full season for our head coach Frank Taggart.

I would like to thank John and acknowledge the hard work he has put into uncovering the historical journey of our Club, It is important that we understand where we have come from, where we are, and where we are going if we are to be here for another 150 years

Steve Morris
Chairman

Preface

My foray into the World of Rugby began in 1976, I was cajoled into turning out for the Extra "A", "Brighton Football Club's" (4th) team. Adrian Biggs, Don Rees and Tony DaVall were to blame.

And from those halcyon days in the Extra 'A's to the 1st XV, I have always been intrigued how a Rugby Club, considered to be one of the oldest Clubs in the World, had the name of Brighton Football Club.

William A. Gibbs (Gibby), who was a leading figure in Brighton Football Club for over five decades, wrote in the 1930s' "It is with regret that our early history has long been lost and forgotten".

My combined love of history and this Rugby Club, was all the impetus I needed to start this journey and try and put the Club's history down on paper, I have included many articles from our early history as this has never been seen or documented before.

Back in 1995 with the help of Roger Lowrie, I was able to produce a few pages of the Club's History for the 128th Season, 1996/97 handbook. Even then I was able to find some early history, the content of which is now on our web site (www.brightonblues.co.uk). I am hoping that this updated version, researched for our sesquicentennial, (150th season), will give you a more in-depth knowledge and understanding into what I believe is a great Football Club.

Speaking as the Club's archivist and historian I have been saddened that in recent years some of our old traditions have disappeared. The use of the club name "Brighton Football Club" (RFU) has slowly but surely been omitted from nearly all correspondence whether it's the local newspapers, match programmes or emails, to the extent that if our minis and juniors were to be asked what is the name of our club, "Brighton Blues" is their answer.

I have been shown a picture and informed that for this year and all future years the 'Club Crest' and red socks have been reinstated, and for the record we were founded as the Shoo Flies in 1868 and established as Brighton Football Club in 1874.

"The Handbook," which was always a great source of information for playing and non-playing members is no longer produced.

I remember being told, when I first played for the second team, that they were not the second team but part of the first team squad, therefore called the Extra First team. I am also pleased to say that this year this is also being reintroduced.

The Club no longer seem to have Club "Rules" ?

Honours Caps, which have been given annually by the Committee since 1885, unfortunately, ceased 2007. And I cannot remember the last time we had a social event, other than the annual dinner.

The 150th Committee, lead by Steve Russell and Sharon Finch have been working on events and games to showcase our Club. I am waiting in anticipation to see the agenda for our 150th season.

The Club of course needs to move forward and there are some fantastic projects on the horizon. However, we should endeavour to strive forward without losing the traditions of one of the select few Clubs, who can truly call themselves a "Football Club". Hopefully this book will give a good insight into our Club and bring back a "Sense of History" to its members. It has taken more than a few years to find, unpick and arrange this historic information, and I hope that in the future, someone will be able to pick up the mantle and continue to add more to this story.

I would like to add that some of the information I have found will not only change the history of Brighton Football Club, but will also have an impact on the history of the game itself. I have attempted to chronologically document the history, concentrating on the hitherto unknown history of the 19th century.

John Honeysett
Hon. Vice President
Club Historian

Introduction

In the late 1960s Mr Norman Bindon of Paignton, Devon began writing letters to several of Britain and Ireland's oldest rugby clubs. Mr Bindon had had the foresight to recognise that a number of these clubs would shortly celebrate their centenaries, as indeed did the Rugby Football Union (RFU) in 1971. Just over a decade later, in 1980, Mr Bindon wrote another letter to Mr Bob Weighill CBE DFC, then secretary of the RFU, offering to share what he had discovered through his enquiries.

Shortly thereafter the RFU received from Mr Bindon 167 books, booklets and assorted documents, put together by as many local club archivists to celebrate and record for posterity the first 100 years of their own club's existence. Mr Bindon's undertaking was the only such corroboration of its kind and his collection now forms a significant part of the World Rugby Museum club history archive, consulted by researchers and academics from around the world on an almost daily basis.

While Mr Bindon's collection was extensive it was not complete and in the absence of an appropriate publication, several venerable clubs were not included, among them Brighton Football Club (RFU). Now, fifty years later, I am delighted that John Honeysett has finally corrected that omission.

This book documents the febrile swirl of mid-Victorian sports clubs that came in and went out of existence almost on a whim. In it John describes the blurred lines between where one club ends and another begins and casts a light on the series of events that might well have dissuaded a less diligent researcher from attempting to write a club history back in the 1960s and 1970s.

John's perseverance has been rewarded with a clutch of important historical discoveries, many published for the first time in these pages and some of which fundamentally challenge existing orthodoxies about how the game of rugby developed.

That Brighton and Sussex were contributors to a wider narrative is now clear. Brighton FC had links to the very heart of the rugby establishment as John demonstrates by the club's long association with late Victorian, early Edwardian movers and shakers such as James Alfred Body, Frank Mitchell and John Birkett.

I hope that you will enjoy this book as much I have and agree that it is story worth telling.

Phil McGowan
Curator, World Rugby Museum

Chapter I

The Early Years of Rugby Football

I have found records that state, at "Rugby College, the 1829 School House team was the first side to adopt a uniform". All their players wore red velvet caps during a match that Princess Adelaide, daughter of the Duke of Saxe-Meiningen (future wife of King William IV), is known to have watched. These velvet caps, together with white trousers and jerseys, became the accepted attire for players although each wore his own favourite colours and carried a personal motto on his shirt. In 1871 for the first English International Rugby match, it was decided to adopt the white shirt and shorts as worn by the "Rugby School".

William IV ascended to the throne in 1830, and his wife Queen Adelaide, with a known interest in the sport, may have insisted on watching another game of FOOT-BALL, and the earliest mention of Football in Brighton, to the best of my research, was at the fourth and last "Grand Fete" to honour the 68th Birthday of King William IV in 1833, which the Queen and the King, attended.

KINGS BIRTH DAY.

At BRIGHTON'S
ROYAL PLEASURE GARDENS
THE FOURTH AND

LAST GRAND FETE

for the season, will take place
THIS DAY, WEDNESDAY, August 21st
Being in Commemoration of the **BIRTH DAY** of his most gracious **MAJESTY**

G. BROWN begs most respectfully to return his sincere and grateful acknowledgements for the numerous remarks of favour which he has received where he has taken the above Gardens, and to inform the Public. that is consequence of the satisfaction expressed by the Visitors at the last Fete, it is proposed to have a fourth, to take place **TO TODAY**, when it is hoped the following arrangements will meet with approbation

PROGRAMME

This Amusement to commence with a
CRICKET MATCH
after which RURAL SPORTS, dancing on the Green, and
FOOT-BALL till sunset,
In the evening the gardens will be illuminated And a great display of
FIREWORKS
(by Mr Jones)

Advertisement found in the Brighton Gazette 1833

In those pioneering days of football, there could have been anywhere from 12 - 30 players on the pitch, for both sides, at the same time. As late as 1866 I found reference to a match in Brighton that was 30 a side, and the forward rushes were reported as contributing to some rather nasty encounters. Hacking, tripping, charging and scragging (tackling by the neck, using the collar) were all within the recognised codes played in most parts of the country.

'Foot -Ball' Thomas Webster 1839

The famous oil painting by Thomas Webster gives a good indication of the game of Foot-Ball played in the early 1800's, however, I'm inclined to think that the game played at His Majesty's 4th Grand Birthday Fete was somewhat more refined?

In Brighton it seems to be the practice to field 12 or 15 players aside. The number of players was determined before the start of each game, according to the particular codes and laws that the Captains decided they would play by. A single goal (which was when the ball was kicked between the posts and above the bar) scored during the game was superior to any number of tries or touchdowns (which was when the ball was placed on or over the try line), which then entitled the player to kick at goal.

Rugby in Brighton was played under the codes and laws of Rugby School (modified), which was a natural evolution considering that "Brighton Schools" had adopted these "Laws" in 1852, as did Fred Lillywhite, in his series of games in 1865-66, which will be made clear in a later chapter. Of course, later the Rugby Football Union (26th January 1871) became the "World Order".

Affiliation to the RFU eliminated the need to find other teams, that played the game according the Rugby College Laws.

I may add that the three senior teams in Brighton in the late 1860's were deemed Hybrid Clubs playing "Football" (Modified) under Rugby College Rules on Saturday and "Football" under Association Rules on Sundays.

Then there has always been that question, "Where does the Brighton Football Club (RFU) stand in thc list of the Oldest Clubs in the World. In one of my many communications with Phil McGowan, curator of the "World of Rugby Museum" at Twickenham. I asked this question and the reply ;

"We don't keep lists of oldest clubs precisely because new information (such as yours) comes to light so frequently. I've attached a document that gives you an indication of some of the clubs that were founded around this time but this is non-definitive and there are likely to be several others. Having said that, Top 10 first open clubs, still in existence, is certainly possible".

So, the foundation date of 1868 is certainly possible for inclusion in the 'Top Ten' list, and the date of 1865... would definitely feature.

'The Roses Match'

Chapter II

The First 'Rugby Football Union'

During my research at Twickenham I was introduced to the 'Football Annuals' of a Mr Charles W. Alcock. It did not take me long to realise that this collection of annuals were the rugby historian's bible, coincidently also starting in1868. Mr Alcock's name will crop up again in the future of Brighton Football Club history and the earliest rugby documented by Alcock, with reference to our locality, was Brighton Schools in 1852 as outlined below.

Brighton Schools

1. **Formed ; 1852**
2. **Membership ; 450**
3. **Ground ; Sussex County Cricket Ground, 200 yards from Hove and Cliftonville Stations, Half a mile from Brighton Station, all London Brighton & South Coast Railway**
6. **Rules ; Rugby Modified**
7. **Administrator ; J.B. Wooley, Captain, The Wick, Brighton.**

I have been reliably informed that in 1850, Brighton and Hove had over 150 educational institutions, and sport in Victorian England was advocated as an important part of a student's well-being. Football was a popular pastime therefore it would seem logical that schools established a code, a set of rules or laws, which allowed these educational establishments to play each other.

J.B.Wooley, the Brighton Schools Board Administrator, appears to have chosen to use the "Rugby College Rules" (Modified). It could be concluded that this was the first "Rugby Football Union". I now have to delve into the whereabouts of this information discovered by Alcock.

Mr J.B.Wooley, inadvertently created a plethora of rugby playing school boys, who in the 1860's will of course mature to rugby playing gentleman. Mr Wooley realised that there was scope to create a "Senior Football Club" and was the instigator in forming two clubs, "The Wick" (Mr Wooley was a Master at this school) and "Brighton Wasps" (1868). It was the trend in the Victorian era to name clubs after either insects, birds or animals, and the formation of "London Wasps" in 1867 may have influenced his choice of names.

The Wick School, Hove

Chronology, would now suggest that my historical search moves on to the formation of the "Brighton Football Club" (ShooFlies) in 1868.

However, at the twelfth hour I received an email from Tim Carder, Historian and Curator of the Brighton & Hove Albion Archives and Museum, that was to change the direction of my research. Tim and I have been liaising for over a year, exchanging information and passing across the odd snippet from newspaper articles. So when Tim sent me an email saying, "John, you may find this of interest", it lead to the discovery of some new and very interesting information.

The email contained a letter from a Mr. J.F.A. Leigh to a Brighton newspaper refuting an accusation about his so-called neglect in a Foot-ball match the week before.

Chapter III

'1866 and all that'

RUGBY and MARLBOROUGH v THE BRIGHTON FOOTBALL CLUB

Sir,---In the report of the above proposed match which appeared in your issue of January 24th, your correspondent states that it was through my neglect that the Club was not represented fully on the ground. Having acted in the capacity of secretary during the whole season, and having had the greatest difficulty in getting our men together for matches and the Club meetings, and having done my utmost (as every member will testify) for the Club, I think that such a remark should not pass unrefuted. The fact is, that I had selected one of the best fifteen in my power, but being unable myself to attend, for important reasons, I merely requested these gentlemen attend for the match, and thought no more of it. My surprise on hearing the result may be imagined, only four men of the fifteen turning up. As I had informed the greater part that I could not be present myself, I do not see how any blame could be attached to me. If your correspondent would in future inquire more into things, before committing his remarks on them to paper, he would be less likely to mislead people in future, as he has done in this case.

Begging the favour of an insertion of this letter in your next impression.

I am yours, &c.
J.F.A. Leigh
Hon Sec, Brighton Football Club.... January 29th 1866

The date January 1866, was this a typing error? My research only started in 1867, on the basis that the Brighton Football Club (ShooFlies) were formed in 1868 and 1867 may produce some information leading to the formation, but it would have never have occurred to me to start my research in 1866.

The following day was spent at The Keep, Brighton's reference library located at Falmer, and lo and behold, in a Brighton newspaper I found the clipping that Tim sent. So my next search was to find the game in question which was played on Saturday 20th Jan 1866 and appeared in the press on Wed 24th Jan.

Brighton Guardian Jan 24th 1866

FOOTBALL MATCH

A grand match of football was announced to take place on Saturday, between fifteen gentlemen of the Brighton Club and fifteen gentlemen of Rugby and Marlborough. But through the neglect of Mr Leigh, who is the captain of the Brighton Club, only four gentlemen appeared. The match had to be stopped in consequence, although Mr Blaker, captain of the schools, had brought up a very able fifteen to meet them. At 3pm a pick-up match was arranged. Messrs Cook and H.C. Blaker selecting the sides, which were as follows:--

W.C.Blake, Esq	*Jno. Cook, Esq*
Oldham, Esq	*Sewell, Esq*
Liptrott Esq	*A. Weekes, Esq*
F. Lui, Esq	*W.C.Austen, Esq*
Gurney, Esq	*G.Wheatley, Esq*
Richardson, Esq	*Peters, Esq*
Sim, Esq	*H.Blaker, Esq*

This proved to be a most equal side, and some fine play was exhibited, although the ground was somewhat saturated. On the side of Mr Blaker, his own play and that of Mr Liptrott and Oldham were especially distinguishable , whilst Messrs Cook, Sewell, H. Blaker, Weekes and Austin equally exerted themselves for the other side.

There was no lack of spectators at the ground, who came expecting to see the exciting match proposed, and who were much disappointed that it did not take place; but no blame can be attached to Mr Fred Lillywhite, who left London on Saturday morning on purpose to attend to the arrangements.

What an amazing and unexpected find, a game played in 1866, so you can imagine my increasing excitement when I found out that this was actually the return match. The first match had been played two weeks previously. So without further ado.

Brighton Guardian Jan 10th 1866

FOOT BALL CONTEST

RUGBY AND MARLBORO' v THE BRIGHTON CLUB

On Saturday last two Fifteens from the above entered the playing ground, at Queens Park, to contend for the honour of victory. The match was made with very short notice, and well know that Rugby (especially) and Marlboro' are greatly distinguished for foot ball players.

The arrangements, notwithstanding the short notice, were all complete and under the management of Mr Fred Lillywhite. Play commenced at 2.15. The Club won the toss, and selected the top part of the ground. The schools were considerably the favourites at starting, owing to their recent performances on their own ground. The winning of the toss. however, made a slight difference, although the wind was against the Club. However, as soon as the armies met it was evident that Rugby and Marlboro' were predominant, for they held possession of the Club's ground nearly the whole of the afternoon, and as near as possible kicked a goal. At four o'clock, time was called and the match was compelled to end in a draw, for the present. Some splendid points of the game was exhibited, and we particularly noticed the hard, long, and well timed kicking of Mr D'Alquin, also the back play and judgement of display by Mr J.A.F. Leigh. Messrs Weekes and Austen were very busy and did good service to their regiment. These were the most noticeable for "good conduct" on the part of the Club. On the side of Rugby and Marlboro', the lively play of Mr J.L. Peters deserves high commendation, his running being remarkably clever. The Messrs Blaker and Cook also greatly distinguished themselves; in fact, the science of the game was never better demonstrated than on this occasion. The ground was attended by many of rank and fashion, and should the remainder of the season, or the days on which these matches may be fixed, prove favourable there will doubtless be a vast number of the fair sex who will avail themselves of the opportunity of passing agreeable one hour at Queens Park.

Arrangements are being made for a County match between Kent and Sussex. Blackheath and Brighton authorities are negotiating, and it will in all probability take place Saturday Feb 3rd. The County will comprise several first class players, including such talent as Mr W. Hudson, the well known "Sussex County Cricket" player, Mr D'Alquin, also a celebrated Foot Ball player, with Mr Hodson at the Brighton College, Mr J.A.F. Leigh, Mr Weekes, Mr C.G. Barnes (Capt of the Brighton College) Mr Austin , Mr Blaker, and several others, among whom no doubt, may be included two or three of the masters of Brighton College. The contest already excites considerable interest and no pain will be spared to collect strength of the county on this occasion

The ground in question was Emmerson's Ground, later Queens Park Cricket Ground, situated between Pankhurst Avenue and St Luke's Church. Solicitors conveyance from this time show that "On 3rd February 1859, Robert Coe's widow Emily, took out a premise lease on the Queens Park Tavern with local brewer William Hallet". By 1866 the licensee is William Emerson whose directory listing of 1871 combines the Tavern with a Dairy and makes reference to the Queens Park Cricket Ground, adjacent at the South West, prior to the construction of housing north of the park in 1890's.

Records indicate that all games played at the Queens Park Cricket Grounds were organised, managed and sponsored by a Mr Fred Lillywhite. He was a famous Cricketer who, followed in his father's (also Fred Lillywhite) footsteps, both of whom played international cricket for England. In 1863 Fred opened a Sports shop in Ship St. as a logical move in his role of supporting local sporting events.

On the 28th January 1866, Lillywhite confirmed arrangements for the first County Foot Ball match to be played between Kent and Sussex.

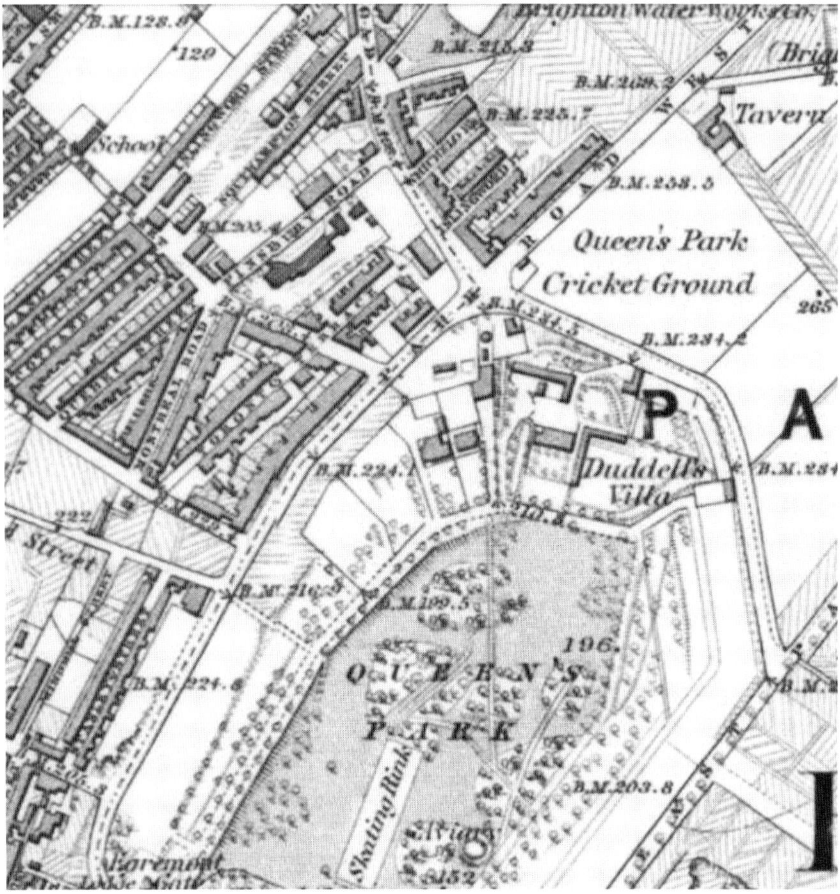

Map of Brighton showing Queens Park Cricket Ground. (1880)

Foot Ball --- We are now enabled to announce that a County Foot Ball Match has been arranged to take place on Saturday next, Feb 3rd, between the counties of Kent and Sussex, the former fifteen coming from Blackheath, and the latter may be seen at Mr Fred Lillywhite's, 41 Ship Street. He has, at present, down the following list:--- The Hon. F.G. Pelham, Rev. E. B. Elliott, A. Bateman, Esq., W.C. Auston, Esq., H.C. Blaker, Esq., W. C. Blaker, Esq., F.N. Foster, Esq., J.F. Leigh, Esq., E. B. Fawcett, Esq., W. Hodson, Esq., A. M. Mills, Esq., W.W. Blunt, Esq., and C.R. Gurney, Esq.

Feb 3rd 1866

FOOTBALL MATCH
THE COUNTIES OF KENT AND SUSSEX

For the first time in our knowledge has a Foot Ball match taken place between Counties,, and this may be attributed to the exertions of Mr Fred Lillywhite, followed up, we are informed, by the assistance of Mr Leigh of the Brighton Football Club, and the gentleman comprising it. The weather was most boisterous; so much so, that all thoughts of play were at one time extinguished. A telegraphic despatch, however, arrived at Lilly's at 3 o'clock stating that the Blackheath gentlemen were on the road, and they hoped to meet their opponents on the field. This (all honour to Sussex) they did, and the necessary arrangements having been completed, Kent won the toss, and play commenced at 4 o'clock. Kent was captained by Mr Paterson and Sussex by Mr H.C. Blaker. The following comprising sides.

SUSSEX
T.S. Baker, Esq.
H.C. Blaker, Esq, (Capt)
W.C. Blaker, Esq.
J.C. Chandor, Esq.
H. D'Alquin, Esq.
F.N. Foster, Esq.
C.R. Gurney, Esq.
J.H.R. Kirby, Esq
J.F.A. Leigh, Esq
A.M. Mills, Esq.
C. Templeton, Esq.
T .Ward, Esq.
A.H. Weekes, Esq.
H.B. Woods, Esq

KENT
F.M. Campbell, Esq.
L.A. Campbell, Esq.
E.L. Dunn, Esq.
C. Fryer, Esq.
D. Lyall, Esq.
J.F. Paterson, Esq. (Capt)
W.C. Scott, Esq.
C.J. Scott, Esq.
W. Smith, Esq
J.V. Walmsley, Esq.
--- Muggeridge, Esq.
--- Millward, Esq.

Kent won the toss, and kicked with the wind, up the hill. Forty minutes of play took place with varied success,----perhaps Kent having a trifle the best of it, they being more of a weighty material.

At 4.40, at the call of the time keeper, a change of sides took place, and Kent soon ran a rouge. It was cleverly done, and at 25 yards, kick at goal was obtained. The play continued until 5:15 when time was called, Kent proving victorious by one goal to Sussex's none. The ground, of course, was in a very slippery state, but some science was displayed by both sides. Mr H.C. Blaker's running was particularly noticeable, as was Mr Layall's for Kent. The goal was admirably kicked by Mr Paterson, there being no dispute as to it going directly over the prescribed limits. Three hearty cheers were given to the winners by the Sussex gentlemen, and Kent, on leaving per bus, for the Old Ship Hotel, returned the compliment, with their Kentish fire , which honour they also did to Lillywhite for his general arrangements. The return match will take place at Blackheath, on March 3rd.

The above Kent side was mainly made up of "Blackheath Football Club" players. I have been in communication with Mandy Allen & Peter Brown from Blackheath F.C. who confirmed the majority of names were Blackheath players. A name that stands out is F. M. Campbell, a very interesting gentleman, who played a very important role in establishing the "Association Football" and the "Rugby Football Union" And I quote:

"Blackheath was a founder member of The Football Association which was formed on 26th October 1863 at The Freemason's Tavern, Great Queen Street, on Lincoln Inn Fields, London with the intention to form a code of laws that would embrace the best and most acceptable points of all the various methods of play under the one heading of "football". Mr Francis Maule Campbell of Blackheath was elected treasurer. At the fifth meeting Campbell argued that hacking was an essential element of 'football' and that to eliminate hacking would *"do away with all the courage and pluck from the game, and I will be bound over to bring over a lot of Frenchmen who would beat you with a week's practice."* At the sixth meeting, on 8 December, Campbell withdrew Blackheath explaining that the rules that the FA intended to adopt would destroy the game and all interest in it. Other clubs followed this lead and did not join the Football Association. In this way the great divide between soccer and rugby took place.

In December 1870 Edwin Ash, the Secretary of Richmond Club, published a letter in the papers which said, *"Those who play the rugby-type game should meet to form a code of practice as various clubs play to rules which differ from others, which makes the game difficult to play"*. This led to a meeting in January and the formation of the RFU.

I have read, on more than one occasion, that it was a surprise that "Bath, Bradford, Liverpool and Brighton etc, were not in attendance at the Pall Mall restaurant for the formation of the R.F.U". I think it was quite possible that the above letter would not have been published in "Provincial" newspapers.

It had become obvious that I needed to systematically work backwards from 1866 to uncover any earlier records mention of the sport in Brighton or Sussex. I came across a very interesting game that took place in late Dec 1865 and to my knowledge the first and probably the documented 30 a side Foot Ball to ever take place in Brighton.

Thursday 28th December 1865

FOOT BALL   MATCH

On Thursday a match of foot ball was played in the Queens Park Cricket Ground, between thirty gentlemen of Hove Club and thirty of Hurst College, the whole of whose names appeared in our last issue. The weather was very favourable for the contest, and there was a fair attendance of spectators to witness the prowess of the various competitors engaged in this now fashionable and invigorating exercise.

The players, most of whom were under twenty years of age, papered on the attired in varied costumes, the predominant being that of a cricketer ; but we fear that many of them stood a fair chance of catching cold by imprudently standing about the grounds in their Summer costumers, and instead of waiting until the word was given to doff their over-clothing for we noticed that many of whom were provided with the ordinary walking suit, which quickly envelope them after they had finished their labours. The game commenced at a quarter to three o'clock, the goals being placed at the extremities of the ground (North and South) and it soon became very evident that the number of players was far too large, for the ball very seldom got free from its adversaries and almost from beginning to end it was being "hustled" by the violent kicks of the players, who, letting out whenever they thought fit, must (in the absence of shin pads) have inevitably injured each other severely in the legs in their endeavour to get the ball from amidst them and "set it going" Again when one player took up the ball and made an effort to run with it towards his opponent's goal, he was instantly pounced upon by the opposing side, who hugged him as would a bear to a man, striving to bear him to the ground, whilst his party used their greatest exertions to move him along (with the ball still in his possession) towards their opponents' goal. It was certainly highly amusing to the majority of the players, but, in our opinion this large number made it a "rough exhibition" of the game of foot-ball, and we will leave our readers to judge of the contest when we state that, at one interval during the "battle" we saw a young fellow in the centre of this crushing "59" borne down to the earth in his white flannel suit (which afterwards assumed another colour, in consequence of the moisture of the ground) and about 6 or 7 others fell upon him amidst a roar of laughter on all sides.

Play terminated a four o'clock, the match ending in a draw, neither party having succeeded in obtaining a goal, although many vigorous and spirited rushes were made by both parties, the match was superintended by Mr F Lillywhite, by whom the ground was well marked. We hope to never see such a large number pitted against each other again, and think that half that number give treble satisfaction...

Then I came across this letter to the Editor of the Brighton Gazette, 4th January 1866, which warrants a mention and appertains to the above game. I consider any views regarding the codes of the game quite poignant pre the formation of the Rugby Football Union.

SIR,--- May I be allowed to say a few words about the account given in your excellent paper of the foot-ball match, played by the Hove and Hurst Clubs last Tuesday. Your correspondent says "they stood a fair chance of catching a severe cold", Does he think that foot-ball players ought to play in their "ordinary walking suit".

Perhaps he would like them to have Inverness Capes on as well. Next he speaks of the players' legs being severely hurt by the "violent kicks of the players unless they had shin pads" Has any foot-ball player ever existed who provided himself with shin pads? Perhaps your correspondent does not know that, at Rugby, by whom rules these clubs profess to play, it is custom to give violent kicks to the shins, but though brutal and very hurtful practice takes place there, Rugbeians never provide themselves with "Shinpads" How does your correspondent intend to make his shinpad? Does he mean them to use Cricket Pad?

Again, how could one player be pushed to the ground by 59 other players unless the "Backs and Half backs" have been playing forward? And I should think that the poor fellow who after having four or five players on him and had to submit to the jeers of the people present would never play foot-ball again. Lastly, this "rough exhibition" of foot-ball is the true Rugby game, and I have never heard of any Rugbeian who was afraid of catching a severe cold. Hoping that I have not trespassed on your valuable space or offended your correspondent.

I remain yours

"ONE WHO PLAYS RUGBY RULES"

The next mention of a Football Contest is this article which ends with the first mention of a Rugby Football match between Brighton and Hove.

1865 Brighton Guardian Dec 29th

FOOT BALL CONTEST

An interesting match announced to be played on Saturday last, was commenced on that day, on Emmerson's ground, the Queen's Park. The weather was very boisterous, consequently the spectators were not so numerous as was anticipated. It was the first match of the kind played in public, and doubtless, the others that have to follow will prove more attractive. The toss was won by Mr Barnes, the Captain of the College fifteen, and the game commenced at 2:30. The arrangements of the ground were admirably carried out under the management of Mr F Lillywhite. Creases of 120yards by 50 yards were marked out, and the flags hoisted on the goal posts, as well as the touch poles. After one hour and twenty minutes of hard play, in which the College obtained two rouges, the rain came on, and the contest was discontinued, the victory and unclaimed India Rubber Prize Foot Ball being awarded to the College A vast number of the Collegians were present, and somewhat assisted their side by aiding the return of the ball to "play", when made out of boundary. This in the future, it is to be hoped will be avoided.

This day, the Brighton and Hove Clubs meet, and the match is expected to be a well contested on. The sides will comprise the following gentlemen :-- 15 of the

HOVE CLUB --- Messrs W.C. Prescott, Beck, F.Levick, W.C.Austin, W,C.Blake, A.Weekes, G.Cox, W.Greenhill, F.Muggridge,, Millward, Abraham, G.Bird, H.G.Turner, W.G.Rigden, and Hayes. 15 of the

BRIGHTON CLUB,---Messrs H.Allen, A.B.Beresford, H.C.Blaker, G.Chandor, T.Ewbank, F.N.Foster, J.F.Leigh, A.M.Mills, H.Philbrick, F.W. Robinson, C.Templeton, H.Thurburn, R.S.Wells, W.E.Woledge, and C.G.Barnes.

At the beginning of December 1865 a game was advertised as the "Grand Foot Ball Match" and reads as if it lived up to that accolade....

GRAND FOOT BALL MATCH

THE BRIGHTON CLUB v THE BRIGHTON COLLEGE

Brighton was somewhat "stirred up" on Saturday last to witness a Foot Ball Contest between the above contending parties and great preparations were made, and the ground was in excellent condition.

The gaiety of the flags, of the most costly description, and the appearance of the goal post and a variety of staves which were placed round the ground for the guidance of the lookers on, --- consisting of a vast number of ladies and gentlemen ---gave the affair an aspect far beyond what might be expected at this season of the year. There were also present numerous carriages during the two hours play.

At a quarter past 3 o'clock, the two fifteens made their appearance in the battlefield; Brighton Club colours, light blue and white; College, mauve. Mr Barnes, the Captain of the College body, won the toss, and selected to kick down. Both sides were very strong, consequently it is difficult to judge which was the favourite. We thought the College men very confident, from the fact of their having the point of "scragging" in their favour, a point, we believe, that will, in future, have to be "considered" It was, however, allowed, and "hacking" was given up, so that "running with the ball" sport was materially stopped by the system of "scragging" or it may be termed "throttling" until the possessor of the ball was compelled to give in by this force. Nearly one hour elapsed before any important point was made, the "mauling" being too conspicuous to afford the visitors a sight of much of the play. However, Mr Barnes very cleverly trundled the ball down by the goal in possession of the College, and the captain, too, who made a rouge, and afterwards kicked the goal in the masterly manner, which naturally brought down immense cheering from the numerous Collegians present. One half hour's more took place, and the game resulted in a victory for the Brighton College. For the Brighton Club, Mr Mills, a splendid player, nearly kicked a goal, but the ball went over the posts. The Club was under the Captaincy of Mr J.F. Leigh, whose expertise and judgement were particularly noticeable, whilst that of Mr Barnes gave evidence of practice.

The prize was one of "Lillywhite and Ward's patent Vulcanised India Rubber Foot Balls".

Next is the write up on the return match between Brighton v Brighton College Dec 20th 1865.

FOOT BALL MATCH

BRIGHTON COLLEGE v BRIGHTON CLUB

The return match between the above took place on Emerson's Cricket Ground, the Queens Park, on Saturday last. The weather was not quite fit for out-door sports, but nevertheless an excellent company was in attendance. The was in good order, and the arrangements for the reception of the gentlemen admirably executed.

The contest excited considerable interest, from the fact that the College having won the first event. Mr Leigh Captain of the Club, had prepared on paper a very strong fifteen, but he was disappointed in three (who absented themselves from duty), and they therefore entered the field with only twelve men. The College won the toss, and selected to play up the ground, and change after 30 minutes play. The Club, at first, had the advantage of getting the ball close to Colleges goal; the latter, however, set to work, and run the ball up towards the Clubs goal, and obtained a touch-down ,--commonly termed as a rouge. Mr Barnes, the captain of the College fifteen, kicked unsuccessfully for the goal four times, and eventually did so with success. Having changed ground, he also run the ball through with much judgement. It will be seen by the points below, that Mr Baddeley also kicked a goal. Therefore, the College won the first and second event, and was presented with one of Mr Fred Lillywhite and Ward's patent Vulcanised India Rubber Foot Ball's--treble-seamed, and manufactured expressly, for the present Foot Ball season is closed, but after the holidays many more match are in contemplation.

The following were contending parties:--

BRIGHTON COLLEGE--- G. Arbuthnot, Esq (rouge), W.L.C. Baddeley, Esq (Kicked a goal), G.C. Barnes Esq, (UK for G 4 kicked goal) J.C. Beattie, Esq, H.W. Blunt, Esq,(back), A.F. Gurney, Esq, C.H.Griffith, Esq, H.H. Harwood, Esq, (Hardback), W. Ireland, Esq,. C. O'Malley, Esq, M. Murphy, Esq, F.G. Lacon, Esq, C.C. Ross, Esq, A.T. Scott, Esq, (back), and J.W. Ward, Esq. (rouge 3 kicked goal).

BRIGHTON CLUB --- W.C. Austin, Esq, (Back), H.C. Blaker, Esq, W.M. Crowe, Esq, F.M. Dixon, Esq, M.S. Fitzgerald, Esq, F.N. Foster, Esq, W.A. Greenhill, Esq, (Absent), C.G. Hilbere, Esq, C.S.C. Horwood, Esq (Absent), J.A.F. Leigh, Esq, (back), C. Templeton, Esq, T. Ward, Esq, (Half-back), A.H. Weekes, Esq, W.E. Woledge, Esq, and H.B. Woods, Esq, (Absent).

Brighton Gazette, Thursday 14th December 1865

On Saturday se'nnight, a most exciting game was contested between the Brighton Club and the College, and although the weather was not so inviting as could be wished there was a goodly sprinkle of the nobility and gentry, including many of the fair sex. The ground was gaily decorated with costly flags, and the goals having being duly pitched, the ball was sent rolling in the play, just after two o'clock.

Mr Barnes, the Captain of the College Fifteen, won the toss, and decided to make for the lower goal ; truly an advantage, Mr A.F. Leigh, as Captain of the Club, met them with his army right pluckily, and the battle had commenced. For about three-quarters of an hour, there was much mauling and "scragging", which was not so much sport to the visitors as when the ball was let loose.

This having been affected, Mr Barnes made way with it for a rouge, and was well followed up by Mr Griffiths, his colleague, who succeeded in kicking a goal, amidst great cheering. Play was again resumed, and Mr Mills, of the Brighton Club, very nearly accomplished a goal, but the "windy instrument" was too high in the air, and was consequently disallowed. Another start was made, and again Mr Barnes succeeded in making a rouge at the top end of the ground, and having placed the ball the allotted space of 25yards from the goal, very cleverly kicked it between.

The Club went gallantly and bravely to work to regain their lost laurels, but time would not admit of it. The match, therefore, terminated at four o'clock, in favour of the College, which caused considerable cheering from all present, The play on both sides was excellent, and much science was exhibited. The two captains also did their duty well.

We have heard much complaint as to the "scragging" system, and doubtless 'ere long that the rule will be erased.

Last Saturday Mr Weeks' 15, and 15 of the Brighton College met on the Queens Park Ground, and a meeting of the "heads of departments" having taken place at Lillywhite's the system of "scragging" was abolished, as was also "hacking", so that merely a "tiger jump" is allowed to get possession of the ball when running.

A good fifteen was brought onto the field, but not powerful enough to compete with the College, whose "playing together" causes them to obtain many points that otherwise would have been lost. The ground not-withstanding the previous wet weather, was in good order, and Mr Weekes having won the toss, the ball was set into play at 2:30. They went to work in real earnest. The College made five rouges. Mr Barnes missed goal three times, having to kick at it at a distance of 25 yards. Mr Scott also missed fire. The last one, however, Mr Barnes accomplished, amidst great cheering, which event decided the match, and Lillywhite's patent prize ball, in favour of the College. The play of Mr Weekes's 15 throughout was good, especially himself, and Mr W.C. Austin (of Wyatt's). An interesting and exciting return contest between the Brighton College and Brighton Club will be played, and, as the College at present are victorious by one match, the "Club" will be "up and doing" on the day.

Going further back I found this advertisement in the Brighton Gazette.

Brighton Gazette, Thursday 23rd September 1865

SUSSEX COUNTY FOOT-BALL MATCHES.

The First of this Series of Matches will take place on the Queen's Park Cricket Ground, on **SATURDAY NEXT,** November 25th. The contest will be

BRIGHTON COLLEGE V THE SCHOOLS OF BRIGHTON

Admission, 6d ; Ladies and Gentleman on Horseback, 1s ; Carriages, 2s 6d. Season and Carriage Tickets may be obtained off Mr FRED LILLYWHITE, 41, Ship Street, Brighton, and Mr EMMERSON, the Queen's Park Cricket Ground. On WEDNESDAY, NOV, 29th, the HOVE CLUB will play the BRIGHTON CLUB

We understand the above Interesting contests have been arranged through the instrumentality of Mr Fred Lillywhite, of 41 Ship Street, and that, by attention to the wants of both the players as well as the visitors and the inhabitants of Brighton and in Sussex generally, the sports will be continued throughout the winter (weather permitting). overcome, by a meeting of the "Heads of Departments" at Lillywhite's, to settle as to the rules by which the games will be played.

The Brighton College rules and the Rugby rules (played by the Brighton Club) have been so altered as to be sanctioned by the Captains. Each side will comprise of 15 players, who are now in strict training for the coming important events, and we have no doubt that the contests will attract a vast number of spectators to the Park between the hours of two and four o'clock. The ground is enclosed, and is situated near the Queens Park, and will be whitened creases(as in Cricket), so as to determine the allotted space for action, and Lillywhite will act as a kind of referee, although it is seldom that such is required where a game is played by Gentlemen strictly in accordance with the rules laid down.

It is only at the time of the immense excitement of obtaining a rouge or a goal that it may likely to occur Captains of Colleges and the Secretaries of Clubs, by communicating with Mr Fred Lillywhite, 41, Ship Street, can arrange for matches to be played.

The above information has only recently been found and it answers more than a few poignant questions. I was aware that Brighton College had its own set of rules and that the Brighton Club played "Rugby" rules. I believe the rules used in this match, and agreed with by all other team secretaries, were "Rugby Modified" rules as played by all schools in Brighton and of course would not be too dissimilar to the laws played by "Rugby" and "Marlborough" Schools.

9th November 1865

FOOT BALL CONTEST

An interesting match announced to be played on Saturday last, was commenced on that day, on Emmerson's ground, the Queen's Park. The weather was very boisterous, consequently the spectators were not so numerous as was anticipated. It was the first match of the kind played in public, and doubtless, the others that have to follow will prove more attractive. The toss was won by Mr Barnes, the Captain of the College fifteen, and the game commenced at 2:30. The arrangements of the ground were admirably carried out under the management of Mr F. Lillywhite. Creases of 120 yards by 50 yards were marked out, and the flags hoisted on the goal posts, as well as the touch poles. After one hour and twenty minutes of hard play, in which the College obtained two rouges, the rain came on, and the contest was discontinued, the victory and unclaimed India Rubber Prize Foot Ball being awarded to the College A vast number of the Collegians were present, and somewhat assisted their side by aiding the return of the ball to "play", when made out of boundary. This in the future, it is to be hoped will be avoided.

It would appear that the game on the 29th November 1865 could be the very first game of "Rugby Football" between Brighton and Hove which ended in a draw?

This day, the Brighton and Hove Clubs meet, and the match is expected to be a well contested on. The sides will comprise the following gentlemen :-- 15 of the

HOVE CLUB --- Messrs W.C. Prescott, Beck, F. Levick, W.C .Austin, W.C. Blake, A. Weekes, G. Cox, W. Greenhill, F. Muggridge,, Millward, Abraham, G. Bird, H.G. Turner, W.G. Rigden, and Hayes.

BRIGHTON CLUB,---Messrs H. Allen, A.B. Beresford, H.C. Blaker, G. Chandor, T. Ewbank, F.N. Foster, J.F. Leigh, A.M. Mills, H. Philbrick, F.W. Robinson, C. Templeton, H. Thurburn, R.S. Wells, W.E. Woledge, and C.G. Barnes.

November 1865

BRIGHTON CLUB v HOVE CLUB

Yesterday (Wednesday) the above two clubs met to decide a "contest of merit." Owing, as we predicted, to the talent engaged on the both sides the match was obliged to result in a draw. It was an admirably contested game, and many points were made on both sides, for which we have not space in our impression of this day of notice. Suffice it to say that two hours play of a most exciting character took place. The Hove Club was under the captaincy of Mr A. H. Weekes and Mr A. J. F. Leigh performed a similar duty for the Brighton Club. On Saturday one of the great contests of the season will be played, weather permitting, between the Brighton Club and Brighton College, who are reported to be in good training for this event.

History to date suggests that both the "Brighton" and "Hove" Rugby Clubs have yet to be founded, but what we do know is that the "Brighton Club" was the 'Brighton Football Club' but the Hove Club was not a predecessor of the current gentleman's 'Hove Club', which was founded in 1882 or the Hove Rugby Club, who were founded in 1952.

The Predicament

Does the "Brighton Football Club" of 1866 have any link with the "ShooFlies/Brighton Football Club" of 1868? Logic would say not, as the ShooFlies claim they were founded in 1868-69, so why not use the earlier date? unless;

a) The original "Brighton Football Club" (Brighton Club) was still in existence, but ceased to function in 1874, thereby allowing the ShooFlies to change their name to Brighton F.C?

b) The ShooFlies merge with Brighton Football Club in 1874?

c) That Brighton Football Club no longer played under the

banner of the "The Brighton Club" and having to change their name they choose the Shooflies?

I came across this in 1872...

"The Shoo-Flies are afoot. Prior to the commencement of a fresh campaign they have held a meeting, at which this now famous football club, on the resignation of the officers of the previous year, the following gentlemen as members of the Committee"

It seems peculiar that the "Shoo-Flies" Football Club, being in existence for only four years, would be classed as a "Famous Football Club"? Mr A.J.F. Leigh, who in his letter (previously mentioned) to the Brighton Gazette, signed himself off as Hon Sec, "Brighton Football Club" however the games that include Mr A.J.F. Leigh as a player refers to the side as "The Brighton Club". Having exhausted my research of Brighton Football Club pre-1865 my research moves on to uncovering more about the "The Brighton Club".

Chapter IV

THE BRIGHTON CLUB

The "Brighton Club" was undoubtedly a "Gentlemen's Sporting Club" based in Brighton. The earliest of the sports that are mentioned as being played by the "Brighton Club" are Cricket, (the main sport) Chess, Sailing, Horse Racing, "Fives", Card Playing! and of course Football". I have since found other sports connected with the "Brighton Club" that are documented as "Clubs within the Club" with Mr Leigh, secrctary of Brighton Football Club, being a prime example of this.

Information on the "Brighton Club" is listed in Chronological order and it might surprise you to know that it goes back to 1791. A date to establish when "Brighton Football Club" was formed within the "Brighton Club" requires further investigation. If we look at the four "Grand Fetes" organised in 1833 to celebrate William IV's birthday, the programme included "Cricket" and Foot-Ball" and logic tells me the participants would be the Brighton Club, but this has yet to be proven.

In the following pages I have attempted to document the sporting activities found with regard the "Brighton Club"

3rd September 1791

The Cricket Match played last week at Brighton, between the County of Middlesex, with Harry Allsop Esq and the "Brighton Club", with Lord Barrymore, was won by the former..

13th September 1791 (Kentish Gazette)

"On Thursday last, the Prince arrived at His Pavilion at Brighton, after a week's absence. The same day and the day following, his Royal Highness with a select party of friends, dined in

his marquee on the cricketing ground, where the second match was played between the "Brighton Club" and Mr Bean's Club, which was won hollow by the former, who beat they adversaries an innings, and more than thirty notches."

Another newspaper article from a year later, September 1792, mentions "The Brighton Club" and a Cricket Match and on this occasion I have decided to transcribe the column in its entirety as it makes very interesting reading ;

Morning Chronicle 3rd September 1792

"Cargoes of unhappy Frenchmen arrive daily at this Port, who get away in the middle of the night in English vessels. Upwards of so many genteel people landed on Monday, and nearly as many on Sunday. They are uniform in their deplorable description of their country. History furnishes no instances of familiar anarchy and distress, nor were such cruel barbarities ever practiced in the most savage nations.

Mrs Fitzherbert, Miss Pigot, Lady Clermont, Lady Ann Fitzroy, with a large party, dined with his Royal Highness the Prince of Wales, and the Duke and Duchess of York, at the Pavilion, at Brighton, on Sunday last, and in the evening the Duke left Brighton for London.

Monday morning at six o'clock a large Ox was put down to roast at the pit near the cricket ground, to which place were sent about 20 hogshead of Ale, and about 2000 loaves of bread--At half past three o'clock they drew Mrs Fitzherbert in her phaeton, at which time their Royal highnesses the Prince of Wales and the Duke of Clarence appeared on the ground.

The Ox was cut up by Mr Ruffell, the butcher, who was dressed on the occasion in white with a mottled cap, and blue and buff ribband round his arms, with a sash over his shoulders---the motto, "Long live the Royal Brothers"

Wednesday morning Mr Burton's packet, from Dieppe brought over 25 foreigners, amongst whom was the Marchioness de Bouille, who came over in the character of a sailor. Another, who was a person of distinction, was brought over in a trunk. The same morning two French sailors brought over a Lady in a open boat for which they had 100 guineas paid them by the Lady's husband. The Prince, Mrs Fitzherbert, and Miss Pigot paid a visit to the Marchioness de Bouille, at lord Clermont's house on the Steyne.

The Cricket match, nine gentlemen of the Mary-le Bone Club with Collins and Purchase, against the "Brighton Club" with Boxall, played on the Prince of Wales's ground at Brighton on Monday, Tuesday, Wednesday & Thursday, fe'nnight, terminated in favour of the Brighton Club.

One day last week, a smuggling cutter, having been closely chased at Sea, in order to lighten her loading, threw in 300 tubs of Spirit overboard, and, by means thereof, escaped her pursuers. The Brighton Fishermen, seeing many of the tubs float on the very rough sea before the town, swam out at the hazard of their lives and saved some of them. Two revenue offices, who looked on while the hardy sons of Neptune buffeted the angry waves for the sake of their favourite grog, endeavoured to seize the fruits of their labour.

But one of them pursuing a woman who had received a tub from her Husband or Brother, fell down a bank and broke one of his legs in a manner that the bone appeared through his stocking. The other, having gone down to the beach in order more effectually to intercept his prey, was hurtled by the crowd off one of the groins, and broke three of his ribs in the fall.

Honest Jack, seeing his foes thus disabled, secured every tub that fell his way, and in his dripping jacket drank confusion to excess".

This previous article is exactly how it was printed in the paper. I'm not sure of the price of a Newspaper in 1792 but whatever it was, it was worth every penny. The following advertisement leads me to presumed that the "Brighton Club" was undoubtedly under the patronage of his Royal Highness the Prince of Wales, which of course made it a very successful Club.

ROYAL CRICKET GROUND

BRIGHTON

"CHALLENGE"

The BRIGHTON CLUB is open to a match against any Club in either of the adjoining Counties

It is no wonder this Brighton Club took on and beat County Teams and played an All-England side four times winning two of their four encounters.

Horse Racing was also on the agenda with the Club supplying a cup and prize money of 100 guineas per annum. Pigeon Shooting was practised at Queens Park Cricket Ground and the Club was also involved with Yacht racing and, "Golf" is described in the following quote,

"This exercise is of all others most conducive to health and longevity; it is not to severe, and is necessarily performed in the open air, and prevention is better than the cure. A Beef steak and a bottle of Port are the Golfers medicine..! We wish the Brighton Club success",

Things changed with the death of the patron of the "Brighton Club", King George IV in 1830, and it would seem that a certain amount of animosity had arisen amongst the Clubs membership. Therefore the dissolution of the Club and the quick reestablishment of a new Club was an obvious way of "Weeding out the bad apples".

Brighton Gazette 8th Sept 1831

THE NEW BRIGHTON CLUB

This Club, which was formed a few months since when the Brighton Club was dissolved, is, likes states and kingdoms a prey for revolution, and already divided in consequence of a serious innovation made on its constitution by the Provisional Committee. The Club was formed by a party of Gentlemen, each of whom was to nominate, if he thought proper, nine friends, who were to be members without ballot ; and with this addition of numbers , the Club was constituted and established, all other persons who might be desirous of joining it, coming under its laws ---- one of which was the usual system of ballot A number of men were proposed, and many were blackballed, we have heard nineteen were thus disposed of in one day. The friends of some of the gentlemen were very much annoyed by their exclusion, on the 24th August the following resolution was passed by the Provisional Committee,

At a Meeting of the Provisional Committee, held this day, it was unanimously resolved, that the committee recommends that at the General Meeting, to be held on Monday 5th day of September next, permission shall be given to Mr Harrington to nominate nine Gentlemen to be members of the "Brighton Club", without proceeding to Ballot ; Mr H, as one of the Committee appointed to form the Club, having had the privilege the same as other members so to do, but of which he could not avail himself, having been unavoidably prevented from attending the Meeting of the Committee on the day fixed for their nomination of Members without a Ballot.

We have heard that the nine gentlemen named had each been previously balloted for and black-balled. In consequence of this proceeding several gentlemen withdrew their names from the Club ; and, we understand, it is intended to establish another New Club at the Albion. Mr Harrington was not the only gentleman who did not avail himself of the opportunity of nominating, which privilege has not, however, been since requested by the others.

The next article I am able to find relating to the "Brighton Club" was found in the Brighton Gazette, 24th May 1832.

ZOOLOGICAL MATCH

FRIDAY NEXT.

NINE MUFFS, with LILLYWHITE and BROWN, against the BRIGHTON CLUB

As this was 1832 this must refer to Fred Lillywhite senior, a famous England Cricketer, who went into a partnership with Mr Brown and opened numerous Sports Shop. When his son took over the business he opened a shop at 41 Ship Street, Brighton. There was no further information found on this 'Zoological Match' and what it entailed. Wikipedia describe the game of MUFFS as ;

"a failure to hold onto a ball that may be reasonably be expected to be caught successfully...."

Hence the term "you muffed it", a mistake..?

In 1832 the "The Royal Cricket Ground" was situated where the current Park Crescent is now built and directly behind the ground, to the left, is "Irelands Pleasure Gardens". In the far right of the picture is the "Fives" (a type of handball) court attached to the Hanover Arms Inn. The road, in the middle distance, stretching up the Hill is Elm Grove,

The "Royal Cricket Ground" & "Irelands Pleasure Gardens"

The Royal Cricket Ground, between Irelands Pleasure Gardens and the Level. c1821

Chapter V

THE "SHOO-FLIES"
(Brighton Football Club)

October 1868 saw the formation of the Shoo Flies. (Brighton Football Club). I am basing this month and date on the second AGM which were held in mid October 1870. I still believe there is confusion on the foundation date, 1868 or 1869, and I am not sure if this will ever be resolved. Three Brighton Gentleman, Charles G. Boxhall, (Later, Colonel Sir Charles Boxhall), William Stuckey (Major V.D.), and F.C. Parsons (Liet-Col T.D.) were the Co-founders.

Charles Gervais Boxall became the first Captain of The ShooFlies

Charles Boxall was a solicitor and his law firm 'Boxall and Boxall' had offices at 22 Chancery Lane, London WC2, but he devoted most of his spare time to the Army Volunteer Movement. He joined the 1st Sussex as a 2nd Lieutenant in 1873 and rose to become Lieutenant-Colonel in 1893 and Honorary Colonel in 1896. His long service in the volunteer movement was recognized by the award of the volunteer decoration in 1894 and his creation as a CB in 1897. Boxall being a specialist in Artillery designed a armoured train (the first one of its kind in Britain) that Brighton Museum has a model of in its collection. The accession register entry states 'experimental trials held at Newhaven, Sussex, May 1894'

Model of the first Armoured Train designed by Charles Boxall, at the Brighton Museum.

Colonel Boxall's funeral was on March 11th 1914, and he was buried at the 'Brighton Cemetery' (Woodvale). It would appear the funeral cortege came down Church Street then proceeded along Lewes Road towards the Cemetery. Judging by the onlookers paying their respect, Sir Charles Gervais Boxall was a very popular resident of Brighton. I will endeavour to search for his grave stone/monument. I'm sure the inscription is very interesting.

There is no doubt that the ShooFlies were an army team as the above founding Gentleman were all reserves serving in the 1st and 8th Sussex Field Artillery Volunteers based at Preston Barracks, Lewes Road, Brighton. The artillery reserves used a Drill Hall, in Gloucester Road, which I'm sure would have doubled as the ShooFlies Clubhouse.

Boxall's funeral cortege, Church Street

Boxall's Cortege at Grand Parade

This former drill hall of the Brighton Artillery Volunteers, with its castellated roof and flagpole still intact, can still be seen at the bottom of Gloucester Road

The artillery volunteers, when first formed, drilled at the Town Hall but they soon got permission to use a corner of the disused Church Street barracks. Having a more permanent base encouraged more people to join, including 60 employees of the Palmer and Green foundry in North Road, which must have included many residents of North Laine. Commander of the artillery volunteers in the late 1860s was Charles Smith Hannington (of the department store), and it was he who in 1869 informed the volunteers that he had acquired the former Eagle Foundry in Gloucester Road and that he was refurbishing it to accommodate the Corps. The Church Street barracks were demolished and the only clue to their former existence is a sign 'Barrack Yard' at the bottom of North Road.

In 1873 as a recognition to his services Charles Smith Hannington was given the title of Honorary Colonel in Chief of the First Sussex Regiment of Volunteer Artillery. The hall was associated with the Royal Artillery until after WW2 and would have been where soldiers bound for the military conflicts assembled. The Sussex Volunteer Rifles also had a home in North Laine establishing

their drill hall at the top of Church St in 1890. I have researched high and low to ascertain why the name "ShoeFlies" was given to this Football Club and with the help of Sally Ward-Lee we have come to the conclusion that the name was taken from a popular "Song and Dance" group of the time. “Shoo-fly” also became a catch phrase in the US and UK in the late 1860's, when a song and dance man named Dan Bryant did a song by that name that became so popular that a “shoo-fly” fad, as H.L. Mencken later noted, “afflicted the British people for at least two years. The only other explanation would be, it's actually a Fly, and "Shoo Fly" was army expression! Unfortunately it was not until 12th October 1871 that the "Brighton Gazette" started to publish information and reporting on games played by the three senior teams that existed in Brighton at the time.

A recently found article written in, Sussex County Magazine,1931 makes for some very interesting reading and I have extracted snippets of interesting and hitherto unknown information.

RUGBY FOOTBALL IN BRIGHTON

The "importation" of players from the London Blackheath and Clapham Rovers, and other sides, was a common practice for even in those days Club secretaries seemed to have been faced with occasional difficulty in getting a complete side together for two matches. Administratively the headquarters of the 'Shooflies' used to be Walter's Wine Bar at the bottom of Spring Street, where committee meetings were held over a dock glass of Sherry and emergency meetings were even known to be held under convenient lamp-posts. Mr Arthur Young, already mentioned, is believed to be one of the earliest secretaries of the Club. He was succeeded in 1872 by Colonel Parsons who held the office for two years. Mr John E. Raven was one of the earliest Captains of the 'Brighton Club'.

The colours of the old 'Shooflies' consisted of a blue jersey with a brilliant reproduction of a "Shoofly" worked into it and a tasselled cap. When the "Shooflies" emerged as the 'Brighton Football Club', the colours adopted included a black and grey hooped jersey. (I have found a contemporary match report stating the jerseys were black and grey quarters). The stockings worn were at one time black but when A.S. Anderson joined the Club in 1901, from London Scottish and became skipper, he introduced the famous scarlet stocking as worn by that Club, and worn by Brighton today.

SHOOFLIES v THE WICK

The first match of the season between the above Clubs was played on the ground on the former, under very adverse circumstances, on Saturday rain falling throughout the match. The toss being won by the visitors, they elected to play with the wind, the Club kicked off. For the first quarter of an hour the side seemed very equally matched, but gradually the extra weight of the Shoo Flies bore the game down into close quarters of the Wick goal. Mr Lewis (Shooflies) was the first to score a rouge goal by a very fine dribble, but the scrimmage failed to produce a goal; and just before half time, Mr Ewbank, by a well judged kick, scored a goal for the Club. On changing goals, the Shooflies again severely pressed their opponents, Mr Lewis again scoring a rouge goal, which also failed in the scrimmage. Thus the match ended in a victory for the Shooflies by a goal and two rouges.

On the losing side we may mention Mr Wooley as playing with great energy, making some exceedingly fine runs and dribbles, whilst for the Club we may mention Messers Lewis, Preston, and Ewbank as playing exceedingly well.

The Shooflies consisted of the following members:-- M.G.C. Dill (Captain), Preston, Lewis, T. Ewbank, L. Ewbank, Purchas, Armytage, Holford, Trist, Elwes, Schneilder and Bordier.

The Wick, of the following:-- Woolley (Captain), C. Haynes, C. Trew, Gladstanes, Palmer, Jackson, Swanston, F. Phillips, Lange, Fabian, T. Haynes and Warner.

I noticed in the above match report, that the "ShooFlies" are constantly being called the Club. Would this be a reference to the "Brighton Club" who were always called "The Club"?

19th October 1871

SHOOFLIES v THE BRIGHTON COLLEGE

The above match was played on Saturday last, on the ground of the former, and resulted after a good hour and a half's of play in a victory to the Shoo Flies by a "rouge goal" to nothing. There was an average number of spectators present. The toss being won by the Collegians, they chose the goal at the Cliftonville end, and gave the kick-off to the Club. From the commencement of the match the college were decidedly pressed, but on changing goals they played in far better form, and worked together in a unmistakable manner. The fine dribbling of their opponents was, however, too much for them, and at about twenty minute before the close of the match M.G.C. Dill by a skilful piece of play, scored a rouge goal for the Shoo-Flies, who, after a somewhat lengthened scrimmage, succeeded in taking the ball through the college goal.

The College twelve, although smaller in size and lighter in weight than their opponents, played as up-hill game in a plucky and determined manner; but not withstanding all their efforts they did not succeed in kicking the ball once behind the Shoo Flies goal line. Great praise is due to the play of H. Wilson, the college captain, as also to that of W.P. Hubbard, F. Cook. and W.W. Robinson, and the goal keeper, whose name we unfortunately did not obtain, but who on more than one occasion did excellent services for the College team.

For the Shoo-Flies all played so well that it is difficult to select the best, but perhaps we may mention J.B. Wooley, T.C. Ewbank,

M.G.C. Dill, E.S. Stashope, W.R. Lee, H.K. Cook, H.J.O. Preston, and C. Bordier, as having done excellent work.

The College team comprised the following :-H. Wilson (Captain), E.P. Barnes, F. Coltam, F. Holmes, W.P. Hubbard, F. Hunter, C. Merlin, F. Pope, W.W. Robinson, F. Schneider, F. Pollard and F. Cook.

The Shoo-Flies, consisted of W.R. Lee (Captain), C, Bordier (Secretary), H.K. Cook, J.B. Wooley, M.G.C. Dill, C. Elves, T.C. Ewbank, H.J.O. Preston, --- Gregson, C. Pollock, E. Pareham and E.S. Stanhope.

Even though the "Shooflies" play the Rugby "modified" rules, this game against Brighton College was obviously played under the "College" rules. These rules were a cross between Association and Rugby College rules and it would be many years before the College change to the "Rugby" code.

Below is a fascinating article found in the Brighton Gazette and definitely worth a mention as the date of 1871 makes this a very early, if not one of the first Football (Rugby Rules) matches in Eastbourne. I'm sure it will of interest to Eastbourne R.F.U.

Brighton Gazette, Wednesday 18th January 1871

FOOTBALL CLUB, --- *During the past week the "Rastipods" have had three meetings on the Eastbourne Cricket Ground, of which the 1st was a pick-up, Mr Podmore's side defeating Mr C. Hayman's.*

Several touch-downs were obtained for the winners by R. Podmore, H. Hayman and Morison, two of which were successfully kicked by E. Vessey. Three touch-downs were obtained by the losers, by E. and L. Jeffery and C. Hayman. Owing to the large attendance on Tuesday, the Alphabet Match was played from "A" to "L", verses the rest, the latter winning with two goals (R. Podmore and J. Van Sommer), and three touch-downs (R. Podmore, two and S. Podmore) ; the losing side getting one goal by E. Jeffrey, and two touch-downs by E. and L. Jeffrey. Thursday was another pick up, G. Podmore's side verses E. Morison's, the former getting three touch-downs, two by G. Podmore and one by Cooper ; while the latter got two, one by E. Morison and one by E. Vessey.

At the conclusion of the match, it was moved, and carried. that the Club should be called "The Rantipod Football Club" It was also proposed by Mr Vessey that Mr G. Podmore should be elected Captain, which was also carried. To-day (Wednesday a match is being played between the Eastbourne Rantipods and the Hastings Amateur Athletic Club, on the Eastbourne Cricket Ground.

After a brief research, I still have absolutely no idea why or what is a "Alphabet Match" ..

SHOO-FLIES V LEWES PRIORY F.C.

On Wednesday, the 15th November 1871, the above match was played in the Dripping Pan, at Lewes, in very wet weather. Both teams were very poorly represented----the Lewes Club playing a man short throughout the match, which however proved a very evenly contested one, ending in a draw in favour of neither side; the ball for most part being kept in neutral ground.

On Thursday last, the Lewes team came to Brighton to play the return match, appearing minus two of their men, whose places were however well filled by members of the Brighton Wasps Football Club.

The ball was started by the home team, who had lost the toss, and consequently held the upper goal, whilst the visitors were guarding the Cliftonville goal. For the first half hour the play was vigorous on both sides, and no decided advantage was gained by either team, but as the time advanced, the play became somewhat tame, and assumed rather an uninteresting character, bar some good runs by Whitefield and Hooper for Lewes, and Worthy and Anderson for the Shoo-Flies.

Half time was called, and nothing scored by either side; immediately however after kick off, Pollock, by an excellent dribble, took the ball into close proximity of the Lewes goal, and Dill who was close behind him, took the ball behind their goal, scoring a touchdown for the Shoo-flies. A most lengthily scrimmage ensued; and in spite of the fine shoving and mauling of Rosseter, and one or two other members of the Lewes team, the Shoo-flies succeeded in taking their ball through their visitors goal, mainly through the fine shoving of Ewbank and Dill. Nothing further of importance was done, and at 4:30 a most interesting match came to a close, in favour of the Shoo-flies by a rouge goal to nothing. For the Lewes Priory, we may mention their captain (Whitfield), Rosseter, Hooper and Lloyd, as playing with great energy; whilst for the Shoo-flies, besides those who have already mentioned, North, Pollock and in fact the remainder of the team, did good service.

The earliest fixtures and results found for either Brighton Wasps or ShooFlies was in "Charles Alcocks Football Annual" 1872.

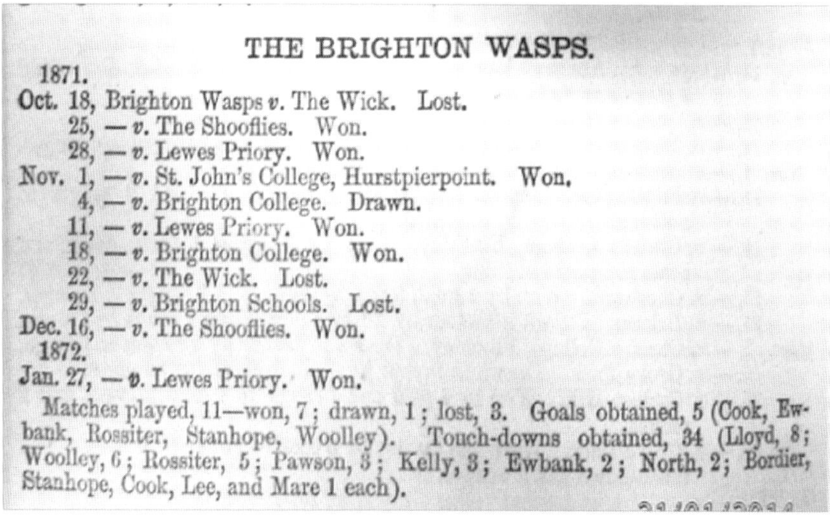

THE BRIGHTON WASPS.

1871.

Oct. 18, Brighton Wasps *v.* The Wick. Lost.
25, — *v.* The Shooflies. Won.
28, — *v.* Lewes Priory. Won.
Nov. 1, — *v.* St. John's College, Hurstpierpoint. Won.
4, — *v.* Brighton College. Drawn.
11, — *v.* Lewes Priory. Won.
18, — *v.* Brighton College. Won.
22, — *v.* The Wick. Lost.
29, — *v.* Brighton Schools. Lost.
Dec. 16, — *v.* The Shooflies. Won.

1872.

Jan. 27, — *v.* Lewes Priory. Won.

Matches played, 11—won, 7; drawn, 1; lost, 3. Goals obtained, 5 (Cook, Ewbank, Rossiter, Stanhope, Woolley). Touch-downs obtained, 34 (Lloyd, 8; Woolley, 6; Rossiter, 5; Pawson, 3; Kelly, 3; Ewbank, 2; North, 2; Bordier, Stanhope, Cook, Lee, and Mare 1 each).

Extract from Alcock's football Annual 1870

In these pioneering days of Rugby, the number of teams were limited to a few schools and Colleges. Other than three previous mentioned clubs, Lewes Priory, Brighton College and St John's College, Hurstpierpoint are the only other clubs playing in Sussex at the time. Charles Alcock was a famous sporting entrepreneur and details of this gentlemen's achievements follow later. However, I will add, he was a Hon Vice President of 'The Brighton Football Club'.

Brighton Gazette October 10th 1872

THE SHOOFLIES

The Shoo-Flies are afoot. Prior to the commencement of a fresh campaign they have held a meeting , at which this now famous football club, on the resignation of the officers of the previous year, the following gentlemen as members of the Committee :-

President, W. Anderson, Esq. Vice-President, H. K. Cook, Esq. Hon Sec, M. G. C. Dill, Esq.

Members non ex-officers, F. C. Allen, Esq. Bruton, Esq. W. Lee, Esq. J. Newton, Esq. E. Purchas, Esq.

The above would indicate that the founding members of the Club had stepped down. However, F.C. Parsons will soon be back on the committee.

THE FORMATION OF THE RUGBY FOOTBALL UNION

The Rugby Football Union was founded in the Pall Mall Restaurant at No 1 Cockspur Street, London, to standardize the rules which also removed some of the more violent aspects of the Rugby School game. The meeting was initiated by Edwin Ash, Secretary of Richmond Club, who submitted a letter to the newspapers in the previous December which read: "Those who play the rugby-type game should meet to form a code of practice as various clubs play to rules which differ from others, which makes the game difficult to play". I have read on two, maybe three occasions, "I'm surprised that Brighton Football Club did not send a representative to the Pall Mall Restaurant" and therefore assume that if the letter had been in newspapers around the country then Bradford, Brighton, Bath, Liverpool etc, may have attended.

The 21 clubs that attended the first meeting, chaired by the club captain of the Richmond Club one Mr E. C. Holmes, included Harlequins, Blackheath, Guy's Hospital, Civil Service, Wellington

College, King's College and St. Paul's School which are still playing today. Other clubs now defunct, or playing under other names, were the picturesquely named Gipsies, Flamingos, Mohicans, Wimbledon Hornets, Marlborough nomads, West Kent , Law, Lausanne, Addison, Belsize Park, Ravenscourt Park, Clapham rovers and a Greenwich club called Queen's House. Many famous provincial clubs, founded before 1871, were not founder members of the Rugby Football Union, though, of course, they became members later; among these were Bath, Bradford, Liverpool and Brighton. Note: Belsize Park were disbanded in 1880 and many players joined Harlequins. A new Belsize club was founded in 1971.

One famous name that was missing though was the London Club Wasps. Somehow they managed to send their representative to the wrong venue at the wrong time on the wrong day. Another version of the story was that he went to a pub of the same name and after consuming a number of drinks was too drunk to make it to the correct address after he realized his mistake

Algernon Rutter (of Rugby and Richmond) was elected the first president of the RFU and E.H. Ash was elected treasurer. Other committee members were: R H Birkett (Clapham Rovers), F I Currey (Marlborough Nomads), W F Eaton (Ravenscourt Park), A J English (Wellington College), J H Ewart (Guy's Hospital), A G Guillemard (West Kent), F Hartley (Flamingoes), E C Holmes (Richmond), and F Stokes (Blackheath). Secretary & Treasurer: Edwin H. Ash (Richmond).

Located in London on the "Texas Embassy" building near Trafalgar Square.

The joining fee and the annual subscription fee for a member club were both set at 5 shillings.

England v Scotland

Brighton Gazette October 17th 1872

SHOO-FLIES V BRIGHTON WASPS

On Saturday, the12th Instant, the first match of the season was played on the Sussex County Ground between the above Clubs.

The Shoo-Flies seem to be rising rapidly to the distance and next year may - and will hope will - find themselves in the first rank of Football Clubs. Saturdays encounter speaks well of them. In the same match last year they will remember, beaten by the unheard of score of fourteen rouge goals. In the present instance the game was drawn after an hour and half of exceeding hard play. Before we describe the match we would give a word of advice to the Shoo-Flies. They might advantageously learn a lesson from their elder brethren, the "Wasps" The great want in the Shoo-Flies play is that they do not "back up" sufficiently. We noticed the ball on several carries taken through the Wasps in good form, but all was lost from the absence of a man to "back up" the player.

Play commenced shortly after three o'clock. The Wasps having won the toss, chose the Eastern goal with the wind against them.

The visitors kicked off and the game commenced in real earnest, though for long without any particular incident, as the sides were so evenly matched.

At 4pm goals were changed, the home team taken the Western goal. The Shoo-Flies were now put to behind their own, having an unfavourable wind and the rain their eyes. However, their greater difficulties inspired them with greater prowess for they soon carried the ball down to their opponents goal which is crossed and Mr C. G. Boxall with great activity obtained a rouge goal for the visitors. The scrimmage that followed was mostly nominal for the Wasps were unable to offer any appreciable resistance to the superior weight of the Shoo-Flies, with Captain, Mr H. K. Cook, ably backed by Mr F. Walker easily forced the ball between the posts; a rouge goal was scored for the Shoo-Flies amidst loud adulations from their partisans. The Wasps were, however, not to be daunted and played up in fine style. Mr Woolley especially distinguished himself by his dribbles and repeatedly passed all the Shoo-Flies "up" players having none but the three "backs" to oppose him. This could not last long, and, as may be supposed, the Wasps soon added a rouge through the instrumentality of Mr Slaughter. They in their turn won the rouge goal with ease, ... making them even with the Shoo-Flies. The following quarter of an hour brought forth nothing, and the game ended in a draw.

We may mention the play of Messrs Woolley, Hooper, Pratt, Baines and Slaughter, as being particular good for the Wasps. The Shoo-Flies were well led by Messrs H. K. Cook, F. Walker, J. E. Raven, H. J. O. Preston. Mr Schneider makes a capital back player and though a small size kicks well. The teams were as follows:-

WASPS --- Woolley (Capt), Daunt, Hooper, Pratt, Baines, Hudson, Semper, Haynes, Slaughter, R. Hooper, F. Shillingford, and Ireland.

SHOO-FLIES --- H. K. Cook (Capt) F. Crunden, M. G. C. Dill, Holford, C. G. Boxall, Chadwick, H. J. O. Preston, C. Shillingford, F. Schneider, F. Walker, White, and J. E. Raven.

We are asked to state that Mr Rigden has most kindly offered his field, lying between Hove and Cliftonville for the use of the Shoo-Flies, which has been accepted. The playing strip for the wasps was "Broad Yellow and Black Hoops" and the "ShooFlies" Grey and Black Quarters... (The first mention of a team strip..!)

The Sussex County Cricket Ground was the venue for all games played by 'The Wick', 'Brighton Wasps' and 'The ShooFlies' as you can see from above we moved to a ground offered by Mr Rigden... as yet I have been unable to ascertain the exact whereabouts

A game played in December against Brighton College makes very interesting reading..!

December 19th 1872

SHOOFLIES V THE BRIGHTON COLLEGE

On Thursday last, these two teams met under much more favourable auspices than in their former match.

The game was played on the College ground, but, according to the rules of the Club. , which resemble the Rugby Union. The College (who play rules of their own) were from the first quite "Off the Grass"? The first quarter of an hour produced many a fight near the College goal, and at last a "touch-down" was obtained by J. E. Raven, whose play throughout was marked. In the consequent "scrimmage" the college goal fell after one of the fiercest encounters we have witnessed.

The College (through their Captain) shortly obtained a "touch-down" but in the ensuring "scrimmage" the Club maintained their goal intact. Amongst the College team, which played a plucky though losing a game, Power and Merlin rendered themselves useful, Woolley and Raven J, were conspicuous for the Shoo-Flies.

We were sorry to note a certain amount of ill feeling showing itself between the rival teams, which broke out loudly more than once. The consequence was, that after two more "touch-downs" had been obtained by the Shoo-Flies, one by J. A. Body who played exceedingly well, and a second by J. E. Raven, the match was prematurely concluded. We must say that the behaviour of the junior members of the College, who witness the game, were not conducive to friendly feeling, and we wonder, that the prep masters, do not restrain such un-gentlemanly and churlish as was exhibited on Thursday.

The match was a victory for the Shoo-Flies by a "Rouge goal," and a "touch-down"

This was "James Alfred Body's" first recorded game for the ShooFlies, and our first English International so it would be poignant time to give his history. In 1872 J.A. Body along with Mr Hilder purchased the "College Brewery" Montague Place, Brighton. On 5th Feb the same year he played his first game for England against Scotland. In Feb 1873 he received his second and last call up from England. Mr J.A. Body joined Brighton Wasps as President in October 1873 which would indicate a falling out between 'Body' and the ShooFlies.

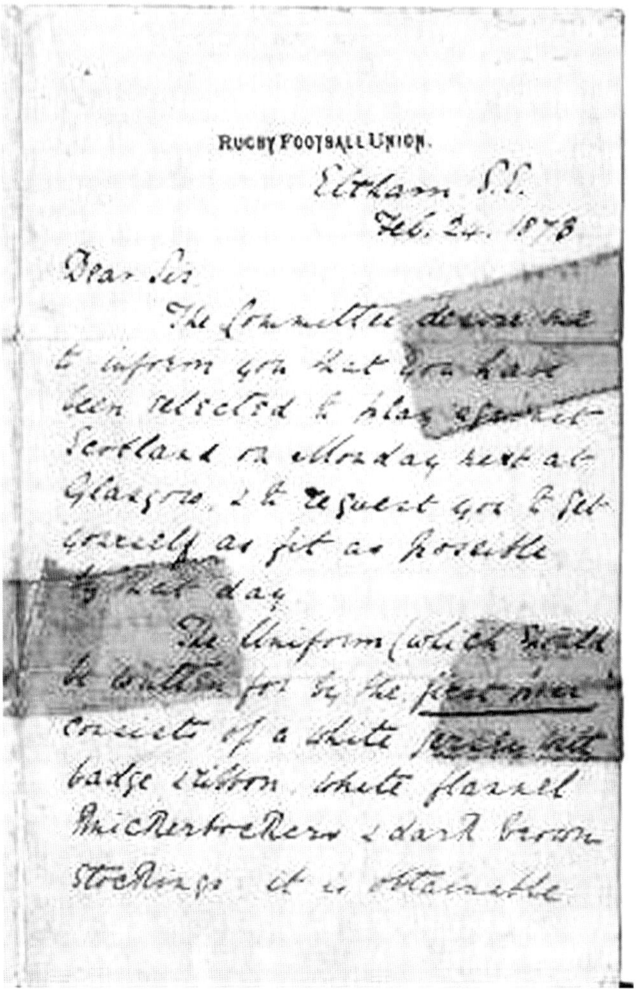

RUGBY FOOTBALL UNION.

Eltham S.E.
Feb. 24. 1873

Dear Sir

The Committee desire me to inform you that you have been selected to play against Scotland on Monday next at Glasgow, & to request you to get yourself as fit as possible by that day.

The Uniform (which should be written for by the players) consists of a white jersey with badge ribbon, white flannel knickerbockers & dark brown stockings if obtainable.

The letter of invitation to Mr J.A. Body indicating his selection for England (Permission of Ivor Body)

England Team 1873, James Body (Front row, second from left)

The AGM of The ShooFlies in Oct 1873,
and the vote to join the RFU.

BRIGHTON SHOO FLIES FOOTBALL CLUB

At the annual general meeting of the Shoo Flies Football Club, held on the 27th ultimo, the (J. E. Raven, Esq in the chair), the following report was read by the Honorary Secretary ---

"It now being the close of the football year, your Committee have to report the result of the past season. On the whole it has been most successful, for although the list of matches won is scarcely as satisfactory as that of the previous year; still we have played many more, and have been much more dependent upon our own members".

"On its own ground the Club compares favourably with others in the neighbourhood, a conclusion which members will doubtless draw from the result of the two matches played with our great rival --- The "Brighton Wasps". "We have also to congratulate the Club on the change of Rules, the popularity of which proceeding may be judged from the almost immediate desire evinced by other local Clubs to follow our example".

"We mention, however, with regret, the loss of two of our late offices, since the continued and unforeseen absence of our late President (W. Anderson Esq.) to resign, and the Vice President".

"As regards the matches played, the actual result of the season is as follows;- Won 5; drawn 8; lost 6, played 19".

"The financial state of the Club is also satisfactorily, as it will be seen that there is a small balance in hand:- Surplus from last year £3 0s 01d; subscriptions for the past season £5 15s 01d; total, £8 15s 01d. Expenditure during past season£7 17s 8d; balance £0 17s 3d".

"In conclusion, the Committee congratulate the playing members, and confidently predict that a greater knowledge of the Rugby Union Rules having been attained, the report of the ensuing season will be even more satisfactory"

On a ballot being taken, J. E. Raven Esq., was re-elected President, Arthur Young Esq., Honorary Secretary, and the rest of the Committee consisted of W. Stuckey, Esq., F. C. Parsons, Esq., and M. G. C. Dill, Esq. The office of Vice President was abolished, and the Committee contracted from seven members to five.

The following proposition was unanimously adopted:- "That gentlemen can be elected by the Committee to play in any match, on payment of an honorary fee" A vote of thanks having been unanimously and enthusiastically accorded to the officers of the previous year and to the Chairman, the meeting was declared to be dissolved.

All communication to be sent to Arthur Young, Honorary Secretary, 4 Junction Road.

Rugby Football and Association Football Fixtures
and Results for 1873-74

THE SHOO-FLIES (Brighton)
Rugby Union Rules

1873

Oct. 4, - v. Sussex County Hospital. Won.
11, - v. Brighton Wasps. Drawn; 2 tries to nothing
18, - v. Wick Club. Won; 3 goals and 5 tries to nothing
Nov 1, - v. Sussex County Hospital. Drawn.
12, - v. Brighton Schools.Won; 1 goal and 2 tries to nothing

	22, -	v. Tonbridge School. Drawn
Dec	5, -	v. Lancing College Drawn ; 2 tries to 1
	10, -	v. Worthing. Won; 8 goals and 20 tries to nothing
	13, -	v. Brighton Wasps. Won; 1 goal and two tries to nothing
	18, -	v. Hasting A.A.C. Won
1874		
Jan	10, -	v. Brighton College (p and p scratch). Won; 2 goals to 1 goal and 2 touch-downs.
	17, -	v. Southdown Wanderers. Won; 1 goal and 1 try to nothing.
Feb	14, -	v. Hurst College. Drawn.
	2	
	8, -	v " Won; 1 goal and 3 tries to nothing.

Total, 18 --- Won, 11 ; drawn, 6; lost; 1
Goals were obtained by Schneider 1, Parsons2, Alban 1, M.Dill1, Total 5 Tries by and Stevens 1 each ; total, 61.

Association Rules

1873		
Oct.	25, --	v. Lancing College. Lost.
Nov.	15, -	v. Ardingly College. Won.
	29, -	v. Worthing . Lost.
1874		
Feb.	21, -	v. Ardingly College. Won

Total, 4 --- won, 2 ; lost, 2. Goals by : Bruton 2, J. E. Raven, 1, R. Dill,1 : Total 8

The game played on Dec 13th against Brighton Wasps, was I believe, the infamous game when:

"These two teams became great rivals and when they met quarter was neither given or asked. The season of 1873 saw The Shooflies beat the Wasps convincingly on two occasions (First game drawn in favour of the Shoo Flies, two "touch-downs" to nothing.). The last game was memorable when on ground sodden with melting snow. Mr G.C. Dill come to blows with J.B. Woolley of The Wasps. It was then that the Shooflies claimed and took the title The Brighton Football Club".

I must also mention the match on Dec 10th against Worthing. 8 goals and 20 tries to nothing! Well, I'm not sure I will see that score line in the near future.

J.E. Raven 15, F.M. Pope 7, Stuckey 6, R. Dill 7, Verrall 5, Hills 5, Wilkinson 3, Catt 3, Scott 3, M. Dill 2, Maitland 2, Mahomed, T. Raven, Alban, Gardner,

Brighton Gazette October 9th 1873

THE BRIGHTON WASPS FOOTBALL CLUB

The third annual meeting of the above Club was held on Saturday last, at 28, Montpellier Street, Mr J. M. Bauton (vice president) in the Chair. After the election of several new members, the Chairman read a letter from the President (J. B. Woolley), thanking the Club for the honour they had done him in electing him as their captain last season and at the same time resigning his office, owing to his now living in London. It appears that the Club during the past year has played sixteen matches, out of which they won ten, lost three, and three was drawn. The Honorary Secretary (Mr F. S. T. Daunt) read a financial statement, which showed a small balance in hand, and then, together with the Chairman, the members of the Committee resigned office. A ballot being taken, Mr J. A. Body was elected president for the ensuing season; Mr J. M. Bauton was re-elected vice president; Mr F. S. T. Daunt Honorary Secretary. Messers C. A. Coke, J. Abbott, F. Schneider, and E. Blair, as four members of the Committee. The first practice of the Club took place yesterday. It was then proposed by Mr F. S. T. Daunt, and seconded by Mr F. Schneider,

"That the Brighton Wasps do now adopt some recognised code of rules, either The Association or The Rugby Union" This was carried unanimously. Then came the important question as to which code was to be adopted.

"The distinction between the two codes is running with the ball, or not running with the ball" After a long discussion as to the merit of each code, it was carried by a large majority that the Club should adopt the "Rugby Union Rules" and that the Secretary be empowered

to enter the name of the Club among those Clubs constituting "The Rugby Union"

A vote of thanks to the Chairman terminated the meeting.

For the benefit of all those who take an interest in the noble game of Football, a list of matches already arranged is appended. Others will follow:-

October 11th, Wasps v Shoo Flies, County Ground; October 15th, Wasps v Hastings, County Ground; October 18th, Wasps v Brighton College, County Ground; October 25th, Wasps v Brighton Schools, County Ground; November 8th, Wasps v Brighton College, College Ground; November 15th, Wasps v A London Scratch, County Ground; November 19th, Wasps v Brighton Schools, County Ground' November 22nd, Wasps v Gypsies, County Ground; December 6th, Wasps v Hurst College, County Ground.

It had become obvious that animosity had grown between the ShooFlies and Wasps, with the then England International, J.A. Body joining the Wasps and the 'Annual Match'...

Brighton Gazette October 23rd 1873

SHOO FLIES v WASPS

The Annual Match between these two rival Clubs took place on Saturday the 11th, on the County Cricket Ground, Hove, and was drawn in favour of the Shoo Flies, two "touch-downs" to nothing. We were sorry to see that neither side depended entirely on its own men for support, the Wasps having imported some "heavy men" from town in "violet and black," whilst two gentlemen in the west, known by "blue and white bars," assisted the Shoo Flies. It would be very much better if this was avoided for the future.

The Shoo Flies, having won the toss, chose to kick with the wind, which slightly favoured the Pavilion, and for some time their goal seemed in danger, but the manner in which they played together began to tell, and the ball was gradually worked nearer their opponents "touch-line" a "scrimmage" taking place close to it, enabled T. E. Raven to run over and touch it down, the wind however rendered kicking at goal an impossibility.

At half time sides were changed, several rushes were made by the Wasps, but without effect. Dill scored a second "touch down" for the Shoo Flies, but owing to an infringement of the Rules the "try" was lost. We may mention Slater, Parker, Abbott and Rossiter, as having done good service for the Wasps.

Wasps - Abbott, Baines, Blair, Coke, Hooper, Parker, Rossiter, Schneider, Slater, Webb, Winslow, and two others.

Shoo Flies - M. Dill, R. Dill, Hirst, MacDonald, May, Nichol, Paraone, Pope, J. Raven, I. Raven, Scott, Stuckey, Young.

A Match was played on Saturday last between 9 men of the Shoo Fly Foot Ball Club, and 12 of the Wick Club, which resulted in an easy victory for the former, 3 goals and 5 touches down being made against 2 touches down.

My research indicates that the "Gentlemen from the West" playing in broad Blue and White Bars were from The Bristol Club, and the "Heavy men in Violet and Black", from out of town were likely to have played for "The Gipsies" J.A. Body's old Club..

To the best of my knowledge the only game published in 1874 was against Tonbridge School.

Nov 19th 1874

BRIGHTON CLUB v TONBRIDGE SCHOOL

The above match took place on Saturday last on the school ground, and after a well played game, resulted in "a draw" in favour of the visitors by four tries and several touch-downs, the ball being only once behind their lines.

Immediately after the school had kicked off, Neild made a splendid run and took the ball almost the whole length of the ground, only to be collared within a few yards of the Schools line. Just before half-time, the school gained their only success by a united effort, which caught one off the visitor's backs napping, and compelled them to touch-down in self defence.

Those who played were, for the Brighton Club;

J. Raven (captain) and Boughton (half-backs), T.H.D. May (three-quarter-back) Verrall and Neild (backs), Grimes, Stuckey, Shillingford, Page, Brownlow, and three others.

Tonbridge School;

Jephson and College (half-backs), Lurkham (captain) (three-quarter-backs) Mulliner and Repton (backs), Carr, Sturgess, Kent, Cameron, Lloyd, Ward, Purley and Patterson.

November 28th 1874 (Brighton Herald)

SERIOUS ACCIDENT AT FOOTBALL

A member of the Mohican Football Club, named Robinson, who was playing with his club against Brighton Football Club at the County Cricket Ground on Saturday, had his leg broken in a general scrimmage which took place. He and another went to kick the ball at the same time and their legs intertwining, Robinson broke just below the knee. He was at once taken to Hospital and the game suspended.

The Mohican Football Club based in Edmonton London, was founded in 1869 and was one of the inaugural 21 Clubs that founded the RFU. In 1873 they moved to Tottenham, then disbanded in 1874 and it could be that this game against Brighton Football Club was the Mohicans finale.

Brighton (late Shoeflies).

1. 1869.
2. 60.
3. Sussex County Cricket Ground, Hove.
4. One mile and a half from Brighton.
5. On the ground.
6. Rugby.
7. F. Cecil Parsons, 31, Buckingham-road, Brighton.
8. Black and grey.
9. Played 12—won 5, lost 4, 1 unfd., drawn in favour 2.

"Alcocks" Football Annual 1875,

BRIGHTON COLLEGE.

Matches played, 12—won, 11; drawn, 1; lost, nothing.

1875.

Oct. 9, —, v. Storrington; drawn.
23, —, v. Worthing (Rugby Union). Won by 7 goals, 12 touch-downs to nothing.
28, —, v. Lancing College. Won by 5 goals to 1 (Buckle, Tyndale, Bond).
30, —, v. Brighton Club. Won by 8 goals to nothing (Bond, Tyndale, (2) Buckle, Edwards).
Nov. 6, —, v. South Norwood Club. Won by 4 goals to none (Buckle, Tyndale, Bond, Wilson).
20, —, v. Hurst College. Won by 3 goals to one (Tyndale, Buckle).
11, —, v. F. H. Adams's Twelve. Won by 2 goals (Barnes, Rudd).
Dec. 15, —, v. Old Brightonians. Won by 3 to none.
18, —, v. South Norwood Club. Won by 3 goals (Wilson, ma., Rudd, Tyndal) to none.
4, —, v. Brighton Club (Rugby Union). Won by 1 goal to 3 touch-downs (Buckle).

1876.

Feb. 18, —, v. Lancing College. Won by 4 goals to none (Tyndale 3, Barnes 1).
—, v. Hurst. Won by 2 goals to none (Gisborne, Rudd).

"Alcocks" Football Annual 1876

"The Shoo Flies Club was formed in 1868 and on a change of name in 1874 The Brighton Football Club was established.

Brighton Gazette Jan 14th 1875

BRIGHTON WASPS v BRIGHTON TOWN CLUB

Notwithstanding the heavy and disagreeable state of the weather on Saturday last week, the Wasps met the lately formed Brighton Town Football Club (late Shooflies) for the first time, and after an hour and a quarter's hard play succeeded in drawing the match in their favour, by making their opponents touchdown in self defence four times successively, they (Wasps) only having only touchdown once at the commencement of the game, when they only had eight men, the remaining team (Including two substitutes) turning up 15 minutes behind time. We must add the Brighton Town men had their full compliment, e.g. fifteen.

Raven having won the toss, Coke kicked off for the Wasps exactly at five past three. The ball for the first few minutes was kept nearly in the middle of the ground, the few Wasps playing very stubbornly against their numerous opponents, but at last the superior weight of the Brighton Town men told against them and were forced to touchdown once in self defence. However, their four other men having arrived, the game wore a different aspect, the Wasps forwards, well backed up by Woolley and H. Rosseter (half backs) succeeded in driving the ball down to their opponents end and a goal kick by H Rosseter made their back touch it down. Soon after this Raven obtained a touch, but it was obtained by an infringement of the rules, and was not allowed by the umpire.

Half time was called and the ball was set in motion, several severe and hard fought scrimmages took place, the Wasps, however, gradually forcing their way down to the Town's Club's end, warming to their work, and playing well together, making up by good play and pluck what they lacked in numbers. Woolley made several grand runs, G. Hooper, R. Rosseter, and the brothers Ellis and Cook also distinguished themselves with good runs. Again the match was renewed, and the same thing happened again, the Wasps forwards sticking well to their work managed to drive their opponents back to their goal line, forcing them to touch-down twice in self-defence. It would be invidious to mention any one of the Wasps forwards more than another, all of them played well, but we must mention J. Woolley and H. Rosseter (half backs) and R. Hooper (back), who made several good runs, as having done excellent service for their Club. For the Brighton Town Club, Cooke (half back), Stuckey, Pope, and Catt played very well.-----Wasps - C. Cooke (captain), R. Rosseter, G. Hooper, F. Ellis, J. Ellis, J. Carry, J. Abbott, Fittock (forward), J. Woolley, and H. Rosseter, (half backs), and R. Hooper, (back).---- Brighton Town Club - J. Raven, (captain), Cooke, (half back), Verral, (back), Pope, Stuckey, Catt, White and several others

BRIGHTON COLLEGE v BRIGHTON CLUB

"This match was played on Saturday, October 30th, on the College ground, and with Association Rules. Whether it was that the captain of the "Club" found it difficult to collect a twelve who would play Association Rules, or from any other cause, we cannot say, but

a more one-sided match could hardly have been, At first the game appeared pretty even. but after the first goal was scored by the College, the Club seemed to fall to pieces...Verrall (Clubs captain) tried hard to pull his team together but to no purpose"

This game highlights the fact that Brighton Football Club was losing its hybrid status and would firmly fall on the side of the "Rugby Rules"

Documented in the Brighton Gazette Jan 27th 1876, I found this very interesting piece;

"A match between the East Sussex Club v Hastings and St Leonards Club, took place at St Leonards Green on Wednesday last, when the former team was the victor, by three goals and three touch downs to their opponents nothing... On Saturday, a match was played on the Brighton's ground, between the Kensington Football Club and the Brighton Football Club, resulting in a victory for Kensington by two goals and a try, to one try. The match was extremely contested"

The Hastings & Bexhill Rugby Club web site stipulates that first game played by Hastings and St Leonards Football Club, which became H&B Rugby Club, was played against Willesden Football Club 10th November 1883. Therefore the Club might be seven years older than first thought.

The game played against Kensington Football Club is their one and only documented fixture against Brighton, and this London Club disbanded in 1905.

It is unfortunate that the newspapers in the late 1870's were devoid of any mention of Brighton Football Club. There is a possibility that the Brighton Club, which were made up of Army Volunteers, may have signed up and joined the expeditionary force to South Africa and participated in the Zulu wars.

Post Script, I did check the names of a list of the soldiers that were at "Rouke's Drift" but fortunately or unfortunately they did not correspond with any of the Brighton players from the previous years. Sorry Andy Rice.

Brighton Wasps continue to play "Football", however, all the matches I have found have been under "Association Rulcs" (soccer). I will conclude that, like other certain Hybrid Clubs, association rules started to dominate and it would seem likely that the so called amalgamation of Brighton Football Club and Brighton Wasps happened due to this evolvement. Players from the Wasps wishing to play under the Rugby Laws joined Brighton Football Club and Brighton Wasps continued playing association football.

In 1879 "The Wasps Football Club" made their first venture to the South Coast, playing "Brighton Collegiate Proprietary School Football Club" first fifteen, which in its self is very interesting as "the game was played, according to Association Rules, at the Race Hill resulting in a double victory for the former, of five goals to none"

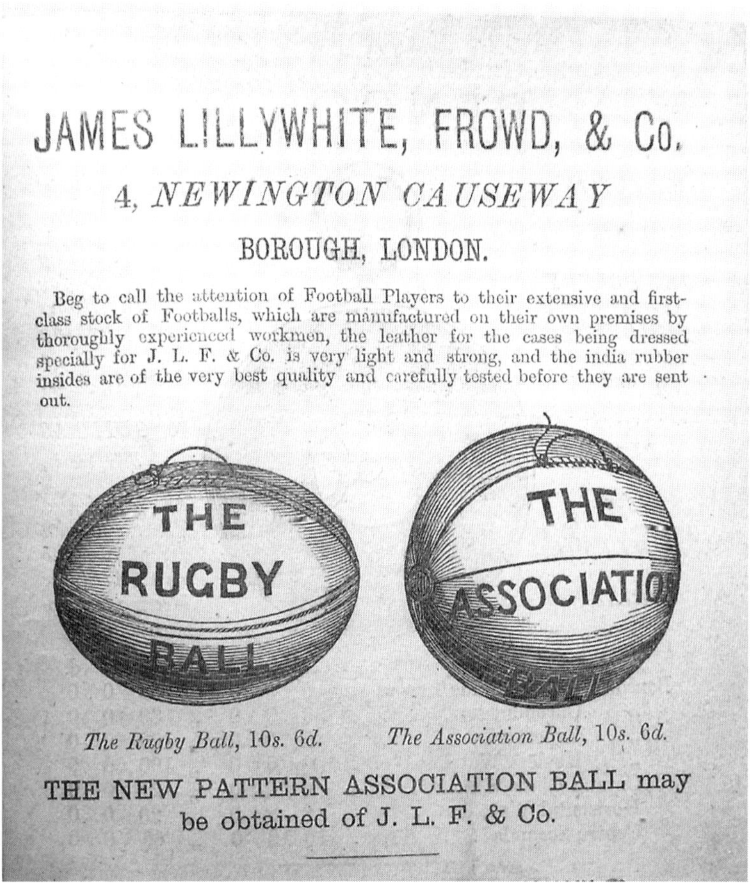

Advertisement from "Alcocks" Football Annual 1879

1880-1900

I must at this stage mention Clapham Rovers F.C. and the "Birkett" family and their association with Brighton F.C. Clapham Rovers were one of the twenty-one London and Provincial football clubs who followed Rugby School rules that assembled at the Pall Mall Restaurant in Cockspur Street and formed the Rugby Football Union on 26 January 1871. Reginald Birkett not only represented Clapham Rovers, but also became one of the thirteen original committee members. Despite his strong ties to rugby, he was known to be "found playing the Association game almost as often as Rugby" and indeed Clapham Rovers, the team he was a member of and captained in the 1871–72 season, steadfastly remained a dual-code club.

Birkett was selected for the first ever international rugby match for England v's Scotland. In this match he scored England's first ever try, although at the time a try did not gain points but rather was the means by which a team was granted the opportunity of converting the try into a point scoring goal. His brother Louis and his son John later also played for England. John Guy Gisberne Birkett played a big part in Brighton's history in the early 1900's but more on that later.

In Dick Tyson's fantastic book "London's Oldest Rugby Clubs" he writes "During the late 80's and early 90's Blackheath, Harlequins, Brighton and Clapham Rovers became close - often swapping players to complement each other teams for important fixtures. And when Clapham Rovers disbanded in 1896 a number of players joined Brighton among them, the famous Birkett family". I must admit I was amazed at the numerous players that ventured across to Blackheath as opposed to journeying down to Brighton, however they did possibly because Brighton would have been classed as a junior side compared to Blackheath.

Thursday 3rd November 1882

FOOTBALL NOTES
BRIGHTON V CROYDON

The game under the Rugby Code between the Brighton team and the Croydon Club on Saturday at Preston Park proved very attractive, notwithstanding the unfavourable elements that prevailed.

There was a large assembly of spectators to watch the very exciting match, many of whom, however, much to their discredit indulged in unsportsmanlike contest on finding the visiting team slightly superior to the home fifteen. This is the fifth match Brighton has played this season, and the only one in which they have as yet to be defeated. A humbler of twelve points to nine, however, is not very serious.

Brighton started well, P.C. Cox in five minutes from the commencement dropping a splendid goal for the home team. Croydon, however, soon showed superiority in passing, though their scrummage work was not so effective, and T. Flint, three quarter back, obtained a try for them which was successfully converted by S. Hubbard, half back.

No further scoring took place before half time was called, at which juncture the visitors had a advantage of one point. The second half was far more exciting. Flint again scored a try for Croydon, which Hubbard duly converted. Almost immediately following this F. Mitchell, forward got behind for Brighton and the effort of E.G.H. North realised a goal. Croydon then managed to add another try to their score and in spite of a creditable struggle on part of the home team, they were, during the subsequent play were unable to reach their opponents score.

Saturday 30th January 1892

BRIGHTON v EALING

The team announced to take part in this Rugby Union match at Preston Park, near Brighton to-day (Saturday) are as follows (kick-off at three o'clock) :-

BRIGHTON,-- F.G. Chichester (back), P.C. Cox, A.G. La Maistre, and F.J. Turnbull (three-quarters backs). F. Mitchell and A. Flateau (half backs), M.F. Voules (captain), B.C. O'Dowda, M. Beves, W.K. Stuart, R.D. Budworth, E.G.H. North, A.M. Brooke, H.C. Wilder and R.P. Wood.

EALING, -- J.C. Highfield, (back), H.R. Bruce (captain), A.D. Crisp and G.E. Fowler (three-quarter backs), H.I. Draper and H. Stocken (half backs), G.M. Edwards, G.G. Williams, H. Simpson, A.C. Tulloch, B. Chambers, M. Stewart, P.A.Lumley, W.P.Martin and E.H. Rouse.

March 1882

THE BRIGHTON CLUB v SALISBURY F.C.

The above match was played at the County Ground on Saturday, and terminated in a victory for the home team by two games and five tries to a goal. Hamilton was the first to cross the line for the Brighton Club, and from the try thus obtained, Curry kicked the first goal. C. Somers-Clark, Smithers, Strachan, Curry and Hodson also got in their opponants quarters, but the place kicks failed in every instance, the chief weakness of the B.F.C. being in this direction. The second goal for the victors was neatly dropped by Strachan, while "S" solitary point was scored by A. Burr.

The winning team consisted of :- G. Edmonds (back), C. Abbottand H. Germain (three quarter backs) C. Somers-Clark (Captain), H.T. Hodson (half backs) A. Mitchell, A. Strachan, F. Stewart, Hamilton, F. Smithers, A.F. Taylor, C.D. Curry, H. Kemball-Cook, C. Money and Grey Temple (forwards).

Next Saturday the Brighton Club travel to Portsmouth to play H.M.S. Marlborough.

BRIGHTON FOOTBALL CLUB

TO THE EDITOR

Sir, -- To prevent misunderstanding, and in answer to numerous enquiries, I wish to state that the Brighton Football Club have no team playing under Association Rules.

Yours &c,
E.SMITHERS, Hon Sec. Brighton F.C.
10, Denmark Terrace, Brighton, Nov 2nd, 1885

The Brighton Football Club was as previously mentioned, initially a Hybrid Club, playing both "Association Rules" and "Rugby Laws" Although the Club affiliated to the R.F.U., and was in fact one of the first to have done so. However, we did continued to play the odd game of "Association" football, right up to the late 1870's.

The above letter to the editor of the "Brighton Gazette" shows that even back in 1885 there was confusion between "Rugby" Football Rules (Laws) and "Association" Football Rules... And of course if you mention "Football" today the world automatically assumes "Soccer".

Confusion then, and confusion now.

3rd January 1889

The Brighton Rugby Club sent fifteen men to Littlehampton to battle the home team who figured in a match of this kind for the first time that day. The visitors won by one goal and a try to a try, but it was as interesting and fast game. Had the Brightonians played their fall strength, there is no telling how the home team would have fared; it's a matter of congratulation that they did not, and further it was wise on the part of Mr secretary not to send a more formidable team.

It was to be approximately 50 years before the two sides faced each other again as, unfortunately, that Littlehampton Rugby Football Club disbanded within a year or two.

The "Brighton Star Rugby Club" of whom something has been heard this season, took a bold step on Tuesday. They had challenged the Brighton Club fifteen to a contest, which had, needless to say, been accepted ; and Tuesday witnessed the game at Preston Park. The Brighton Club were not strongly represented, but the team utterly roasted the Stars.

They asserted their superiority everywhere and scored 29 points, or rather seven goals and eight tries to nil. The Stars had no chance of scoring, and without going into details, I would unhesitatingly say that they will long remember their contest on New Years Day.

I would assume that the Town wasn't "big enough for the both of us"

9th February 1886

BRIGHTON FOOTBALL CLUB

At the Gloucester Hotel on Saturday evening, the Brighton Football Club entertained the Worthing Football Club at a Smoking Concert. The large room of the Hotel was filled with a numerous and select company, and the programme was exceptionally well carried out, A pianoforte selection was played by Mr H.J. Parkin, and songs were sung by Messrs G.M. Barling, T. Bayley, F.W. Madden, G. Hallett, F. Parsons, W. Stuckey, A. Sters, and R. Nicholson, Mr R.O. Thompson gave a capitol recitation. The Captain of the Club presided: and the arrangements for the comfort of those present were, as usual most satisfactory, and reflected great credit upon Messers; Gregory and Smallwood, the popular proprietors of the Hotel.

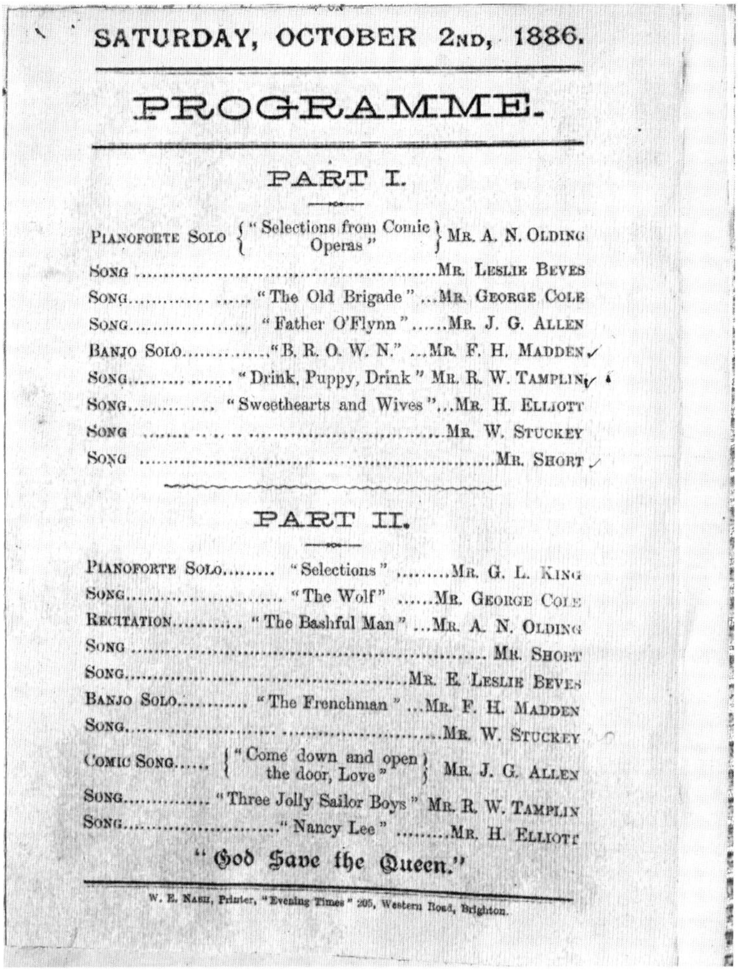

SATURDAY, OCTOBER 2ND, 1886.

PROGRAMME.

PART I.

PIANOFORTE SOLO { "Selections from Comic Operas" } MR. A. N. OLDING
SONG .... MR. LESLIE BEVES
SONG.................. "The Old Brigade" ...MR. GEORGE COLE
SONG.................... "Father O'Flynn"......MR. J. G. ALLEN
BANJO SOLO..............."B. R. O. W. N." ...MR. F. H. MADDEN
SONG.................. "Drink, Puppy, Drink" MR. R. W. TAMPLIN
SONG.............. "Sweethearts and Wives"...MR. H. ELLIOTT
SONG .... MR. W. STUCKEY
SONG .... MR. SHORT

PART II.

PIANOFORTE SOLO......... "Selections" ....MR. G. L. KING
SONG........................... "The Wolf" ......MR. GEORGE COLE
RECITATION........... "The Bashful Man" ...MR. A. N. OLDING
SONG .... MR. SHORT
SONG...MR. E. LESLIE BEVES
BANJO SOLO........... "The Frenchman" ...MR. F. H. MADDEN
SONG...MR. W. STUCKEY
COMIC SONG...... { "Come down and open the door, Love" } MR. J. G. ALLEN
SONG.............. "Three Jolly Sailor Boys" MR. R. W. TAMPLIN
SONG........................."Nancy Lee" ....MR. H. ELLIOTT

"God Save the Queen."

W. E. NASH, Printer, "Evening Times" 205, Western Road, Brighton.

Even though the quality of the two "Smoking Concert " programmes, held at the Gloucester Hotel, leaves a lot to be desired, their rarity and age, (October 2nd & 30th 1886), make their inclusion in this history well deserved.

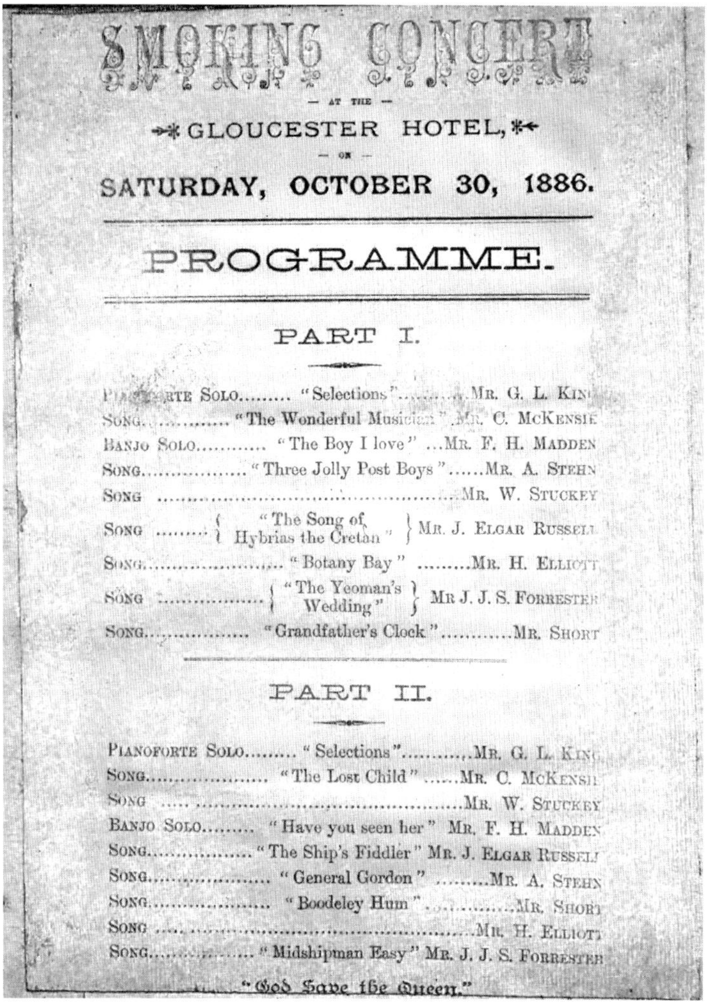

SMOKING CONCERT

— AT THE —

GLOUCESTER HOTEL,

— ON —

SATURDAY, OCTOBER 30, 1886.

PROGRAMME.

PART I.

PIANOFORTE SOLO	"Selections"	MR. G. L. KING
SONG	"The Wonderful Musician"	MR. C. MCKENSIE
BANJO SOLO	"The Boy I love"	MR. F. H. MADDEN
SONG	"Three Jolly Post Boys"	MR. A. STEHN
SONG		MR. W. STUCKEY
SONG	"The Song of Hybrias the Cretan"	MR. J. ELGAR RUSSELL
SONG	"Botany Bay"	MR. H. ELLIOTT
SONG	"The Yeoman's Wedding"	MR J. J. S. FORRESTER
SONG	"Grandfather's Clock"	MR. SHORT

PART II.

PIANOFORTE SOLO	"Selections"	MR. G. L. KING
SONG	"The Lost Child"	MR. C. MCKENSIE
SONG		MR. W. STUCKEY
BANJO SOLO	"Have you seen her"	MR. F. H. MADDEN
SONG	"The Ship's Fiddler"	MR. J. ELGAR RUSSELL
SONG	"General Gordon"	MR. A. STEHN
SONG	"Boodeley Hum"	MR. SHORT
SONG		MR. H. ELLIOTT
SONG	"Midshipman Easy"	MR. J. J. S. FORRESTER

"God Save the Queen."

I notice that Mr W. Stuckey, one of the founding members, is still participating. Maybe we should contact Worthing Rugby Club and attempt to emulate this evening for our 150th! Joking apart, I do remember when more than a few Rugby Clubs had a Piano. Dare I say "The Good Old Days" in fear of being ridiculed.

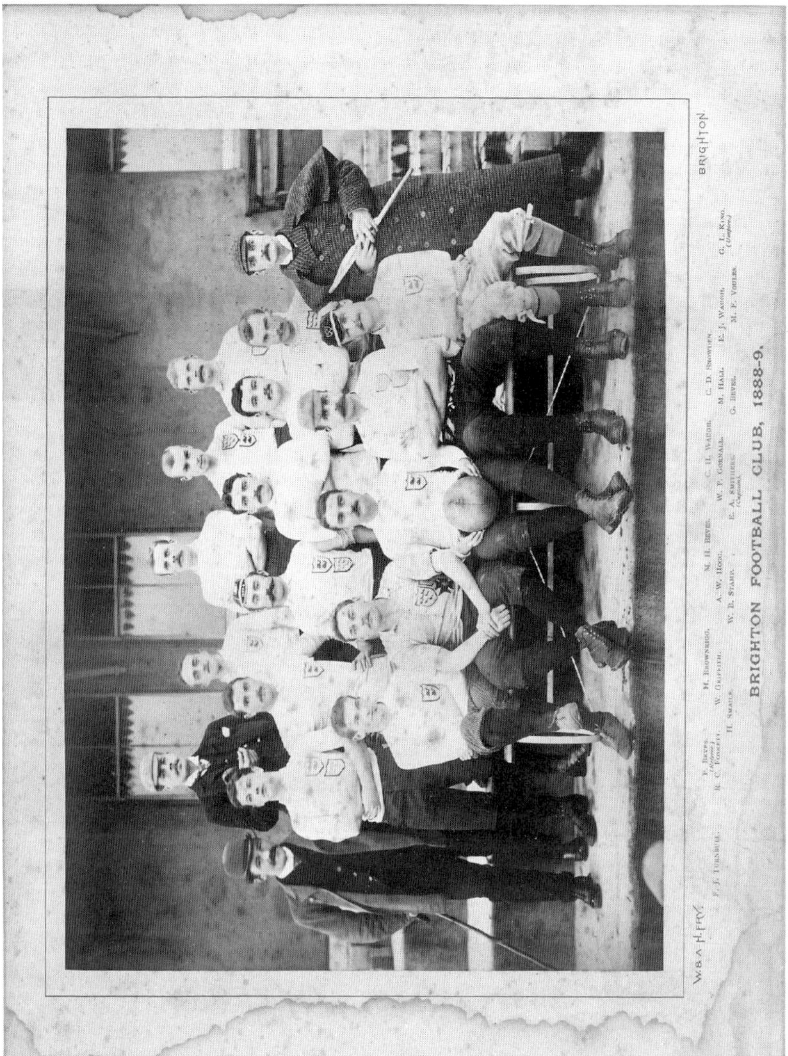

Brighton Football Club 1888-89

Brighton Football Club 1888-9, is the oldest known photograph in existence and I'm glad to say in the ownership of the Club. Unfortunately due to the Club's nomadic existence, trophy hunters and a general lack of enthusiasm, numerous historical artefacts have slowly but surely disappeared over the years.

Brighton Football Club 1889-90

I am very grateful to Henry Smith, a Vice President, and Ivor O'Mahoney, a past Club Trustee, Treasurer and Vice President, who purchased this photograph at a Christies "Football Memorabilia" auction in March 2000, and subsequently donated to the Club.

SUSSEX RUGBY UNION.

The annual general meeting of this Union was held on Saturday evening at the Crown and Anchor Hotel, Preston Park, Brighton under the presidency of Mr. H. Beves. The report and balance sheet were adopted. The former showed that during the past season four matches had been lost and one won; that Hastings Club had become defunct, but that a second club had been formed at Worthing. A great improvement had been effected in the finances, the statement of accounts showing a balance in hand of £4.5s 11d. The following officers were elected for the coming year. Viz:- President, Mr. W.S. Simpson. Hon Sec, Mr A. C. Borlase: Hon Treasurer, Mr W. Stuckey.

Committee:- Brighton – Messers. M.F. Voules, S. Matthews and E. A. Smithers.

Herford House:- I. H. Pedlar. A. D. Green, and H. T. Mieblechurch
Worthing: - G. I. Evans, J. W North and Dr. Bernard.
London: - F. H. Gunnery, C. J Hill and C. D. Snowden.

The following matches were announced:-

Nov. 2. – Sussex v. Eastern Counties, at Brighton.
Nov. 16.- Sussex v. South Midlands, at Bedford.
Nov, 23 or 30 – Sussex v. Hants, at Worthing.

It was also decided to endeavour to arrange matches with Surrey, Middlesex and Kent to take place after Christmas. An offer from the Bradford Club to meet Sussex at Brighton in November, 1893 was accepted.

Sporting Life – Saturday 16 January 1892

UNDER RUGBY RULES
BRIGHTON v. OLD DOVORIANS

In this match, which is to be played in Preston Park, Brighton, this (Saturday) afternoon, between the Brighton Union and the old Dover College Boys' Club, the teams are announced as follows:-

BRIGHTON. – F. G. Chichester (back). F. J. Turnbell and W. E. Ellis (three-quarter backs). F. Mitchell and A.D, Green (half backs), M. F. Voules (captain). B. C. O'Dowda, H.H. Perry, E. G. H. North, A. J. Brown, H. C. Lancaster, R. P Woods, S. Stuart and R. D. Budworth.

OLD DOVORIANS. – C. B. Pike (back), W. R. Hunt, D. Fagan and H. Wood (three-quarter backs), V. B. Avery., F. Wilde (half-backs), R. W. Hunt, W. Long, J. Brown, A. Shepherd, S. B. Hulke, F. E. Gunter, R. M. Bird, P. J. James W. B. Hulke.

Kick-off at 2.45 p.m

Sussex Agricultural Express – Tuesday 20 December 1892

BRIGHTON v UPPER CLAPTON

(RUGBY) – *This match was played in Preston Park on Saturday, in the presence of a large number of spectators. The result was a victory for the visitors by one goal and two tries (nine points) to nothing. Teams:-*

BRIGHTON:- R.P Wood, back; H. H. Perry, P. C. Cox. and A. D. Green, three-quarter backs; C. H. Stewart and B. M. Lannowe, half-backs; M. F. Voules, R. D. Budworth, E. G. H. North, L. S. Richards, M. H. Beves, F. Mitchell, B. C. O Dowda. J. J. Steinitz and A. Northern (forwards).

UPPER CLAPTON. – M. P. Ladell, back: F. T. Stokes, J. C. Bond and W. J M'Ghee, three-quarter backs: D. Hughes-Morgan and F. R Lloyd. Half-backs G. Sparkes, captain; H. Greenfield, W. E. Bailey, G. B. Wickes. C. H. Wickes, T. Jones, W. Hammond, C. Helder, and G. Thompson (forwards).

I've included the above fixture because it's the only game I can find against Upper Clapton, who I may add, at this time were a top class side with fixtures against Rosslyn Park, Old Merchant Taylors, Saracens, London Hospital and Wasps etc.

The season 1891-92 saw Upper Clapton achieve amazing results ; Played 21, Won 17, Draw 2 and Lost 2. The match above was a good result by "Upper Clapton" when you consider that there were four internationals in the Brighton team ; R. D. Budworth, E. G. H. North, F. Mitchell, B. C. O Dowda.

"Upper Clapton made up the Backbone of the Eastern Counties side, hence, they would sometimes play host to 2000 spectators. (London's Oldest Rugby Clubs, Dick Tyson)

Bromley & District Times – Friday 11 March 1892

BRIGHTON v SIDCUP

A good Rugby game was played between Brighton and Sidcup at Brighton on Saturday. The home team proved too strong for their visitors, and got across their goal line three times, and had they been as successful with the place kicks Sidcup would have had a tall score against them. As it was, Sidcup, by scoring a goal, only lost by one point

Thursday 16th February 1893

BRIGHTON v EASTBOURNE

Notwithstanding the uninviting and miserable condition of the weather on Saturday last, a large gathering of spectators defied the elements to turn them off the sodden turf or deprive them of their pleasure (?) In watching the game under the Rugby Union between Brighton and Eastbourne. With the ball coated in slimy mud, and the ground sufficiently slippery to render it almost impossible to secures ones footing, accurate play was impracticable.

The Eastbourne team included some sturdy fellows, and although beaten by a goal and four tries (15 points), to nothing, they, under more favourable circumstances, would probably have given Brighton even more trouble than they did on this occasion. During the first half, Brighton gained three tries through the instrumentality of E.G.H. North, R.D. Budworth and H.H. Perry respectively, whilst after the intervening space, M.F.Voules, and F. Mitchell got behind, the latter being converted by the dashing three-quarter back, P.C. Cox, who, with Perry, was responsible for some capitol passing.

The Rev C.N. Roberts, three-quarter, was most prominent amongst the visiting team.

Brighton Gazette – Saturday 7 April 1894

PRESTON PARK RUGBY FOOTBALL CLUB

Representatives of this club attended the annual meeting of secretaries, held on Thursday at Anderton's Hotel, London, and arranged a strong list of fixtures for next season, including the following clubs, who are booked to play in Brighton:- Old Blues, West London, Saracens, Dulwick Park, Old Leysians "A", Kingston, Royal Veterinary College, Clapham Park, Croydon, St. Andrews and Eastbourne. This club hope to secure a pitch in Preston Park next season, and since games under the Rugby code seem to form the greatest attraction in the Park the Recreation Grounds Committee will no doubt see their way to grant this. The Preston Park Rugby Club is not a very long standing; neither has it as yet been very successful in its fixtures, but there is plenty of enthusiasm and perseverance amongst its governing body which can hardly fail to meet with ultimate and well-deserved success. The possession of a pitch in Preston Park would undoubtedly increase the club's popularity.

Again it is surprising that another Rugby team has established itself within Brighton. I am aware the Brighton F.C. had established a second team, the "A's" as there was a time when Brighton supported three Clubs, and maybe Brighton Football Club, was unable to run or organise three or four sides on a weekly basis..?

Brighton Gazette – Thursday 27th September 1894

BRIGHTON FOOTBALL CLUB, A.G.M.

There was a fairly good attendance at the annual meeting of the Brighton (Rugby) Football Club, held at the Imperial Hotel on Monday evening. As usual, it was presided over by that well-known patron of the Rugby Code, Mr. A. C. Borlass, and was of a harmonious and happy character. There were present besides the chairman, Messrs M. Beves, N. Beves, H. B, Burfield, F. G. Chichester, L. F. Duckworth, H. G. Giffard, G. S. Godfee, L. Homes, A. E. Smithers, F. W. Welch, H. Waugh, and R. P. Wood (hon.sec), with most of whose names the Rugby football enthusiast is no doubt familiar. The reports as to the clubs doings last season, presented by the secretary was extremely gratifying. Of 28 matches played, 16 were won, eight lost and four drawn; whilst the club scored 14 goals and 40 tries (185 points) against 11 goals and 18 tries (109 points) by their opponents. The balance sheet was not all that could be desired, but the balance on the wrong side was smaller than that of last year. The report and balance sheet were adopted.

The election of officers for the coming season resulted as follows: - President, Major-General Richards; Vice-President, Mr C. C. Bailey, Mr A. C. Borlase, Mr. J. M. Kidd, Mr G. L. King, Mr E. Knott, Mr E. A. Smithers, Mr W. Stuckey and Mr F. Tooth; Captain, Mr R. D Budworth; Hon. Secretary, Mr R. P. Wood; Hon. Treasurer, Mr E. A. Smithers; Committee, Mr M. Beves, Mr F. G. Chichester, Mr L. F. Duckworth, Mr E. H. G. North and Mr L. Holmes; and representatives on the County Committee, Mr M. Beves, Mr L. Holmes and Mr E. A. Smithers. I think it will be generally admitted these gentlemen constitute a fine body of officers, and the club is to be congratulated upon retaining the services of R. D. Budworth, who so ably captained the team last year, and also the services of R. P. Wood, than whom it would be difficult to find a more energetic and hard-working Hon. Secretary.

RUGBY FOOTBALL MATCH at the COUNTY GROUND

Teams representing Sussex and Eastern Counties respectively, meet at the Sussex County Ground, Hove, Saturday afternoon, in the presents of a fairly large number of spectators.

The following were the teams:-

SUSSEX:- J.F. Lane (Preston Park), back; F.G. Lawrence (S.W. Borderers), L.F. Duckworth, P.C. Cox (Brighton) and C. B. Fry (Blackheath), three-quarter backs ; C. Wells (Brighton) and J.E. Roberts (Preston Park), half-backs ; M.H. Beves and R.D. Budworth (Brighton), W. Falcon (Blackheath and Brighton), H.B. Jeffery (Pembroke College, Cambridge) B.F. O'Dowda (Brighton), R.B. Hayes (Old Merchant Taylors), E.M. Chrishop (Preston Park) and B.C. Hartley (Brighton) forwards

EASTERN COUNTIES:- H. B. Brandt (Harlequins), back ; R.C. Merrifield (Ipswich), J.C. Horsley (Hammersmith), R. Powell (Ipswich), G.A.G. Atterman (Saracens), three-quarter backs,; H. Cooper (Ispwich), and S.C. Norton (Ilford Wanderers), half-backs; D.P.D. Duckworth (late Oxford University), J.D. Whittaker (Harlequins), Dr Martin IChelmsford), R. Hamblin-Smith (Ipswich), R.Mills (Ipswich), A. Whitmoore (Ipswich), R.L. Whittaker (Harlequins), and W.T.A. Bears (Saracens).

The weather was fine and the ground in good condition. It soon become evident that Sussex were the more powerful set of players. The home team were almost continuously the aggressors, and only once or twice during the first half did the visitors break away. Ten minutes from the start, Wells secured a try for Sussex, but Duckworth failed in the place kick. The players had scarcely resumed operations when Roberts, smartly seizing the ball from the scrum, got behind for the home team ; the work of converting easily accomplished by Duckworth. Sussex continued to press, and Fry, who was doing admirable work for his County, obtaining possession of the ball, made a splendid dodgy run and secured a try, but O'Dowda was unsuccessful with the place kick. Cox, who was in great form, still further improved matters a few minutes later, getting behind in very smart fashion. Duckworth easily converted. Thus, at half time Sussex had a lead of 16 points to nothing. The visitors played up a little better upon the resumption, but all their attempts to score failed. Towards the end, Sussex completely out-played them, and added no fewer than 18 points. Two tries were scored by Lawrence and converted by Duckworth and Cox, and O'Dowda and Fry each got one behind, the former's try being improved upon by Cox, whose place-kicking was marked by considerable skill. The visitor's weakness was chiefly in the three-quarter back division, Powell being the only player to distinguish himself to any particular degree.

The result of a very one-sided game was :--

SUSSEX :- Five goals and three tries (34 points)
EASTERN COUNTIES :- Nil.

As you can see the above match was a very one-sided game. This may be reflective of the quality of the Brighton players in this Sussex side. Let me give you a insight into these players.

R.D. Budworth
England International 1890-91
Played for Barbarians 1891
C. Wells
Played 6 games for The Barbarians, 1894-97
W. Falcon *(Blackheath and Brighton)*
Played for England XV v Yorkshire.
Played for the Barbarians, 1894-97
B.F. O'Dowda
New Zealand International - 1901
Played three games for the Barbarians, 1898
B.C. Hartley
England International -1901-02
Played 19 matches for the Barbarians, 1900-04

30th September 1899

BRIGHTON RUGBY FOOTBALL CLUB

Last evening the annual meeting of this Club was held at the Imperial Hotel, Queens Road, Brighton. Mr A.C. Borlase presided, and ther were also present Messrs W.J. Bowe, H.P. Boughton, Lloyd, R.W. Fox, G.S. Godfree (hon.sec), H.L. Gifford, T.R. Harper, E.T. Mitchell, V. Pelton, A.V. Richardson, and T.O.Ruthven.

The Honorary Secretary submitted the annual report and balance sheet. The report stated that last season was one of the most successful in the history of the Club. Twenty-three matches were played, fifteen won, four lost and four draws. Seventeen goals and 36 tries were scored, against 6 goals and 16 tries, or 185 points to 76 by opposing teams. The general account showed a balance in hand of £21 1s 5d due to the treasurer. The enclosed receipts last year only amounted to £3 3s. Taking the two accounts together, there was a balance of 17s 1d due to the treasurer.

The Club was thus in a better position than last year, when there was a balance of £11 due, this having been paid. On the motion of Mr Ruthven, seconded by Me Gifford, the report and balance sheet were adopted.

Mr Godfree proposed the re-election of Mr A.C, Borlase as President, and, in doing so, alluded to the keen interest that the gentleman had for many years shown in the Club/Mr Ruthven seconded the motion, which was carried unanimously.

The Vice-Presidents were re-elected, with the addition of Mr R.P. Wood, Mr B. Brook, and Mr A.C. Coster, Mr P.G.H. Broadbent was re-elected captain, and Mr T.O.Ruthven was appointed vice captain in the place of Mr G.C. Morphett, who is with the 1st Sussex Regiment at Malta. The committee was constituted of the following gentlemen:- Messrs M.H. Beves, D.J. Bowe, M. Black, H.L. Gifford and T. Smith.

The Chairman moved the re-election of Mr G.S. Godfree as Hon Sec, remarking that he had proved himself a worthy successor to Mr R.P. Wood. Mr Godfree, interposing, said he would be willing to act again if he were afforded assistance. Mr Godfree was re-elected hon secretary, and Mr T.R. Harker was elected assistant hon Secretary.

Messrs Beves, Broadbent and Smithers were appointed delegates to the Sussex County Rugby Union; and the Hon Secretary reported that Mr B.Brook, the referee of the Club, had been elected member of the London rugby Union Society of referees.

The Hon Secretary presented a list of twenty five fixtures for the ensuing season, the first being against the Polytechnic at Preston Park next Saturday. A vote of thanks to the Chair concluded the meeting.

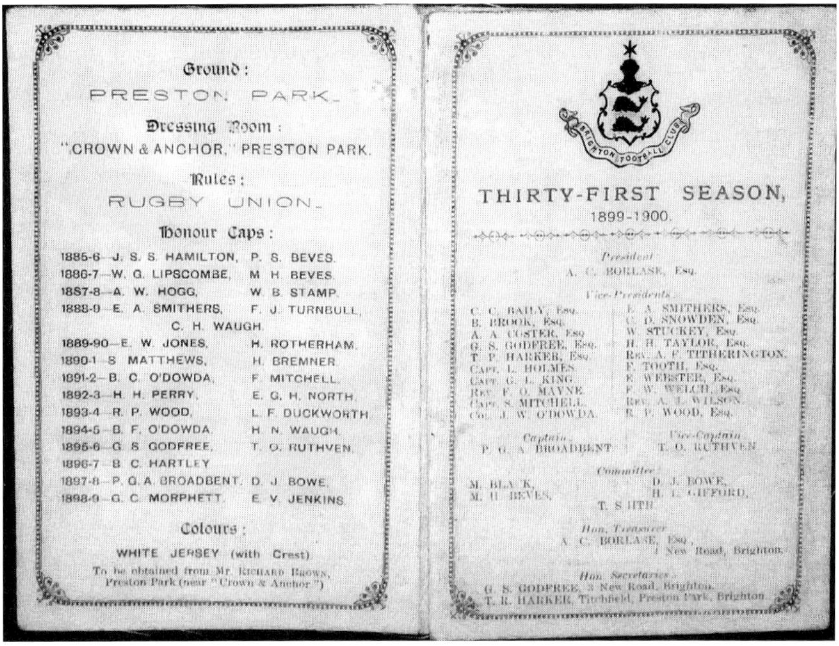

Ground:
PRESTON PARK.
Dressing Room:
"CROWN & ANCHOR," PRESTON PARK.
Rules:
RUGBY UNION.
Honour Caps:

1885-6	J. S. S. HAMILTON,	P. S. BEVES.
1886-7	W. G. LIPSCOMBE,	M. H. BEVES.
1887-8	A. W. HOGG,	W. B. STAMP.
1888-9	E. A. SMITHERS,	F. J. TURNBULL,
	C. H. WAUGH.	
1889-90	E. W. JONES,	H. ROTHERHAM.
1890-1	S. MATTHEWS,	H. BREMNER.
1891-2	B. C. O'DOWDA,	F. MITCHELL.
1892-3	H. H. PERRY,	E. G. H. NORTH.
1893-4	R. P. WOOD,	L. F. DUCKWORTH.
1894-5	B. F. O'DOWDA,	H. N. WAUGH.
1895-6	G. S. GODFREE,	T. O. RUTHVEN.
1896-7	B. C. HARTLEY.	
1897-8	P. G. A. BROADBENT,	D. J. BOWE.
1898-9	G. C. MORPHETT,	E. V. JENKINS.

Colours:
WHITE JERSEY (with Crest).
To be obtained from Mr. Richard Brown, Preston Park (near "Crown & Anchor.")

THIRTY-FIRST SEASON,
1899-1900.

President
A. C. BORLASE, Esq.

Vice-Presidents.

C. C. BAILY, Esq.	E. A. SMITHERS, Esq.
B. BROOK, Esq.	C. D. SNOWDEN, Esq.
A. A. COSTER, Esq.	W. STUCKEY, Esq.
G. S. GODFREE, Esq.	H. H. TAYLOR, Esq.
T. P. HARKER, Esq.	Rev. A. F. TITHERINGTON.
Capt. L. HOLMES.	F. TOOTH, Esq.
Capt. G. L. KING.	E. WEBSTER, Esq.
Rev. F. O. MAYNE.	F. W. WELCH, Esq.
Capt. S. MITCHELL.	Rev. A. L. WILSON.
Col. J. W. O'DOWDA.	R. P. WOOD, Esq.

Captain. P. G. A. BROADBENT
Vice-Captain. T. O. RUTHVEN

Committee.
M. BLACK, D. J. BOWE,
M. H. BEVES, H. L. GIFFORD,
T. SMITH.

Hon. Treasurer.
A. C. BORLASE, Esq., 4 New Road, Brighton.

Hon. Secretaries.
G. S. GODFREE, 3 New Road, Brighton.
T. R. HARKER, Titchfield, Preston Park, Brighton.

The earliest fixture card known 1899 - 90

Chapter VI

BRIGHTON FOOTBALL CLUB 'BARBARIANS'

I have said previously that I had no idea what I may unearth in my quest for the history of this Football Club, and so far it has been quite mind boggling and very exciting. If you can envisage that the Brighton Football Club (RFU) had absolutely no idea that any Brighton players were invited to represent the Barbarians Football Club then it would be remiss of me not to delve into the history of some prominent players. I have listed, or should I say attempted to list, all the Brighton players that were invited to adorn that famous "Barbarians" shirt. But first, a brief history of the Barbarians Football Club.

In 1889 William Percy Carpmael (Clapham Rovers, later Blackheath) organised a tour with Clapham Rovers in which the team faced five or six clubs in the Midlands and Yorkshire areas. The following year he created and toured with the "Southern Nomads" and on 8th April 1890, at Leuchter's Restaurant in Darley Street, Bradford, Carpmael took his Southern Nomads for a meal to put forward his idea of a touring rugby club. Later that night, at the Alexandra Hotel, the 'high-spirited' team agreed to Carpmael's plan and the Barbarians were formed. His idea was to create a touring team that would play the provinces in holiday times and would not only contain Englishmen but players from Scotland, Wales and Ireland.

I will endeavour to list the Brighton players in chronological order. I have painstakingly cross referenced Brighton players with the honours caps from the Barbarians Football Club, but it is unlikely to be complete.

Richard Dutton Budworth

(17 October 1867 – 7 December 1937) was an forward who played club rugby for Brighton and international rugby for England, 1890-91. In 1890 Budworth became one of the original members of the Barbarians Football Club, played five games in 1891 and one game 1892.

A very early photograph of the "Barbarians" and R.D. Budworth, top row. far right

Cyril Wells:

Played for The Barbarians, 1894 - 3 game, and 1897 - 3 games.

Cyril Wells

Eustace Herbert Guest North:

Another Brighton player who is classed as an original member of the Barbarians invitational team who played for Oxford University and England. Played three games in 1891.

Eustace Herbert Guest North. Standing middle back.
1889 Oxford Varsity Team.

W. Falcon. (Blackheath and Brighton)

Played two games in 1894, three games in 1896 and one in 1897. Played for England XV v Yorkshire, caps were not given for this game.

Frank Mitchell:

Was born in Yorkshire in 1872 and was schooled at St Peter's School in York captaining the school side at Rugby and Cricket for two years before moving to Brighton where he took up employment as a schoolmaster, I believe at Lancing College.

Frank Mitchell also won a Brighton honours cap in the 1891-92 season. The same season he became the Club's Hon. Secretary, he gained a double Cambridge Blue and was captain of Rugby and Cricket at the University. He played for England as a forward against South Africa, was on the Barbarian Committee, the Kent CCC and served as a Lieutenant in the York Dragoons. He fought at Bagshot and Shwartz Koffeafontain in South Africa, won the Queens Medal and was promoted to Lt Colonel. In his spare time he wrote a book about the game Rugby Football, in the Hamilton Library series.

Cambridge University Rugby Football Team 1894 - 95

Back Row (L-R): A.F.Todd, S.J.Lawry. 1st Row: C.Dixon, W.G.Druce, R.Griffiths, S.P.Bell, H.B.Taylor, W.Falcon. Sitting: L.E.Pilkington, F.Mitchell, W.E.Tucker (Captain), E.Field, L.B.Giblin. On Ground: W.L.Bunting, P.G.Jacob.

Not only a double blue, F. Mitchell can claim the very rare distinction of not only captaining Cambridge University Cricket Eleven but also Rugby Football Team in the same year. Educated at St Peter's School York, he had proved his ability in both games during a stay of two years at Brighton, before he went in to residence at Caius College Cambridge. His record as a Cricketer as well as a footballer during the last two years has been particularly brilliant. Selected for every English international, he has shown himself to be one of quite the best forwards of the day in Rugby Football. Very clever with his feet he dribbles well, but in addition he passes and runs with all the skill of a three-quarter. In addition he is a fine place kick.

Mitchell went on to play for Blackheath and won six caps for England between 1895 and 1896, as a forward, and was recognised as a very strong member of the pack. He also kept goal for Sussex at soccer.

Brighton Gazette 5th May 1894

Mr F. Mitchell, the Cambridge freshman, late secretary of the Brighton (Rugby) Football Club, has already done wonders with the willow this season. On Wednesday he made another centuary (136) against Selwyn for Caius. He has now made as many as 711 in seven innings, being twice not-out ; he has, therefore, the extraordinary batting average of 142. His best efforts were 203 not out, 143 not out, and 136. His career will be watched with the greatest interest by his Brighton admirers.

B.F. O'Dowda;

New Zealand International - 1901. Played three games for the Barbarians, 1898.

B.C. Hartley;

England International, 1901-02. Played 19 matches for the Barbarians, 1900-04.

Bernard Charles Hartley "Jock" played for Brighton Football Club in the mid 1890's and gained his honours cap in our 28th Season, 1896-97. He left Brighton to further his education, firstly to Dulwich, and then in 1897 Jesus College, Cambridge. At Cambridge he won three sporting "Blues" as a student, one in rugby and two in athletics for the hammer. The one "Rugby" Varsity Match was in 1900. By the time Hartley made his international debut, on 9 March 1901, he was representing Blackheath despite still being at Cambridge. His first cap for England, at Blackheath in the 1901, was a Home Nations Championship encounter against Scotland. England lost the match 18-3, but Hartley finished his international career with a win when he played his second and final match for England on 15 March 1902 at Inverleith, in a victory over Scotland. Although his international career was behind him Hartley had a long relationship with the game of rugby throughout his life. In 1900 he was offered a place in the invitational touring team, Barbarian F.C. scoring the only Barbarian try in their 3-9 loss to Newport in the 1901 Easter tour. In the 1903-1904 Barbarian tours he was made team captain and would later become Honorary Secretary of the club.

In 1907 he became Cambridge University RUFC's representative on the Rugby Football Union and in 1923-24 he was on the committee of National Selectors for the England national team. In 1938, Hartley was given the role of manager of the British Isles team for their 1938 tour of South Africa which they lost the series 2 - 1.

Bernard Hartley left of middle, bottom row

1904 Barbarians Team, Bernard Charles Hartley; Middle row, Centre

He served in the British Army, during World War I, as a Lieutenant in the Hertfordshire Regiment. Wounded in action, Hartley was employed by the War Office and rose to the rank of Major. In 1927 he was awarded the Civil Division of the Order of the British Empire and in 1947 he was awarded the Military Division of the same award. In 1947-48, Colonel Bernard Charles Hartley became the thirty ninth (39th) President of the Rugby Football Union.

John Guy Giberne Birkett;

There are many players who would warrant the title of the most famous player to have ever played for Brighton Football Club (RFU), subjective of course, but John Birkett must be up there. He was born in Richmond Surrey on 27th December 1884. The son of Lizette Crunden and Reginald Birkett. He had a older brother, Gerald Halsey Birkett (1883) who also played for Brighton, and I may add, for quite a bit longer than John, but obviously Adrian Stoop didn't see in Gerald what he saw in John.

I could not talk about J.G.G. Birkett without first mentioning, John Birkett's father, Reginald Halsey Birkett. He was an important figure in the formation of the Rugby Football Union. Reginald was the representative of Clapham Rovers, who were one of the twenty-one London and suburban football clubs that followed Rugby School rules that assembled at the Pall Mall Restaurant in Cockspur Street and formed the Rugby Football Union on 26 January 1871. He became one of the thirteen original committee members. Despite his strong ties to rugby he was known to be found playing the Association game almost as often as Rugby and indeed Clapham Rovers, the team he was a member of and captained in the 1871–72 season, steadfastly remained a "Hybrid" football club. Birkett was selected for the first ever international rugby match for England v's Scotland in 1871. In this match he scored England's first ever try, although at the time a try did not gain points, but rather was the means by which a team was granted the opportunity of converting the try into a point by kicking a goal. In 1879-80 Birkett was a member of the Clapham Rovers "Association" side who won the F.A. Cup

At this stage in Reginald's life he is still, according to the 1871 census, living with his parents in Westminster. R. Birkett gained one International Association Football cap for England in 1879 as a Goal Keeper. According to the 1881 census, Reginald B. is a hide brokers clerk, visiting the Crunden's (one of the daughters will be his wife in the near future, so he presumably was engaged to her). They lived at 5 Marlborough Place in Brighton and had four servants.

Dick Tyson in his fantastic book "London's Oldest Rugby Club's", states, "During the late '80s and early 90s Blackheath, Harlequins, Brighton and Clapham Rovers became close - often swapping players to complement each other's teams for important fixtures. And when the Clapham Rovers Rugby Football division disbanded in 1896 a number of players joined Brighton - among them the famous Birkett family. Louis Birkett, Uncle of John, also gained an International Rugby cap for England. Unfortunately, Louis like Reginald never played for Brighton. Reginald died in 1898 and at his inquest it was stated that 'Birkett' was delirious from diphtheria, and while being helped into bed he suddenly leapt through the window, falling a distance of twenty feet and smashing his skull. He died in a few moments and a verdict was returned that he committed suicide while delirious."

If you are walking past 5 Marlborough Place, (close to the "King & Queen") in Brighton, look up about twenty feet at the window, and pause for thought.

Reginald Birkett (Highlighted)

John Guy Giberne Birkett and Gerald Halsey Birkett were both pupils at Haileybury College in 1901. John furthered his education and attended the Imperial Service College.

John Birkett joined Brighton Football Club in 1903 with Gerald following a few years later. John gained a honours cap in 1904 - 05 which was also the year he was voted on as Vice Captain, and he was re-elected Vice Captain for the 1905 - 6.

It was after the Brighton v Harlequins game, in that season, that Adrian Stoop persuaded him to take part in the Harlequins F.C. trial games at Wandsworth Common. Birkett initially regarded himself as a half-back and after attending the trials, he was selected for the team.

At the time, the Harlequins' talisman Adrian Stoop was beginning to implement a change in the way in which back play was structured and which itself would become the template for how rugby union backlines are organised today. Stoop wanted to see the ball moved quickly across the three-quarters and out to the wings, for a quicker style of play.

The ball would leave the forwards, via a position Stoop termed the scrum-half, and then outward to the wings. Stoop saw in Birkett the ideal build and skills needed for a centre in this new format, and this became Birkett's position for the rest of his career. Birkett came into the England side in 1906 after England had suffered a seven match losing run.

Playing Scotland at Inverleith, Birkett took up his position at centre and with Stoop also in the side as half-back the first glimmers of the new back play was seen at international level. In this match England overcame Scotland, putting an end to their losing streak and tries were scored on both wings. Five days later in Paris, Birkett was involved in the first England-France match, again a win for England. Birkett became a regular in the England side and in 1908 captained the side to a defeat against Wales in Bristol. He lost the captaincy but kept his place and in the 1910 and 1911 Five Nations Championships he was captain on four consecutive occasions.

The 1910 championship was also one in which England became the first Five Nations champions and Birkett scored twice in the match against Scotland. During his international career he played 21 times for England and at the time of his final match in Paris he was England's record cap holder. He was also the record try scorer with ten. Ironically he never captained his club-side. However he never lost his place in the Harlequins side and was part of the generation that witnessed the move to the new Twickenham Stadium.

He played in the inaugural match on 2 October 1909 at what is now the home of English rugby. In this match he had the distinction of scoring the first try at the new stadium, echoing his father's distinction of having scored England's first ever try in 1871. I have read that John Birkett finished his playing career back at Brighton Football Club, but this has yet to be substantiated.

17th April 1915   Barbarians v Wales XV

On 17th April 1915 he played for The Barbarians v Welsh XV at Cardiff Arms Park in what was termed a "Military International" between Wales and England, designed to boost recruiting for the newly formed Welsh Guards and to raise money. Wales fielded a near International team with only one uncapped player (Dan Callan of the Royal Munster Fusiliers). The Barbarian side had 12 Englishmen , 2 Irishmen and 1 Welshman (South African International Joseph Partridge). He scored a try and the match, won by the Barbarians 26 - 10, raised £200.

In World War 1 he was a captain in the Royal Field Artilliery and was mentioned in dispatches no less than 18 times. On the 30th May 1918, he was decorated with the "Ordine della Corona d'Italia" (Order of the Crown of Italy, 5th Class, Knight),

In 1915 he married Elsie Allen and had a son John Brian who would later become a Brigadier and serve in the Second World War. John Birkett served as a captain in the Army Claims Commission for England between 1943 and 1946. He died on 16th October 1968.

Ernest Dye Galbraith Hammett;

Played one game for the Barbarians on 14th April 1922 (English International, Eight matches,1920-1922).

Ernest Dye Galbraith Hammett, at the age of 29, gained his first International Cap in 1920 against Wales in Swansea, finishing with a total of eight caps from 1920-22. Hammett joined "Brighton Football Club" in 1922 and played his first game for Brighton against the "National Provincial Bank" in October of that year. Hammett was picked for the Great Britain side that toured Argentina in July and August 1927, and played in the first three tests, but missed the last, and was the top test scorer with 40 points.

Ernest Hammett passed away in Hove in 1947.

C.D. Aavold, E.D.G. Hammett and E.G. Taylor
(cover on the Argentine magazine "El Grafico")

Gary F. Halpin ;
Played two games in 1995, and two 1996.
And scored a total of 25 points!

Chapter VII

1900 -1910

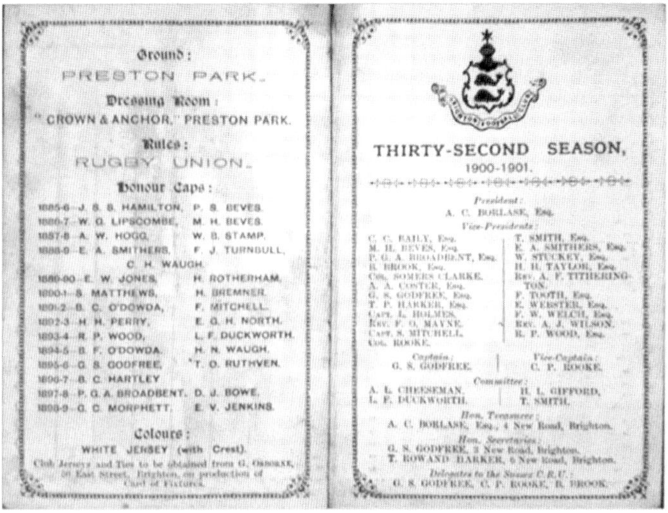

Ground:
PRESTON PARK.
Dressing Room:
"CROWN & ANCHOR," PRESTON PARK.
Rules:
RUGBY UNION.
Honour Caps:
1885-6—J. S. S. HAMILTON, P. S. BEVES.
1886-7—W. G. LIPSCOMBE, M. H. BEVES.
1887-8—A. W. HOGG, W. B. STAMP,
1888-9—E. A. SMITHERS, F. J. TURNBULL,
C. H. WAUGH.
1889-90—E. W. JONES, H. ROTHERHAM.
1890-1—S. MATTHEWS, H. BREMNER.
1891-2—B. C. O'DOWDA, F. MITCHELL.
1892-3—H. H. PERRY, E. G. H. NORTH.
1893-4—R. P. WOOD, L. F. DUCKWORTH.
1894-5—B. F. O'DOWDA, H. N. WAUGH,
1895-6—G. S. GODFREE, T. O. RUTHVEN.
1896-7—B. C. HARTLEY
1897-8—P. G. A. BROADBENT, D. J. BOWE,
1898-9—G. C. MORPHETT, E. V. JENKINS.
Colours:
WHITE JERSEY (with Crest).
Club Jerseys and Ties to be obtained from G. OSBORNE, 98 East Street, Brighton, on production of Card of Fixtures.

THIRTY-SECOND SEASON,
1900-1901.

President:
A. C. BORLASE, Esq.
Vice-Presidents:

C. C. BAILY, Esq.	T. SMITH, Esq.
M. H. BEVES, Esq.	E. A. SMITHERS, Esq.
P. G. A. BROADBENT, Esq.	W. STUCKEY, Esq.
B. BROOK, Esq.	H. H. TAYLOR, Esq.
Col. SOMERS CLARKE.	Rev. A. F. TITHERINGTON.
A. A. CONTER, Esq.	F. TOOTH, Esq.
G. S. GODFREE, Esq.	E. WEBSTER, Esq.
T. P. HARKER, Esq.	F. W. WELCH, Esq.
Capt. L. HOLMES.	Rev. A. J. WILSON.
Rev. F. O. MAYNE.	R. P. WOOD, Esq.
Capt. S. MITCHELL.	
Col. ROOKE.	

Captain: G. S. GODFREE. | Vice-Captain: C. P. ROOKE.

Committee:
A. L. CHEESEMAN. | H. L. GIFFORD,
L. F. DUCKWORTH. | T. SMITH.

Hon. Treasurer:
A. C. BORLASE, Esq., 4 New Road, Brighton.
Hon. Secretaries:
G. S. GODFREE, 3 New Road, Brighton.
T. ROWAND HARKER, 6 New Road, Brighton.
Delegates to the Sussex C.R.U.:
G. S. GODFREE, C. P. ROOKE, B. BROOK.

BRIGHTON FOOTBALL CLUB

The annual meeting of the Brighton (Rugby) Football Club was held at the Imperial Hotel, Queens Road, on Monday evening. Mr A.C. Borlase presided, and there was also present, Messrs B. Brooke, A.S. Cheesman, L.F. Duckworth, H.J. Gunn, W.G. Hooper, G. Livingstone, W.A. Newcombe, H.M. Penfold, C.P. Brooke, T.O. Ruthven, R. Sandland, F.C. Smale, T.Smith and G.S. Godfree and T.R. Harker (hon sec).

Mr T.R. Harker read the annual report which was as follows:- The past season of the Club has been one of the most unfortunate that has been experienced for some years by circumstances quite beyond our control.

At the commencement of the season ten of our best players left for service in South Africa, including G.C. Morphett (one of the most brilliant players Brighton has ever had)

D. Horsford, E.V. Evans, H.W.P. Lippert, A.V. Richardson, E.R. Willmer, H.L. Gifford, and others, and efficient substitutes not being forthcoming, the club was never able to put the same fifteen into the field for any successive matches....

This is a poignant extract from a clipping of the 1900-01 A.G.M. We have established that Brighton Football Club was formed with army volunteers and this was still the case in 1899 hence the fact that *"10 of our best players left for service in South Africa"* the Boer War. And I'm glad to say, my research tells me all 10 returned.

Post Script, The committee were further incensed by a player "Stolen" by the "London Welsh"..!

March 20th 1902

BRIGHTON FOOTBALL CLUB
VISIT OF BLACKHEATH "A"
FROM FIELD TO CONCERT ROOM.

One of the most popular fixtures of the Brighton Rugby Football Club during the season is that with Blackheath "A". It always proves an immense attraction, and the meeting of the teams at Preston Park on Saturday, as we anticipated, draw a large crowd of spectators. Blackheath had a fine team, and from the character of the exchange during the first few minutes the outlook was not very bright for the home team.

The Blackheath three-quarter-backs indulged in some very smart passing, and their dodging runs kept those in charge of the defence on the qui vive. The Brightonians, however, tackled cleverly, and in the scrummages were extremely tenacious, so that danger was for a time averted.

W.G. Hooper figured conspicuously in a strong attack subsequently made upon the Blackheath goal, but was floored just as he seemed certain to score a try. A penalty kick was awarded to the home team, but they failed to make use of it. Then the play became fast and exciting, the ball being carried from end to end. The visitors, who had slightly the best of the contest, about twenty five minutes from the start, secured a try through the instrumentality of C.A. Priday, but,

C.G. Brandram failed to convert. G.S. Godfree, A.E.Y. Trestrail, A.S. Anderson, and Hooper each made good attempts to put Brighton on equal terms, but the interval arrived with the visitors leading by three points to none. Shortly after the resumption, Anderson made a capital run for Brighton, but was collared just as he was becoming dangerous. The Brightonians pressed for some time, but were ultimately driven back and Blackheath became aggresive, with a better result, P.P. Terry getting behind and Brandram converting easily. Eight points to the bad, the home fifteen played up with great determination, and W.D. Harris managed to score a try. A keen contest, which afforded much pleasure to the spectators, terminated in a victory for the visitors by one goal and one try (eight points) to one try (three points).

PRESENTATION OF HONOURS CAPS

In the evening the visitors were invited by the Brighton Club to a "smoker" at St James's Restaurant and spent a very jolly time. The president of the Club (Mr A.C. Borlase) presided over a large company, including several old members of the Club in Colonel Somers Clarke, Lieut-Colonel Cecil Parsons, Captain Holmes and Councillor E.A. Smithers.

The PRESIDENT during the evening proposed the health of the Blackheath team, and, in acknowledging the compliment, Mr BEECHING (the captain) spoke in appreciative terms of the hearty reception they had had from the members of the Brighton Club. He concluded by proposing the health of Brighton Football Club, and Mr G.S. Godfree (Captain) suitably returned thanks on behalf of the Club.

Honours caps awarded by the committee were next presented by Mr Godfree to Messrs A.E.Y. Trestrail, A.S. Anderson and H.C. Brown.

The health of the old members was submitted by Mr Anderson and acknowledged by Colonel Somes Clarke, and the Hon Sec, (Mr W. Graham Hooper) and the "Press" were also toasted.

A capital musical programme was sustained by Mr C.L. Borisoon (piano), the Rev Cuthbert, E.T. Wills, Mr C.T.A Hankey (Cello), Mr J.B. Wilkinson, Mr E.F. Caston

(Violin solo), Mr C.E. Pocock, Mr A.S. Anderson, Mr A.E.Y. Trestrail, Mr C.C. Ward, and Mr W.J.E. Verrall. Mr C.L. Borisoon was the accompanist.

Brighton Society 3th April 1903

After having played during the afternoon a capital game with a strong team of the "Harlequins" (from London), which resulted in a draw, the Brighton Football Club gave a "Smoking Concert" last Saturday evening in the large room of the Unicorn Hotel, at which about a hundred members and friends were present.

BRIGHTON FOOTBALL CLUB

ANNUAL

Smoking Concert

WILL BE HELD AT THE . . .

UNICORN HOTEL, NORTH STREET,

BRIGHTON, on

Saturday, April 4th, 1903.

At 7.45.

Chairman - THE PRESIDENT (A. C. BORLASE, Esq.) 159 1/-

Mr A.C. Borlase presided, and among those present were Mr A. Stewart Anderson (the Captain of the Brighton Club), Mr W. Graham Hooper (honorary secretary), Mr G.S. Godfree, Mr C.L.Borissow, Mr C.O. Ward, Mr A.E.Y. Trestrail, Mr Crowder, Dr Liebstein, Mr Carmichael, Mr D.F.S. Smith, Mr W.J.E. Verrall, Mr George Cole, and many others, including the majority of the "Harlequins" fifteen, who were making a weekend visit to Brighton, and appeared to be in capitol spirits after the afternoon battle.

In the course of the evening three "Caps of Honour" were presented by the captain to Messrs H.T. Oliver, G.C. Roff, and A.B. Wrey for their good play during the past season, and each recipient made a speech in reply, and was greeted with great shouting. Later, a still wilder demonstration took place when "The Health of the Captain" was honoured, the whole company standing, most of them on chairs and the remainder on tables, and all singing and shouting. Mr Anderson deserves all his popularity, for he has made an excellent captain, and has also been invaluable as a place kicker ; and the pleasent speech in which Mr Godfree proposed the toast, winding up with presenting the captain with a case of pipes from the members, did not contain a word of praise that was too high. The Captains reply was short and modest, and excited a renewal of the demo.

The Chairman proposed "The Health of the Harlequins", welcoming them that evening as an old and honoured London Club that had in the past possessed members whose names were "household words" in the football world, such for example as A.E. Stoddart and C.M. Wells ; and again "the air was laid with sound" Mr A.C.T. Veasey responded, and in the course of an amusing speech expressed the emphatic opinion that Brighton was the Queen of Watering places and that of all the clubs the "Harlequins" had ever met the Brighton Football Club contained the most agreeable men and the best players --- declarations which were, of course received with great applause. "The Health of Mr Graham Hooper" was proposed by the same gentleman and "honoured" by the Harlequins" with enormous vocal energy ; and in response to the toast of "The Brighton Club", which had been proposed by one of the visitors, Mr Borlase said "he had greatly admired the form shown by the team this afternoon, and hoped often in the future to see them play as well"

It should be added that the record of the Club for the past season, as read out by the Captain, was as follows:-- They have played 21 matches, of which they had won 14, drawn 3, and lost only 4 ; and they had scored 54 goals and 35 tries (373 points) against 10 goals and 20 tries (100 points) by their opponents.

The record was as Mr Anderson said, one of which they had every reason to be proud.

The musical part of the evening was worthy of the occasion, through the excitement in the air rendered it rather difficult for either vocalist or pianists to do themselves justice.

Mr Borrissow set the ball rolling with a pianoforte solo, a selection of popular airs, which were promptly taken up by the audience and warbled ; Mr C.O. Ward sang a couple of songs ; Mr Trestrail and Mr Anderson gave a comic duet from "The French Maid" ; Mr W.J. Steers sang a couple of comic songs ; Mr D.F.S. Smith, Mr W.J,E. Verrall, and Mr H. Parker also contributed. The proceedings terminated shortly before Eleven with the singing by all of "Auld Lang Syne" and "God Save The King"

Evening Argus, 5th December 1903

Mr H.T. Olliver, who recently succeeded that sterling player, Mr A.S. Anderson, as Captain of the Brighton Football Club, may be warmly and deservedly congratulated upon the successes the team have achieved under his command, in the last three matches

In the first match, in which he acted as "skipper", Brighton defeated Charing Cross Hospital by 59 points to none, in the second, Brighton scored six points to four, registered by Westminster Hospital; and on Saturday his team realised 28 points to nothing against University College Hospital ---- the three matches giving an aggregate of 92 points, scored by Brighton, against four by their opponents.

The above advertisment came from the Brighton Gazette 1901,

In Messrs W.L.A. Lennard, J.G.G. Birkett, and C.F. Nanson the team have a fine trio of recruits, and the old players are, at present, on the top of their best form.

The Oxford University Rugby team are spending a few days in Brighton, training for their match with Cambridge University, at Queen's Club, Kensington, tomorrow. The Brighton Football Club courteously made arrangements for the Dark Blues to use their ground at Preston Park on Friday and Saturday, and will assist them this afternoon in a final practice on the same ground".

From what I can ascertain from the fixture cards, the Headquarters of Brighton Football Club was at the "Crown & Anchor", Preston Road from 1891 to 1939.

The earliest photograph taken outside the "Crown & Anchor" 1905-06

Charles William Alcock

The Fixture Card for 1903-04 caught my eye when I saw "C.W. Allcock" as a Vice President!

"The" Mr Alcock, the man who's "Football Annuals" from 1868 kept myself and many others at the Twickenham Rugby Museum, reference library, occupied for hours on end.

So who was Mr Charles William Alcock?. If you are a sportsman with a passion for either Cricket, Football or Rugby, then please read about this great man.

"Described by the official historian of the Football Association as 'the forgotten father of English sport', Charles William Alcock was arguably the central pillar of London's sporting establishment in the fourth quarter of the 19th Century. Surprisingly, this pioneering sports administrator and journalist qualifies as a Mackem having been born at 10 Norfolk Street, Sunderland, on 2 December 1842.

The son of a ship owner, the Alcock family had moved a few streets to 17 John Street by the time of the 1851 census.

In 1855, Charles followed his elder brother John to Harrow School where both developed a passion for football. On leaving school, together they formed the Forest Club in Epping in 1859.

By 1861, the entire Alcock family had moved south, taking up residence in Essex. Now described in the census as shipbrokers, John and Charles, were near neighbours of the Kings Head Inn in Chingford and lived in a house called 'Sunnyside'. Whether the house name was chosen as a reminder of the family's roots in Sunderland's Sunniside district, or a was remarkable coincidence is, for the moment, unknown.

1863 was an eventful year for the two brothers. John attended the inaugural meeting of the Football Association at the Freemasons Tavern in Great Queen Street, London, while Charles took the lead in founding the Wanderers which made its home at the Oval and supplanted Forest as the leading Old Harrovian football club.

Charles was elected to the FA committee in 1866, aged 23. He became secretary in 1870 – a position he held for twenty-five years. Almost immediately, he was involved in organizing the first unofficial international football match between England and a 'Scotland' team made up largely of ex-public school Scots living in London. The match, which ended 1-1, was played at the Oval on 5 March 1870.

By 1871, now married with a son and two daughters and declaring himself to be a journalist in the census, Charles had made his home in Rosendale Road, Norwood in a house possibly called 'Grassendale'

For the 1871-72 season, and drawing in part on his experience of the 'Cock House' inter-house knock-out competition at Harrow, he devised the FA Cup as a competition open to all football clubs. Not content with simply organising the tournament, he also captained the Wanderers team that won the inaugural final – also played at the Oval – on 16 March 1872. (Wanderers went on to win the Cup five times between 1872 and 1878.)

At the same time that he was pioneering the FA Cup and international football, Alcock also became the first paid secretary of Surrey County Cricket Club. Appointed in 1872, he held this post for the rest of his life.

Known to have played rugby for Blackheath – then one of the leading proponents of alternative form of football – with his influence at Surrey, he may well have been involved in the staging of the second rugby international in history: England's first ever home match was played at the Oval on 5 February 1872.

Back on the football field, Alcock refereed the first official football international – a nil-nil draw between Scotland and England played on 30 November 1872 at the West of Scotland Cricket Club near Glasgow. He also fostered relations with the longer-established Sheffield Football Association, paving the way for the eventual adoption of a common rulebook.

As well as becoming the first president of the Referees Association, Alcock also managed to find the time to serve as president of the Surrey FA, vice-president of the London FA, chairman of the Richmond Athletic Association and vice-president of Royal Mid-Surrey Golf Club.

At Surrey, Alcock assumed responsibility for arranging the first cricket test in England: England verses Australia match played at the Oval in 1880. Two years later, the Australian demolition of England that gave birth to the Ashes legend also took place on Alcock's watch.

Alcock was living at 36 Somerleyton Road, Brixton when, in 1881, he was granted a testimonial by the FA Committee 'in consideration of his having been the founder of the Association game'.

As football grew in popularity, tensions arose between the ex-public school amateurs who dominated the Football Association and clubs mainly from the Midlands and the North who were calling for a more professional approach to the organisation of the game. With his cricketing experience of managing relations between 'gentlemen' and 'players', Alcock helped to prevent football splitting in the way rugby eventually divided into union and league. However, the 2005 Burns report on the governance of the FA confirms that some of these tensions continue to exist to this day.

By 1891, Alcock, his wife, four daughters and three domestic servants had moved to Heathlands in Kew Road, Richmond. (His son had died as an infant.)

Thanks to Alcock, most of the big FA fixtures came to the Oval up to 1895. Improvements funded by these revenues helped secure the ground's status as a test venue. Surrey were also successful on the cricket field under Alcock's stewardship, winning eight county championships between 1887 and 1895.

In addition to his multiple roles in sports administration, he was also a prolific and ground-breaking sports journalist and publisher. In his twenties, he wrote for The Field and The Sportsman before founding specialist magazines such as the Football Annual, Football magazine and 'Cricket'. Alcock's books included Football; the association game (1890) and Surrey Cricket; its history and associations (1902).

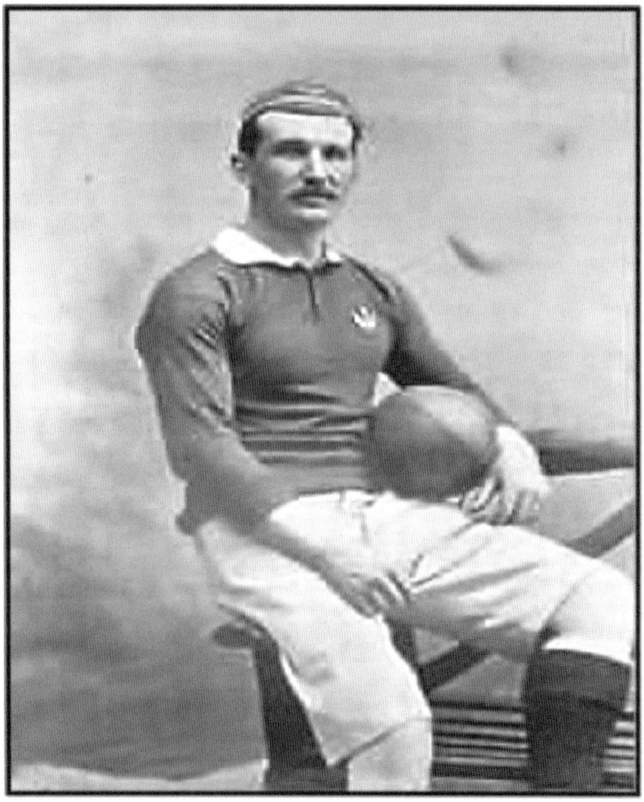

Charles William Alcock

Charles William Alcock lived at 7 Arundel Place, Brighton until his death, aged 64, on 26th February1907.

FOOTBALL RUGBY

Yesterday's results

The International Match

Victory to Brighton F.C.

1903

The international match yesterday in Saint-Cloud between Brighton Football Club and Stade Francais was not brilliant. We could expect much better from this meeting, which brought together two excellent teams that have long proven their worth.

It must be admitted that Stade Francais was, yesterday, much inferior to its reputation, and regret that this team did not play against Brighton FC just as it had done in its last matches against the Bordelais and The Racingman. Apart from a few players, who alone have led almost the entire game, it would be difficult to relight the Stadist's line. The front line, even, the previously reputed famous front line, seemed to me yesterday disunited, and especially little disposed to work seriously.

I want to admit that the English team was not the first to come, but at home and in full, the Stade Francais should have triumphed easily, instead was beaten by 3 points to nothing.

An unfortunate incident marked this meeting. The spectators, composed mostly of friends of the Stadist's, thought it their duty to spit at the referee, Mr. Brook, who had come especially, not to be spat at, but to arbitrate the game. We even asked the blue and red to leave the field. It is a very bad thing, unworthy of real sportsmen; if the referee is not happy, for any reason whatsoever, it is easy to deprive himself of his services in the future, without encouraging a team to be missed by all the laws of politeness in abandoning the party.

I do not think that Mr. Brock was biased to the point of not blaming them so harshly; I prefer to think that in England the referee enjoys only a moderate reputation. That said, let's go to some details about the game.

The Half-Day Promenade

Remarkably and remarkably well, the match starts exactly at the time indicated. This is a good achievement at S.F. The kickoff went to the Parisians, and immediately the SF threatened the opposing goal; by a few kicks Brighton clears, and the game is confined to the 50 meters.

On a pass set up by Brighton, S. Cagninacci intercepts very skillful, but the ball, fat, escapes and falls from him. The English, who excel in the foot work, constantly move the game, and after a few well-managed dribbling came back near Parisian's goals.

In a penalty, Brighton nearly missed a goal; very well served by their halves, the ball is very often with the English who, despite their efforts, cannot keep it, as their men are marked by three quarters of opponents. Bruneau, very nice player, saves several times Paris goals; Forsyth tries in turn a few chances but with no appreciable result. Once when the ball came out of a melee, on the side of the Parisians, resulted in a three-quarter pass on pass was intercepted at the very moment it was going to succeed. Poirier passing his ball to an opposing team. Half time whistle was blown.

Recovery

The recovery, the front row of the Stads give a vigorous rucking, which brought them progressively closer to the English goals. The dribblings begin again, and as the English are excellent, they are quickly released.

Bruneau, in possession of the ball, charges and would have score but he falls three meters from goal.

It takes a free kick at Brighton F.C. to clear, and the game is in the middle of the field. On a nice kick from Cagninacci, who followed his ball in well, the Brighton responded quickly and it is he who marks the test; the goal is not successful. This result has the advantage of encouraging the S.F. to work seriously, Bruneau, Forsyth and Neurisses struggling terribly, and it is not their fault if the effort does not result in much.

On the other occasion, Bruneau escapes, but cannot succeed. Another escaped from Forsyth, who passes at Santos Cagninacci, we thought might be a successful attempt, but an unfortunate one forward to Forsyth was whistled. The S.F. is not happy neither are the supporters, who challenged the referee's whistle, but he does not seem to care.

The faults now multiply, the game is tightening more and becoming less and less beautiful.

Nothing else remains of interest before the whistled end. The Brighton F.C. work done by 3 points to nothing.

The teams were composed:

B.F.C. - Arrieres: T. Schmity; three-quarters: W. G. Hooper, J. J. Gardiner, G. S. Golfree, L. A. Goldfree; semis. J.G.G. Birkett, W.L.A. Lennard; avante; H. T. Oliver (Cape), T. W. Ruthven, C. F. Nanson, H. C. Lycell, H. E. Ward, R. T. Holmes, W. J. Borlase, J. E. Whittall.

S.F. - Back: Mr. B. Mulligan; three quarters: M. Bruneau, S. Forsyth, Neurisse, S. Cagninacci; half: B. Galichon, C. Luherre; fronts: J. Muir (Cape), Ch. Beaurin, J. Tolson, P. Gaudermen, S.A. Verges, G. Jerome,

When I approached Stade Francais regarding this game, I was meet with a dismissive but courteous reply, as I am sure they receive letters like mine on a regular basis. However when I produced the above photograph (this photograph is/was unknown in the World of Rugby) everything changed and I was directed towards Frederick Humbert, a author and a great authority on French rugby, who informed me that the majority of records at Stade Francais (pre 1905) have unfortunately been lost in a fire. The Club had no idea that this and the previous game in 1902, (Brighton Football Club lost nine points to three) ever took place. In fact they had no idea that players from both sides of this game would again face each other in Paris, in what was the first France v England International in 22nd March 1906.

Saturday 24 September 1904

BRIGHTON RUGBY CLUB

The Brighton Rugby Club have arranged an attractive programme for the season. The matches in the following list, with a few exceptions, will be played at Preston Park:- October 1st, Old Whitgiftians; 8th, Civil Service; 18th, Surbiton; 22nd, Streatham; 28th, Guilford. November 5th, Kingston; 20th, Charing Cross Hospital. December 3rd, Westminster Hospital; 10th, University College Hospital; 17th Tunbridge Wells, at Tunbridge Wells; 31st, Saracens. – 1905: January 7th, Hong Kong and Shanghai Bank; 14th, Ilford Wanderers; 21st, Upper Clapton; 28th, Hammersmith. February 4th, Christ's Hospital, at Horsham; 11th Tunbridge Wells; 18th, United Services, at Portsmouth; 25th Harlequins "A". March 4th, Sutton; 11th. Haileybury Wanderers; 18th, Roslyn Park "A"; 25th, Blackheath "A".

At the annual meeting, held on Wednesday evening at the Imperial Hotel, Mr A. C. Borlase presiding, Mr G. S. Godfree, hon. Treasurer, presented a balance-sheet, which showed a deficit of £9 2s 9d. Special efforts are to be made to secure more subscribers. Mr Leonard Holmes was reappointed President of the club, and the vice presidents were re-elected with the addition of presidents were re-elected, with the addition of Mr H. T. Olliver and Mr. G. W. Millard. Mr T. O. Ruthven will captain the fifteen, Mr J.G.G. Birkett being vice-captain, Mr W. G. Hooper, hon. Secretary and Mr. G. B. Godfree hon. Treasurer.

At this A.G.M. Mr John Guy Giberne Birkett became the Vice Captain and the following season 1905-06 was re-elected. Following the success of the two games against Stade Francais, a letter was sent to the "Racing Club" enquiring into whether a fixture was possible, and the reply is below. It was decided at this A.G.M. that John Birkett, along with others, would form a sub-committee to arrange the proposed match with the "Racing Club" (Paris) in Brighton.

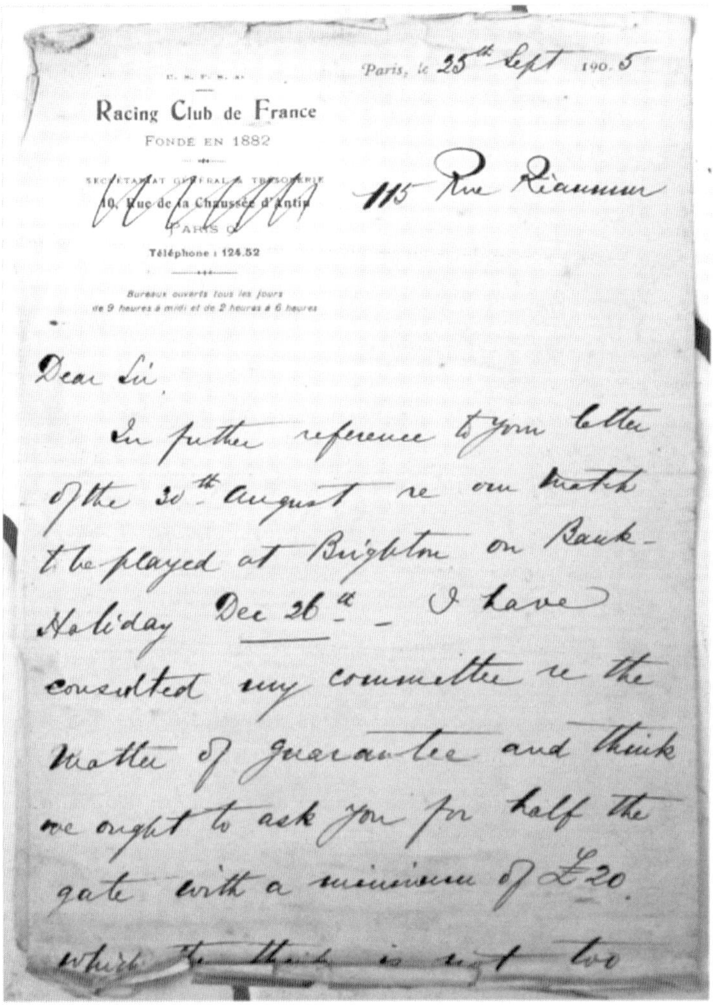

Paris, le 25th Sept 1905

U. S. F. S. A.

Racing Club de France

Fondé en 1882

Secrétariat général & trésorerie

10, Rue de la Chaussée d'Antin

Paris 9e

Téléphone : 124.52

Bureaux ouverts tous les jours de 9 heures à midi et de 2 heures à 6 heures

115 Rue Réaumur

Dear Sir,

In further reference to your letter of the 30th August re our match to be played at Brighton on Bank-Holiday Dec 26th – I have consulted my committee re the matter of guarantee and think we ought to ask you for half the gate with a minimum of £20. which we think is not too

A full transcription of the letter is as follows; (and you may notice Mr C.W. Alcock gets a mention).

Dear Sir

In further reference to your letter of the 30th August, re our Match to be played at Brighton on Bank Holiday Dec 26th. I have consulted my committee re the matter of guarantee and think we ought to ask you for half of the gate with a minimum of £20, which they think is not too much to ask. I think if you take the Sussex County Cricket Ground you would get a good crowd, being a Bank Holiday and believe our Club is getting pretty well known now in England.

I might mention that the last time we visited England viz; the year before last to Northampton & Bedford, they had 10,000 spectators at Northampton & 7,500 at Bedford, (and it was not a holiday at Bedford).

The great thing of course is that the match is well advertised. C.W. Alcock of Arundel Road, Brighton, whom I know pretty well & often correspond with could I believe help you in this matter, as I believe he is corespondant for one or two papers, as he always writes to me to know about our matches.

Capt Southwell, Fitz Gerald would also advertise in the "Sporting Life" for you as he is their corespondant for Rugby this Winter

Believe me
Yours truly
Cyril F Ruthford

ps Your last card dated 23rd Sept, has just come to land after I had written this letter

Unfortunately my research leads me to believe that this game never took place, even though letters were sent to the "Greyhound Stadium" and there is a letter in the archives of Brighton & Hove Albion asking to use the "Goldstone Ground" and according to Fredrick Humbert a letter exists in the minutes of the 'Rugby Football Union' regarding the financial requirements of the 'Racing Club'.

Thursday 11 April 1907

CLOSING MATCH AT PRESTON PARK

The Brighton Rugby Club on Saturday met the Harlequins team at Preston Park and brought a memorable season to an end with a rather ignominious defeat. The visitors played a forceful game, and from the outset it was seen that they were the stronger team. Brighton, however, was the first to score, Wheeler getting behind for Brighton, the try being converted by Gardiner. This seemed to spur the Harlequins to further efforts, and before the local men could gather themselves together after their brief success. Lambert had rushed through and scored a try, which he converted, and this equalised. This was the forerunner of a long succession of goals. At half-time the score stood at 23 points to 5 in favour of the visitors. As in the first half, Brighton also opened the score in the second venture. Sage touching down, though Gardner failed to convert. Then the Harlequins started again, and when the final whistle went the scores stood at: Harlequins, 11 goals, 3 tries (64 points); Brighton, 1 goal, 1 try (8 points),

After the match, the Rugby Club sat down to dinner at Booth's Restaurant, East Street, when Mr A. C. Borlase presided.

After the Chairman had submitted the loyal toast, Mr G. Cole gave "The Brighton Rugby Club." in the course of which he congratulated the club on the true sportsmanlike spirit and harmonious feeling which animated the members. Continuing, he said that they had been heavily handicapped by the loss of some of their best players and for this reason the past season had not been one of the most successful they had experienced. But he hoped, in conclusion, they would have much greater success and prosperity.

Replying, Mr J. J. Gardiner said that the scoring records of the club during the season did not adequately represent their performances, for several of their matches had only been lost by very narrow margins, while they had beaten such strong teams as the London Scottish and the Wasps.

In his concluding remarks Mr Gardiner said that honour caps were awarded to Mr J. C. Medhurst and Mr J. Nathan.

"The Hon. Sec" was given by Mr H. T. Oliver and Mr W. Graham Hooper briefly responding. In the course of his remarks he said that the past season, with one exception, was the most unsuccessful they had experienced for a long time. They played 18 matches, of which 7 were won and 11 lost, and had scored 140 points to their opponents 250.

"The Chairman" and "The Press" were also toasted and this brought an enjoyable evening to a close.

It's rather amusing, and somewhat "tongue in cheek", that Mr G. Cole, during his speech alludes to the fact that Brighton have been *"heavily handicapped by the loss of some of their best players"* with the legend himself J.G.G. Birkett leaving to join Harlequins a few years previous. This move to Harlequins undoubtedly earned John Birkett, with almost immediate effect, his first England Cap.

Saturday 03 April 1909

ENGLISH v FRENCH AT RUGBY

The Easter arrangements at Brighton include a Rugby match between the Brighton Club and the Rugby Club Compiegnois. This will be played at Preston Park on Easter Saturday, the kick off being at 4pm. The French team come from Compiegne, a town of about 16,000 inhabitants, situated about eighty miles North-East of Paris.

It is principally composed of old players of the College of Compiegne, and is recognised as a first class team in France. This year they have had a most successful season; having played 18 matches, of which 14 have been one won and two drawn, and they have scored 358 points against 60. Among the Clubs which they have played this year have been Havre Athletic Club, with whom they drew at Compiegne, and whom they beat at Havre by eight points three. They have also drawn with the Sporting Club Universitaire de France, a well known Paris Club. They have also easily beaten the Olympic Lillois (Champions of the North) and the Racing Club de Reims (Champions of Compagne); also the Association Sportive Francais.

In addition they have been champions of Picardy, for three years in succession. Their colours are Navy Blue with vertical Red banding, black knickers, Blue stocking with Red tops. The team that will visit Brighton, is as follows: Full back, Sauvageom; three-quarters, Chetclat, Daert, Seves (Captain), L. Godart; half-backs, Granier, J.Godart; forwards, Boutonnet, Havy, Felabre, Moulinet, Delachapelle, Bomeil, Jouve, and Molaye ; reserves, Coutte (half-back), Huches, Boudoin and Verval (forwards). The match will be proceeded by the boys' match between boys of Elm-Grove School (Reds v Blues), the kick off being at 3pm. A great deal of interest is being taken in the French match, and arrangements have been made for special trains from various parts of the County.

You may not be aware that 'The Glade of the Armistice' in the Compiègne Forest was the site of the signing of two armistices; those of 11th November 1918 and 22nd June 1940. Hitler specifically chose the location of the second, and had the original signing carriage moved from Paris to Compiègne, as an irony for the defeated French.

Chapter VIII

A Poignant Decade
1910 - 1919

As this was such a poignant decade I came across a limited number of fixtures in 1910-1912.

We played local sides, Eastbourne, Hastings and Worthing however, fixtures against London sides were few and far between.

In the season of 1912-1913 one fixture was reported where Brighton were trounced by Eastbourne, 38points to 0...!. The clipping went on to say, "was due to Brighton's depleted team”. So I can only envisage the depletion of the team was due to the numerous reservists that played for Brighton. As I explained earlier was initially made up of Army reservists from Sussex Artillery and Sussex Rifles Volunteers.

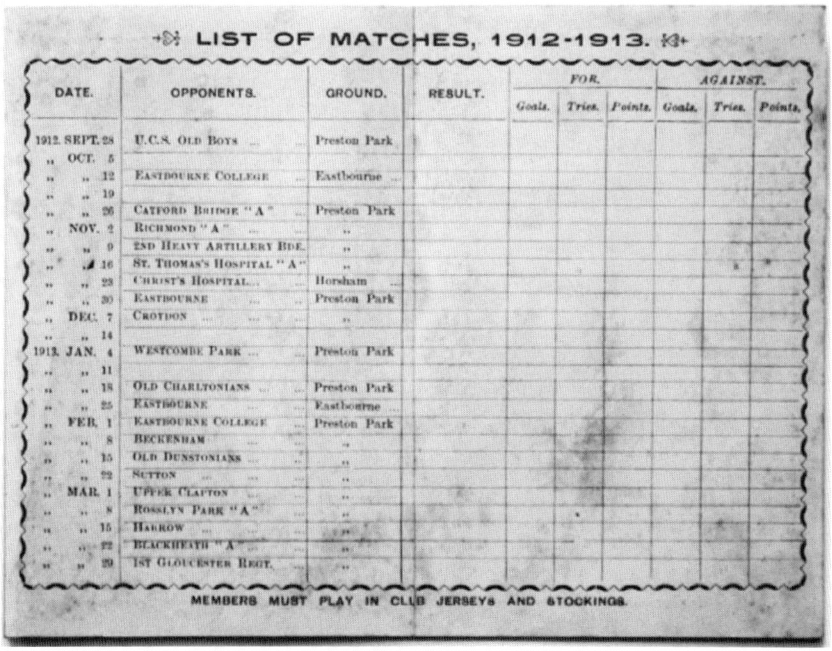

LIST OF MATCHES, 1912-1913.

DATE.	OPPONENTS.	GROUND.	RESULT.	FOR.			AGAINST.		
				Goals.	Tries.	Points.	Goals.	Tries.	Points.
1912. SEPT. 28	U.C.S. OLD BOYS	Preston Park							
„ OCT. 5									
„ „ 12	EASTBOURNE COLLEGE	Eastbourne							
„ „ 19									
„ „ 26	CATFORD BRIDGE "A"	Preston Park							
„ NOV. 2	RICHMOND "A"	„							
„ „ 9	2ND HEAVY ARTILLERY BDE.	„							
„ „ 16	ST. THOMAS'S HOSPITAL "A"	„							
„ „ 23	CHRIST'S HOSPITAL	Horsham							
„ „ 30	EASTBOURNE	Preston Park							
„ DEC. 7	CROYDON	„							
„ „ 14									
1913. JAN. 4	WESTCOMBE PARK	Preston Park							
„ „ 11									
„ „ 18	OLD CHARLTONIANS	Preston Park							
„ „ 25	EASTBOURNE	Eastbourne							
„ FEB. 1	EASTBOURNE COLLEGE	Preston Park							
„ „ 8	BECKENHAM	„							
„ „ 15	OLD DUNSTONIANS	„							
„ „ 22	SUTTON	„							
„ MAR. 1	UPPER CLAPTON	„							
„ „ 8	ROSSLYN PARK "A"	„							
„ „ 15	HARROW	„							
„ „ 22	BLACKHEATH "A"	„							
„ „ 29	1ST GLOUCESTER REGT.	„							

MEMBERS MUST PLAY IN CLUB JERSEYS AND STOCKINGS.

1912 - 1913, fixture card

Sat. Dec. 19th 1914

Official Programme. **Price One Penny.**

GOLDSTONE GROUND HOVE.

Great Rugby Match

— IN AID OF —

"NORTH SEA FLEET"

Under the Patronage of

Lady Jellicoe and General Sir J. Ramsay.

Shoreham Camp v. Barbarians (Service Team)

BARBARIANS (Black & White.)

FULL BACK.

J.L. Urquhart

[illegible] (Yorkshire).

THREE-QUARTER BACKS.

LIEUT. G. G. ZIEGLER, [illegible] (Cambridge), [illegible], LIEUT. G. A. VAUGHAN

HALF-BACKS.

*PTE. H. COVERDALE (Blackheath and England). PTE. L. R. BROSTER (Guy's Hospital and Oxford).

FORWARDS.

*LIEUT. M. C. HARRISON (United Service and England). LIEUT. J. B. BOSHER (Rosslyn Park). *CORPL. IAN PENDER (London Scottish & Scotland). [illegible] (Leicester).

PTE. M. P. ATKINSON (London Hospital). [illegible] (Guy's Hospital). PTE. G. KIDMAN (Guy's Hospital). PTE. G. HOPKINS (Leicester).

T. M. E. Baillie

KICK-OFF 2.30 P.M.

FORWARDS.

PTE. E. W. MANN (Northampton). [illegible] (Northampton). CPL. J. H. MARTYN (Rosslyn Park). CPL. [illegible] (Northampton). J. Brooks

CPL. L. SKIMPTON (Northampton). CPL. L. DUDBRIDGE (Stroud). LIEUT. H. GRIERSON (Rosslyn Park). CPL. J. J. LAWSON (Gloucester).

HALF-BACKS.

Corpl. M. G. Davies

CPL. H. WILLETT (East Midlands). LIEUT. B. H. HOLLOWAY (Cambridge University).

THREE-QUARTER BACKS.

PTE. J. GILLHAM (Bedford). LIEUT. C. H. MARTYN (East Midlands). *LIEUT. E. R. MOBBS (Capt.) (Northampton and England). CORPL. E. G. BUTCHER (Devonshire).

BACK.

LIEUT. R. GURNEY (Bedford).

SHOREHAM CAMP (Blue and White)

* INTERNATIONALS

(P.T.O.

The above programme was passed to me by Julie Searle with the compliments of 'Shoreham Fort', (which is well worth a visit), and unfortunately after searching many newspapers I can only conclude this information may have been restricted, as I could find nothing additional

The organiser of the above match and Captain of the 'Shoreham Camp' team was Edgar Mobbs, who organised a number of Barbarian matches in 1914 as part of his morale boosting/training campaign.

Edgar Mobbs

The outbreak of war in 1914 found him as manager of the Pytchley Auto Car Company at Market Harborough, having followed his father into the motor industry. He was then contemplating emigration to Canada. When he attempted to enlist in August of that year Mobbs was initially refused a commission as, at thirty three, he was over the mandated age limit.

Not a man to allow a trifling matter like this to get in his way, he joined up as a private soldier and raised his own unit of 264 men as 'D' Company, 7th Battalion, Northamptonshire Regiment. 'D' Company included many Rugby players, including E R Butcher, captain of Devon, and H Willett, captain of Bedford.

Wounded and at home

Mobbs arrived in France in September 1915, and took part in the Battle of Loos. In March 1916 he was promoted to Major and in April 1916 took over command of the 7th Northants, later being promoted to Lieutenant Colonel.

He was wounded by shrapnel in August 1916 while taking part in an attack on Guillemont during the Battle of the Somme.

After two Mentions in Despatches in 1916, Mobbs was awarded a DSO in December 1916 for his work as a Battalion Commander. The 7th Northants suffered severe casualties during the Battle of Arras in April 1917. He was wounded at Messines on 7 June 1917, but returned to the Battalion on 26 June.

On 29 July 1917 while in his headquarters in Canada Street tunnels near Zillebeke, Edgar, hearing of the loss of officers from the walking wounded, decided to lead the Battalion from the front. He moved to Shrewsbury Forest and was killed in action on 31st July at Lower Star Post while attempting to bomb a machine gun that had trapped a detachment of his Battalion. The Battalion history says 'The fact that his body could not be recovered and buried, as all ranks would have wished, was perhaps a good thing, as it helped keep alive his memory in the Battalion, and inspired in everyone the resolve to avenge his death and to end the war that had already caused so much misery and suffering'. It is reported that of the 400 or more volunteers that served in 'Mobbs Own' Company, only 85 survived the War. On 10th February 1921 the first Edgar Mobbs Memorial Match was played at Franklins Gardens, Northampton between two of the great rugby loves in his life, East Midlands and the Barbarians. This memorial match was an annual fixture at Northampton, but in 2007 was transferred to Goldington Road, Bedford. In 2012 it was agreed that the match will now be played alternate years at Northampton and Bedford and for the 2013/14 season it will be played at Northampton.

With kind permission of Olney & District Historical Society

A poignant extract from the minutes of Annual General Meeting September 1919

"After a lapse of five years owing to the war, the members of Brighton Football Club (RFU) held a General Meeting at the Royal Albion Hotel.

The Balance Sheet for 1914-15 was submitted by the Hon Treasurer (Mr E. M. Taylor) who reported that in 1915 the club had a balance in hand of £10 11s 10d., and the then committee decided that £5 should be devoted towards the buying of Rugby balls for the troops in France.

The Chairman observed that the Committee thought the better course would not to send the footballs to any particular regiment at the Front, but to forward them through a London centre.

The Chairman also mentioned that within six months of the outbreak of War 15 members of the club went to the Front, and of that number, five had made the supreme sacrifice. They were Messrs

P.W.Johnson (their Captain), W.F.Keay (the Vice Captain), M.Brewer, L.Colbourne, and Rhys-Evans --- all good sportsman who nobly answered the call and whose loss they deeply deplored"

A British First World War poster encouraging Athletics to follow the example of rugby players and enlist in the armed forces.

The Obituaries of P.W. Johnson & Wilfred Farrar Keay

Dorking and Leatherhead Advertiser – Saturday 29 May 1915

"Second Lieutenant P. W. Johnson, 3rd the Queen's (Royal West Surrey) Regiment, who was killed on May 19th, at Richebourg, was the second son of Mr. and Mrs. W. B. Johnson of The Maples, Orpington, formerly of Blackheath. He was educated at the City of London School, and was captain of the Brighton Rugby Football team. He enlisted in the ranks of the Royal West Kent Regiment in September last, and in December was gazetted to the Special Reserve of the Queen's. He went to the front in January last".

Sussex Agricultural Express – Friday 06 October 1916

Lieutenant Wilfred Farrar Keay. King's Own Yorkshire Light Infantry, youngest son of Alderman Amd Mrs. H. W. Keay, of Elms Meade, Eastbourne, was killed on September 16th. He was educated at Eastbourne College, and took up an appointment in the Inland Revenue Land Valuation Department. He received his commission in November 1914, and was promoted lieutenant and adjutant, in May last. He had had 12 months service in France and was present at the battle of Loos. He played Rugby both for his College and for the Brighton Rugby Football Club, and obtained his county cap. He was born in 1888 and married last September. Ethel, daughter of Mrs Leason and the late Thomas Leason of Red House, Redditch.

1920-1925

"Sussex Daily" Sept 1920

BRIGHTON RUGBY CLUB

52nd ANNUAL MEETING

The 52nd annual general meeting of Brighton Rugby Football Club, was held yesterday evening at the Royal York Hotel under the Chairmanship of the President. Mr A.A. Coster, -- Remarking that the Club was one of the oldest in the country, the Chairman said that from a playing point of view it did not enjoy a very successful season last year, but after five years of war that was all to be expected. This year he hoped for better success.

The Treasurer (Mr E M Taylor) presented the balance sheet, which started with a balance in hand of £5 11s 10d, dating back to 1916, and showed at the present time a balance of £6 2s 5d, while also one or two pounds were subscribed before the meeting. The balance sheet was adopted.

APPOINTMENT OF OFFICERS

Mr G.S. Godfree proposed that Mr Coster again be elected as President, remarking that they had never had a keener gentleman in that position. The proposition was carried amid applause,. On the motion of Mr Graham Hooper, the Vice Presidents were elected en bloc, with the addition of, Mr H. Preston, D. Brooks, H.S. Moore, W.W.Philips and C. Jackson. The following offices were also appointed ; Captain, Mr W.A.Gibbs ; Vice-Captain, Mr P. Evans, Treasurer, Mr E.M. Taylor; Executive Committee, Messrs, Graham Hooper, Vaughan, Lee, H.F. Taylor now vacant owing to the resignation of Mr Wormald, the filling of the position of secretary, which was referred to the Committee, The President proposed a vote of thanks to Mr Wormald for his untiring work in connection with the Club. Mr Wormald pointed out that although the Club only won four of it's matches last year, scoring 108 points against its opponents 151 points, the games were contested in a sporting spirit and greatly enjoyed.

Among the new members enrolled was Mr V.C.W. Jupp, the famous County Cricketeer, who had turned over from the soccer code. A vote of thanks to Mr Harry Preston for his kindness in allowing the use of room, which closed the meeting.

"Argus" Sept 1920

The Brighton Rugby Club, which is one of the Oldest in the country, and now the only one in Sussex (Eastbourne not started since the War) is now entering its 52nd season, and with the exception of the war period, has not missed one.

The matches in Preston Park are the envy of many London Clubs who have visited Brighton for many years. As will be seen by the fixture list, there are only a very few away matches, a point worth consideration in these days of expensive travel.

The Club has produced Nine or Ten Internationals, has played in France and received visits from French Clubs, and also from Trinity College, Cambridge.

There will be practice in Preston Park on Saturday September 25th at 3:30.

It was mentioned in the 52nd "Annual General Meeting" that a newly enrolled member was a "Famous County Cricketeer" Mr V. Jupp. This was confirmed by the Argus a few weeks later.

"Argus" Sept 27th 1920

MR. JUPP AND AUSTRALIA.

Sussex Amateur Unable to Go.

Mr. Finlay, Assistant Secretary of the M.C.C. Cricket Club, this morning received a message from Mr. V. C. W. Jupp, the Sussex amateur, regretting that he found it impossible to join the England team for Australia. Hitch, the Surrey fast bowler, will go instead of Mr. Jupp.

Mr V.C.W. Jupp, had obviously been picked to play for Brighton on that Saturday..!!

1920 Jubilee Dinner menu and Ticket

"Daily Express" Oct 1920

BRIGHTON RUGBY ALL ALONE

The Brighton Rugby Football Club is peculiarly placed in that it is the only one outside school fifteens playing the handling code in Sussex.

Brighton are in their fifty second season and the fixture list includes games with Blackheath "A", Old Alleyaians "A", O.M.T. "A" (Old Merchant Taylors), Wasps, Old Blues,and other prominant teams.

Only two matches will be played away from home, one of them being Eastbourne College, being tomorrow.

A very rare survivor, a poster from the 1920's

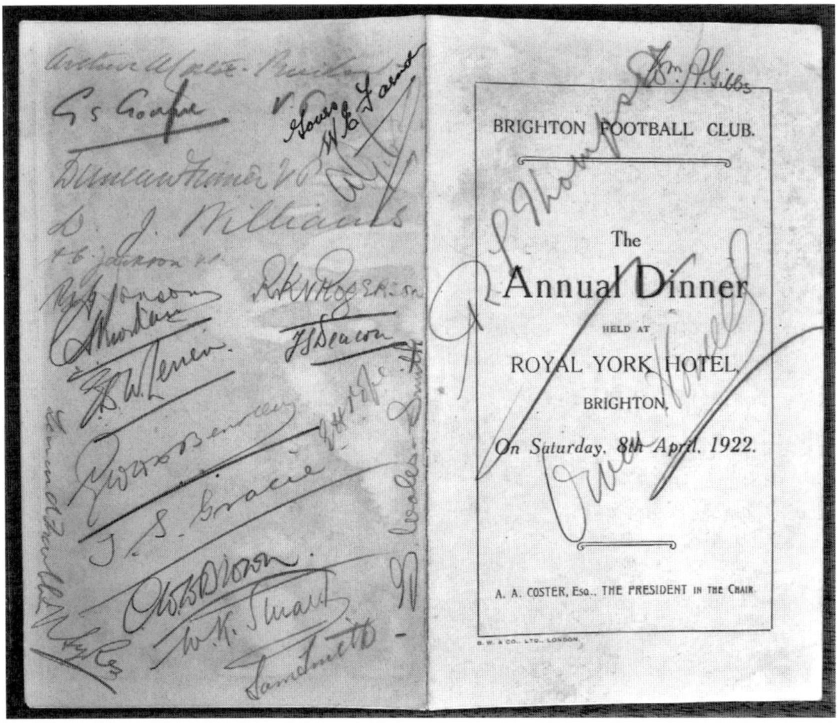

During my research I have encountered many name "famous" with their association with " Brighton Football Club" and then, to encounter a "Menu Card" signed by these Gentlemen is quite amazing

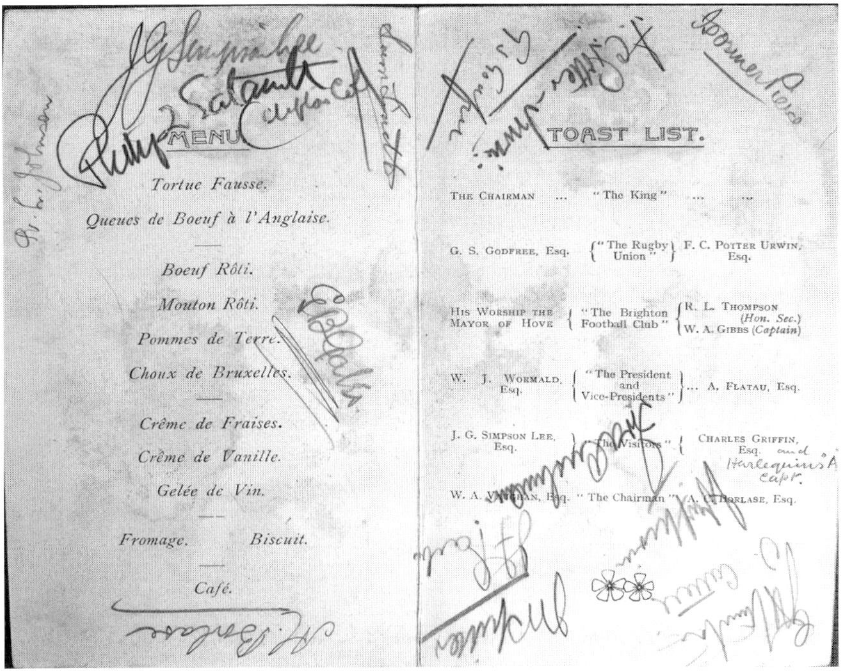

MENU

Tortue Fausse.

Queues de Boeuf à l'Anglaise.

—

Boeuf Rôti.

Mouton Rôti.

Pommes de Terre.

Choux de Bruxelles.

—

Crême de Fraises.

Crême de Vanille.

Gelée de Vin.

—

Fromage. *Biscuit.*

—

Café.

TOAST LIST.

THE CHAIRMAN ...	"The King"	... ...
G. S. GODFREE, Esq.	"The Rugby Union"	F. C. POTTER URWIN, Esq.
HIS WORSHIP THE MAYOR OF HOVE	"The Brighton Football Club"	R. L. THOMPSON *(Hon. Sec.)* W. A. GIBBS *(Captain)*
W. J. WORMALD, Esq.	"The President and Vice-Presidents"	... A. FLATAU, Esq.
J. G. SIMPSON LEE, Esq.	"The Visitors"	CHARLES GRIFFIN, Esq.
W. A. VAUGHAN, Esq.	"The Chairman"	A. C. BORLASE, Esq.

While reading an article in the Argus, dated 19th September 1922, in which the headline was "FOOTBALL" followed by two sub headings "SUSSEX RUGBY UNION RE-STARTED" and "BRIGHTON CLUB PROSPECTS", it was of interest to read that Mr E. Hammett, the English International, has recently been elected a member, and I quote ; " I promise to play whenever possible".

Earlier in the year on the 21st January, Ernest Dyer Galbraith Hammett played his final game for England and three months later on14th April 1922, E.D.G. Hammett played his one and only game for the 'Barbarians F.C.',

BRIGHTON FOOTBALL CLUB 1868 2018 RUGBY FOOTBALL UNION

The above "Advertisement" was for a return Match against Brighton. Unfortunately I have not been able to find the report for this match, however the first game against Brighton in January is on the next page.

Daily News Monday 14th January 1924

RUGBY FOOTBALL

Littlehampton's Display at Brighton

Brighton entertained for the first time the latest recruits in Sussex to the "handling code". The start was a little late and the home side was a forward short for some twenty minutes, when H.H. Thyer filled the vacancy. The home side defending the South goal got going first with a combined run by Stiff and Skeggs, but play ruled generally in the visitors "25" when Skeggs getting possession landed a lovely drop goal.

From the restart, Hare got away on the wing, but was well collared by Fanshaw, and play in mid-field was the order. Good dribbling by Bentley and a pick up and break through by Stiff carried the ball back to the visitors "25" and later they were forced to touch down, Williams and Skeggs were prominent by good tackling.

VISITORS TOUCH DOWN

Littlehampton now had a "look in" and Boulton by clever dribbling forced Richards to touch down. The pressure was kept in the home "25". A free brought relief with a fine kick to the half-way line by Skeggs. The home "3"'s combined well and after the ball had changed hands seven or eight times, Densham made a great effort to get over but just failed. The visitors came again with a rush to be forced back by good long touch kicking. Fanshaws cross kick went astray but Stiff gaining the ball put to touch at the "25". A brief invasion to the home "25" was the next item and here Stiff lost his jersey and play was very "ragged" hereabouts. Bembridge was playing a good game at the back for Littlehampton.

C. Thompson had the bad luck to mistake the dead ball line for the goal line and so lost a certain try. Littlehampton were kept on the defence, but the home side not to be denied, Stiff got over for the first try wide out, the kick by Skeggs from a difficult angle failed. Half time ; Brighton 1 drop goal, 1 try (7 points) ; Littlehampton nil.

The second half opened with very "scrappy" play, wherein

Fanshaw securing the ball got over in the corner. Densham's kick failed to reach. Good dribbling, a forward rush, and following up saw Bently going over for the third try. Skeggs landed a fine goal from this. The passing of the home three-quarters was often erratic, and promising movements broke down for this reason. C. Thompson, who is keen and a very fair scrum half broke through with fine dash to see his efforts wasted by his faulty passes. Passing in one's own is not to recommended. The tackling was better than last week, but it is still too high and the packing of the forwards was also too high.

BRIGHTON RAIDS

Densham and Bentley were prominent in a forward rush to the visitors "25" but Bembridge cleared. A strong run by Stiff, Williams and Fanshaw carried the exchanges to the goal line, but play went back into the home half with a good kick bt Gough. Brighton made another raid which Bembridge cleared with difficulty. R. L. Thompson went down to a forward rush and broke up the movement. The home threes got going again andended with Young getting over.. A good shot at goal by Skeggs just failed. Another promising movement resulted in Williams getting over, but he did not touch down corrctly, and so another certain try was lost. A brief invasion to the home "25" forced a touch down, but form the drop out Fanshaw gained pssesion at half way raced down and scored behind the posts for Skeggs to add the extra points.

The final whistle went immediately after.

Score ;--
Littlehampton nil
Brighton..... 2 goals, 1 drop goal & 3 tries (23 points)

Littlehampton are to be congratulated on getting together what appears to be the making of a good side, and considering many of their players are quite novices to "rugger" it speaks well for whoever is responsible for their instruction. Of the home side, Richards had a fairly easy task. The three-quarters were good at times but not convincing. More understanding is required between the half backs, and the forwards should get down quicker. Next week the 1st XV journey to Porstmouth to meet in the return game the strong team of

H.M.S. "Fishgard" The "A" team will entertain Storrington College, and are promised fixtures on most Saturdays, the 1st XV are away from home.

Brighton:--

B. Richards, R.D. Young, L.A. Stiff, A,C.N. Williams, Lieut Fanshaw ; R.L.D. Skeggs, C. Thompson ; G.W.H. Bentley (captain) J.H. Densham, Lieutenant Bramwell, R.L. Thompson, N.F. Edwards, L. Fairburne, R.L.D. Herbert, H.H. Thyer.

Littlehampton:---

H. Bembridge, L.Hare, V. Scorer, C.A.R.M. Bolton, S.H. Hicks; S. Heard-White, J. Campbell ; C. De Byne, G.F.H. Gough (captain) W. Holmes, G.A. Burnard, L.E. Le Meitre, J.W. Mek, R.V. Cobden, R. Bacock.

Referee ; Mr R.C. Holloway.

This game was reported as the first time these two sides met, however as mentioned earlier, on the 3rd January 1889 :---

The Brighton Rugby Club sent fifteen men to Littlehampton to battle the home team who figured in a match of this kind for the first time that day. The visitors won by one goal and a try to a try,

!920 - 21 Fixture Card, Enclosure Ticket and Rule Book

I had mentioned earlier, in the Club's history, that we were initially linked with the Royal Artillery. This article, published in 1925, confirms that even after 57 years since the Club's formation the lineage is still there.

Monday 25th March 1925

BRIGHTON v 19th BRIGADE ROYAL ARTILLIARY

The Brighton Club should have been playing the Royal Dental Hospital, at Greenford, but they "scratched" on account of a cup match, so a game was fixed up with the 19th Brigade R.A. who are stationed at Preston Barracks, and as eight of the officers of their XV are members of the Brighton Club, while several of the men have assisted one or other of the Clubs XV's, during this season, a keen game was expected.

The Gunners kicked off towards the North goal, but very scrambling play followed, in their half, Lieut Everett defending well and putting to touch with good length kicks, which gave the Gunners a footing in the home half. By good dribbling the Brighton forwards re-claimed the ground lost, and carried play to the visitors "25" where Osbourne took a "free" for off-side, but from an awkward angle his shot went wide. A.C.N. Williams broke through beautifully, but his pass was not accepted, and a few minutes later a cross kick to the left was fielded by Skeggs, and a score seemed certain, but the passing broke down at the critical moment. Osbourne then Beavis, both made strenuous efforts to get over but with no avail. A "free" to the Gunners was taken by Lieut Morley, but failed to reach, and an even first half ended with the score sheet blank.

The Only Try

The R.A. attacked at the outset of the second period and were almost in, but a break away by Osbourne brought relief and the scene was transferred to the visitors "25" where Williams, picking up the ball in a ruck of players, ran well and passed to Skeggs, who, in turn, parted with the ball at the right moment, for Beavis to "cap" the movement with a try under the bar. From the easiest of positions Skeggs failed to convert, the ball hitting the cross bar and rebounding. Very keen tackling on both sides checked many three quarters run. Dr Davis at scrum half, was playing very well for the Gunners. Nearing the end, a good run by the home threes looked dangerous, and Lieut Everett only just managed to bring Forge down in time to avert a score. With a good kick to touch near the flag, Bentley kept the Gunners on defensive, but by good footwork their forwards headed by Lieut Inglis got down to half way, and set up a counter attack, which was frustrated by B. Richards making two good tackles, Osbourne broke away but was grassed.

One of three 'Honour Caps' the club has in its possession, The 1921-1922 cap belonged to G.W.H. Bentley. The other two caps are 1903 - 04 (T. Smith) and 1938 - 39 (J.C. Lord)

Chapter IX

THE GOLDEN YEARS
1926 -1929

I have heard a few times that the Brighton Football Club had its best ever season in 1926-1927. I discovered a newspaper cutting from the Sussex Advertiser in 1927 which documented everything from that season. I will transcribe it in its entirety.

Sussex Advertiser 1927

RUGBY FOOTBALL
Brighton Club
Review of the Season

The 58th season of the Brighton Football Club will rank as the very best in every respect in the Club's long history. With the ever-growing number of playing members it is becoming well nigh impossible for a Club situated as the Brighton Club is to supply them with games, because of the lack of playing space.

Three XV's were put out on 16 Saturdays, four on two Saturdays and two on Wednesday afternoons, and during the season 120 players took part in the games. Of these, 11 played in the three XV's, 16 in the 1st only, 14 in the "A" only, 15 in the "B" only, 19 in the 1st and "A", 1 in the 1st and "B", and 38 in the "A" and "B".

The 1st team called on 47 players in their 28 games ; the "A" XV 82 in 24 games ; and the "B" 65 in 16 games. The 1st XV Captain, J.G. Simpson Lee, and B.W. Richards, were the only two players who played in all 1st XV matches.

The Club record is as follows:--

	P.	W.	D.	L.	Points For	Points Against
1st XV.........	28	26	0	2	621	121
"A" XV.......	24	15	1	8	284	141
"B" XV.......	15	5	1	9	109	103
Extra XV....	3	2	0	1	36	26
Totals....	70	48	2	20	1050	391

The Club's 1925-6 record was as follows.

P.	W.	D.	L.	Points F.	Points A.
45	22	4	19	577	435

For all teams 78 matches were arranged; of these seven were scratched and one abandoned. Never before have as many as 28 games been played by the 1st XV. The greatest number before and since the war was 24. In numbers of wins 26 is by a long way the record. The following gives the past five seasons' results:

	P.	W.	D.	L.	Points For.	Points Agst
1922-23......	21	7	...	14	133	397
1923-24......	24	14	1	9	313	261
1924-25......	23	20	...	3	332	125
1925-26......	23	14	3	6	311	172
1926-27......	28	26	...	2	621	121

Although more games were played the scores of the 1st XV's opponents was the lowest registered since the war

A combined fixture list for 1922-23

Photograph taken before the Brighton v Saracens match in Preston Park, result was draw 0-0, a terrible wet and muddy day, Nov 19th 1927.

A CLUB RECORD

The 1st XV have a record which will be hard to beat. W. L. Tiffen, who filled the wing position after Lieutenant C. D. Fanshaw left, created a Club record by scoring 40 tries in one season, making the 120 points a post war record. His six tries in one match also constituted a post-war record. Tiffen's 120 points was only one point short of the opponents total for the season.

G. C. Mophett scored eight tries in one match in 1899-1900, and that was his total for the season. The total was also the greatest number scored by one player during that season. In 1902-03, W. D. Harris recorded 151 points for the season, scoring 15 tries, and converting 51 of 54 goals during that season and dropping one goal. He was often skipper of the side.

THE SECRET OF THE SUCCESS

The wonderful success was not anticipated at the beginning of the season, but in spite of many changes, the greater part of the side was able to turn out with great regularity, especially for the forwards, who have been the mainstay of the side. None worked harder than the popular Captain J.G.S. Lee, who set his side a very fine example. Roy Lee, L. Fairburne, J. F. Hamptom, W. H Stapley, A. J. E. Taylor, N. P. McFarlane, E G. Shrubbs, and A. G. W. Penney, were consistently good. C. A. Osborne, at scrum half, was better than ever. A. C. N. Williams, his partner, was rather inconsistent in attack, but his defence was very good. All who played at full back did pretty well, but as the score indicates, the full backs had a fairly easy season. R. Lee and C. A. Osborne played in all the Championship games for Sussex, and eight others played for the County.

CONTRASTS

In only five games did the 1st XV, fail to reach double figures, whereas in only two did the opponents achieve this, they being Worthing and Westleigh. Brighton crossed their opponents line twice or more in 27 games but their visitors failed to respond at all with a try in eight games and once only in 11. All the games, with the exception of perhaps one, were played in a true sorting spirit and were thoroughly enjoyed by both players and the big crowds of *spectators. No serious injuries were sustained by players. Honours Caps were awarded to A.J.E. Taylor, N.P.McFarlane, and A.D. Robinson.*

Following the very successful season of 1927-28, that allowed Brighton to expand their fixture list to include first class teams, "Neath" being one of them, journeyed to Brighton for the first fixture between these two sides in November 1928, and were given a mighty reception and a fantastic weekend.

1st XV RESULTS

Appended are the 1st XV results. Of the 28 matches played, 26 were won and only two lost, those against Worthing and Sutton:-

	Points					
	For			Agst		
Opponents	G.	T.	Pts.	G.	T.	Pts.
Crawley (h)…………	7	4	47	…	…	…
Eastbourne Col. (a)…	4	3	28	1	…	5
Blackheath "A" (h)…	1	5	20	1	1	8
Upper Clapton (h) …..	3	2	21	2	…	8
H.M.S. "Fisgard" (h)..	5	7	46	1	…	5
United Services (a)….	5	4	36	…	…	…
Brighton College (a)..	…	2	6	…	1	3
Leytonstone (h)……..	1	2	11	1	1	8
Worthing (a)………...	…	5	15	…	1	3
London Welsh "A" (h)	1	1	6	…	1	3
Old Brightonians (h)….	3	5	30	…	1	3
Crawley (h)…………...	3	9	42	…	1	3
Old Alleynians "A" (h)	3	3	24	1	…	5
United Services (h)…...	5	6	43	…	1	3
Ealing (h)……………...	…	7	21	1	…	3
Hastings & Bexhill (a)..	3	3	23	…	…	…
Eastbourne College (h).	1	7	26	…	2	6
Worthing (h)…………	1	1	8	3	…	13
Mid sx Hosp "A" (h)…	3	9	40	…	…	…
Crawley (a)…………..	1	2	9	1	…	3
Sutton (h) ……………	1	…	5	2	…	9
H.M.S "Fisgard" (a)….	1	2	10	1	1	8
N.P.Bank (h)…………	4	5	35	…	…	…
Catford Bdge "A" (h)...	2	1	13	…	1	3
Harlequin "A" (h)…….	1	2	10	…	1	3
West Herts (h) ………	2	2	16	…	2	6
London N. Zealanders (h)	…	4	12	…	…	…
Westleigh (h) ……………	2	2	16	2	…	10

Team photograph of Brighton Football Club 1926-27, taken outside the Club's headquarters, the "Crown & Anchor" Preston Road.

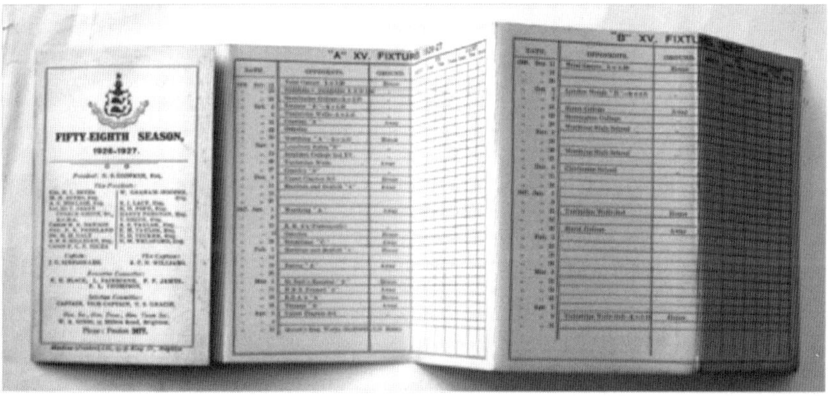

Unusual pull out fixture card for 1926- 27

The Welsh Affair'

Sussex Daily News, 17th November 1928

THE RUGBY GAME
The Visit of Neath.

The Brighton Rugby club have given Brighton a wonderful advertisement. At the moment there are 30 or so Welshmen in Neath singing the praises of the "Queen of Watering Places".

Brighton played Neath, the famous Welsh 15, in Preston Park on Monday afternoon. Neath are the champion side of Wales, and it was a feather in the cap of the Brighton club to bring such outstanding exponents of the game to Brighton to play a match of such first class importance. It will enhance the Brighton club's prestige.

Neath won by 2 goals and 6 tries (28 points) to a try (3 points). But that is besides the point. So well did the Brighton club arrange the social side of the visiting parties programme that every Neath player and official was sorry to leave Sussex. From the time they arrived at Brighton Station on Sunday midday until they left again on Tuesday morning, the visitors were right royally entertained.

The Brighton Club president (Mr W. Graham-Hooper), councillor Harry Preston (Vice President), officials, players, and supporters of the Brighton Club were on the platform to receive their guests on Sunday. The Neath party were agreeably surprised and even overwhelmed at the reception. Private cars took the visitors to the War Memorial where the Neath secretary placed a wreath.

A move was then made to the Royal Albion Hotel, where the two clubs toasted each other at councillor's Preston's invitation.

A party of 50 sat down to lunch at Mutton's as the guests of Mr Graham-Hooper, and later the visitors were shown over the Royal Pavilion. In the evening they visited the Academy Theatre, West Street, at the invitation of the general manager, Mr J. B. Binmore.

The Neath party impressed as a band of superbly built young sportsman. Their captain, Tom Evans, is a footballer of the finest type, and the men under him follow his example. Thus the match between Brighton and Neath at Preston Park Cricket Ground was a

model sporting match. Threatening weather spoilt the attendance, but those who braved the elements were rewarded with a great game.

The Sussex forwards did very well, and held their own in the tight scrums in surprising fashion. The home three quarters, however, were outclassed by the brilliance of the Neath threes!!.

Nothing finer has been seen in Brighton rugby circles than the sprinting for the line by Dan Jones. Time and again his speed left him a clear run for a try. Brighton's try was scored in great style by H. M. Holman, he swerved around two opponents and went over the line in much the same way as he did against Middlesex, at Hastings, on the previous Wednesday. J. F. Hampton failed to convert, although the kick was from in front of the post.

The place kicking of Neath left something to be desired. Neath would have done better on a wet ground, but, as it was, Dan Jones was troublesome enough. The Neath halves played a great game and got the ball from the scrum every time. And the passing of Owen to Reynolds was a revelation. Prior to the match, both teams and officials were presented to the Mayor and Mayoress of Brighton (Councillor and Mrs. H. J. Galliers).

A visit to Neath?

After the match Neath were the guests of the Brighton club for tea.

The Neath secretary, Mr Archy Morris MBE. proposed that Brighton would beat Edgware on the following Saturday, and hinted that negotiations were already in hand for Brighton to visit Neath in the near future. He assured Brighton that Neath would endeavour to equal the warmth of the welcome they had been given in Brighton. He also hoped that Neath fixture visit to Brighton will become an annual fixture.

"Never before" said Mr Morris " have we been received as we have been received by you jolly fine Brighton sportsmen".

After tea, Neath looked in at the Brighton boys club where the warden (Mr A. E. Tyrer) had arranged a physical training and boxing display for their benefit. The boys of the club were eager to get the autographs of the internationals in the Welsh party and particularly that of skipper Tom Evans, who is ex amateur heavy weight boxing champion of Great Britain.

In the evening, both teams and officials visited the Regent Dance Hall at the invitation of the general manager, Mr R. H. Ainsworth. The Neath men thoroughly enjoyed themselves. The commented on the variety of Brighton's attractions, and all expressed their intentions to go back to Wales and tell of Brightons amenities.

Neath Honours Cap 1931-32, which I believe was presented to J. Owens

There was a muster of Brighton officials and players at Brighton station on Tuesday morning to say "au revoir". Before entering their train, the Welsh party surprised all who did not know them by singing several unaccompanied glees. Their harmony was delightful.

Mr Graham-Hooper was at head of the Brighton party from the first to the last. He entertained Neath from Sunday to Tuesday, in this he was ably assisted by Mr J. G. Simpson Lee (Brighton Club captain), Mr W. A Gibbs (Brighton Club secretary) and Mr R. L. Thompson (Sussex County Secretary).

The Brighton club are to be congratulated on the success of their enterprise.

Rugby Football Weekly, April 6th 1929

Brighton F.C. (RFU) 1928-29
60th (DIAMOND JUBILEE SEASON)

An interesting feature of this year is that Brighton will celebrate their Diamond Jubilee next Saturday, when a dinner will be held in the evening. The Brighton Club was founded sixty years ago as a result of a match between two local Clubs called, The Wasps and The Shooflies, respectively. It was felt that there was no room for two Clubs in the same town, so it was agreed that they should amalgamate under the style and title of "The Brighton Football Club". Early records are somewhat scarce, but, J,E. Raven K.C. was the first Captain, and Lieut-Col. Cecil Parsons was the Hon secretary about the season of 1870-71.

For the greater part of the Club's existence before the War only one team was run, with an occasional mid-week side, but the Club carried on until the end of the 1913-14 season, and resumed operations in September 1919, Brighton then being the only Rugby Club in Sussex apart from the Schools.

The early seasons after the War were somewhat troublesome , but a few old members kept interest alive in the game, with the result that gradually the difficulties were overcome, the membership grew, and the Club was able to turn out three teams, a number which has increased to four.

In its Diamond Jubilee season the Club has suffered its worst blow in the death of the President, W. Graham-Hooper, who played three-quarters and was Hon Sec for twelve years, also representing Sussex. The great handicap which the Club has to face is the lack of a suitable ground, but strenuous efforts have been made and are still being made to achieve this end.

Brighton was the first English Rugby Club to tour in France under the new regulations of the Rugby Football Union, for touring sides abroad, as on December 21st 1902, they met Stade Francais at the Parc des Princes, where the home side won by 9 points to 3.

Many well know players have represented the Club, and others have rendered it long and faithful service.

The Beves family have been connected with the Club for forty years, "M.H." being the captain for four successive season from 1893to 1897. A.C. Borlase, first played in 1869, was hon secretary in 1883 and has also been President. G.S. Godfree, the acting President has held every office in the Club both on and off the field, and has played in every position. He has been with the Club and rendered yeoman service for nearly forty years. The Club has played on its on its present pitch for roughly fifty years, three years before Preston Park was bought by the Brighton Corporation.

A few of the notable players who have assisted the Club include F. Mitchell, B.C. Hartley, E.G.H. North, A. McDonell, J.G.G. Birkett and R.D. Budworth. Mitchell being the Hon Secretary in the season 1891- 1892.

Coming to the present season, while the results have perhaps not been so good as the two previous years, the first team have not done too badly, having played 23 games, of which they have won 15 and lost 8, with a total of 409 points, against 216.

The hard grounds early in the season caused a number of "crockings" and then the frost in mid December all through February, coupled with the influenza epidemic, made it difficult to get fit sides together. The fixture list has been strengthened, but owing to the above reasons 36 matches (for various reasons) have been scratched during the season.

J.G.S. Lee, who is the Captain for the third year in succession, is the only pre-war member still playing and has not missed a game for two successive seasons.

The Brighton Club has rendered valuable service to Sussex County both on and off the field.

No record of Brighton F.C. (RFU) would be complete without a few words about their energetic and enthusiastic hon secretary and hon Treasurer, W.A. Gibbs, Gibbs joined the Club from Northampton in October 1911, played for Brighton up till the outbreak of the War, was Vice Captain in 1919-1920 and Captain the following season. Since 1922 Gibbs has been a "general utility man" of the Club. He has been Hon Sec and Hon Treasurer from 1923 up to date, in addition to being match and team secretary until this year. The Brighton Club owes a debt of gratitude to its Hon Secretary and Hon Treasurer.

Spectators at Preston Park 1928

The Brighton Football Club
(R.F.U.)

Members' Season Ticket
1929-30.

Admit to Ground and Stands
(not centre section)
AT
HOVE STADIUM.

A Member's Season Ticket, for the "Greyhound Stadium", were averaging a gate of 1,000, a 50% drop from their 1927-28 Season

1930 -1939

Due to the success of the latter part of the 1920's, our fixture list increased in quality including two Welsh teams, Aberavon and Neath.

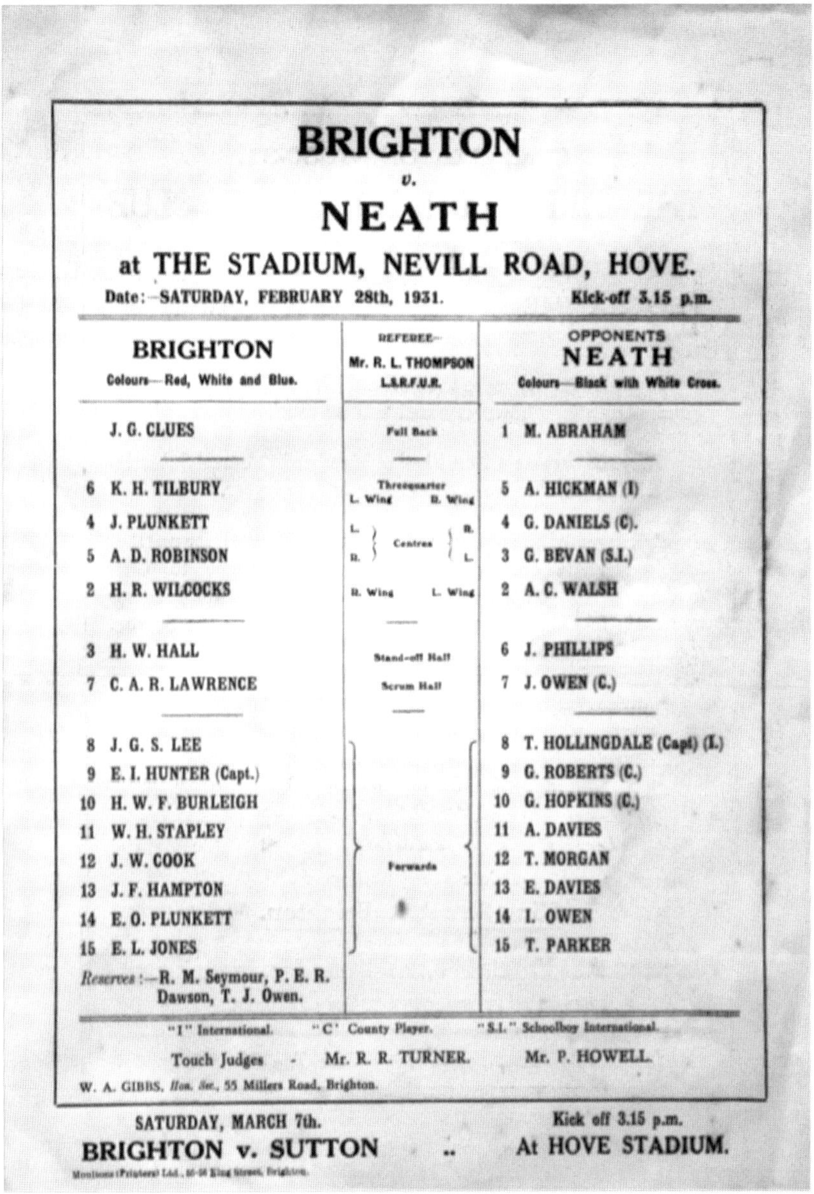

BRIGHTON

v.

NEATH

at THE STADIUM, NEVILL ROAD, HOVE.

Date:—SATURDAY, FEBRUARY 28th, 1931. Kick-off 3.15 p.m.

BRIGHTON Colours—Red, White and Blue.	REFEREE— Mr. R. L. THOMPSON L.S.R.F.U.R.	OPPONENTS NEATH Colours—Black with White Cross.
J. G. CLUES	Full Back	1 M. ABRAHAM
6 K. H. TILBURY	Threequarter L. Wing / R. Wing	5 A. HICKMAN (I)
4 J. PLUNKETT	L. } Centres { R.	4 G. DANIELS (C).
5 A. D. ROBINSON	R. } Centres { L.	3 G. BEVAN (S.I.)
2 H. R. WILCOCKS	R. Wing / L. Wing	2 A. C. WALSH
3 H. W. HALL	Stand-off Half	6 J. PHILLIPS
7 C. A. R. LAWRENCE	Scrum Half	7 J. OWEN (C.)
8 J. G. S. LEE	Forwards	8 T. HOLLINGDALE (Capt) (I.)
9 E. I. HUNTER (Capt.)	Forwards	9 G. ROBERTS (C.)
10 H. W. F. BURLEIGH	Forwards	10 G. HOPKINS (C.)
11 W. H. STAPLEY	Forwards	11 A. DAVIES
12 J. W. COOK	Forwards	12 T. MORGAN
13 J. F. HAMPTON	Forwards	13 E. DAVIES
14 E. O. PLUNKETT	Forwards	14 I. OWEN
15 E. L. JONES	Forwards	15 T. PARKER
Reserves:—R. M. Seymour, P. E. R. Dawson, T. J. Owen.		

"I" International. "C" County Player. "S.I." Schoolboy International.

Touch Judges - Mr. R. R. TURNER. Mr. P. HOWELL.

W. A. GIBBS, *Hon. Sec.*, 55 Millers Road, Brighton.

SATURDAY, MARCH 7th. Kick off 3.15 p.m.

BRIGHTON v. SUTTON .. At HOVE STADIUM.

Saturday 28th February 1931, Brighton v Neath, (Tom Evans, pictured) Greyhound Stadium, Hove

"Brighton Football Club & Neath Rugby Football Club taken at Preston Park before their encounter"

In 1928/1929, Tom Evans led Neath to the Welsh championship again. They set a Welsh record of 930 points and wing Dan Jones established a world record 59 tries. Despite a drain of players into rugby league ranks, Neath carried off the Welsh title twice in succession in 1933/1934 (led by Arthur Hickman) and 1934/1935 (led by Glyn Daniels)

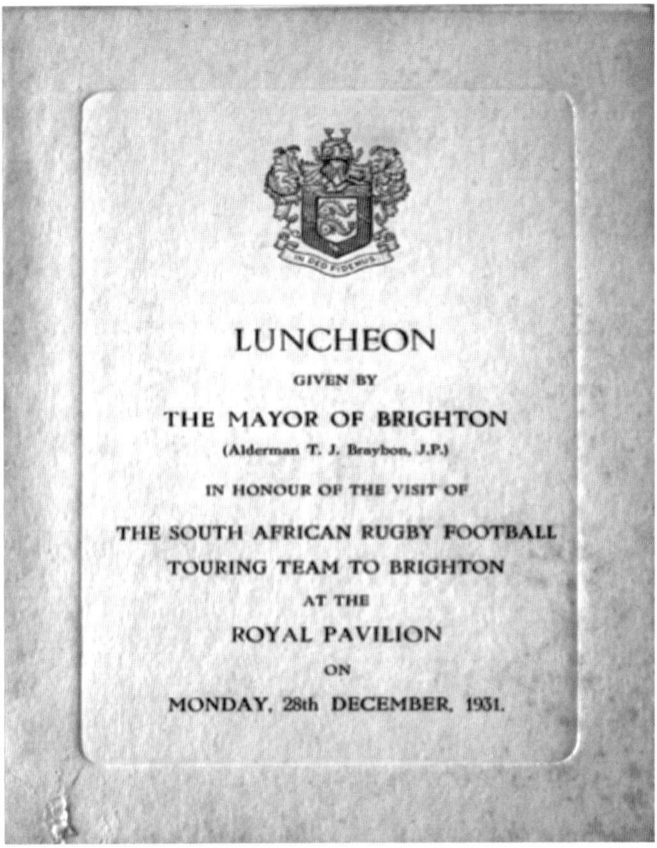
LUNCHEON
GIVEN BY
THE MAYOR OF BRIGHTON
(Alderman T. J. Braybon, J.P.)
IN HONOUR OF THE VISIT OF
THE SOUTH AFRICAN RUGBY FOOTBALL
TOURING TEAM TO BRIGHTON
AT THE
ROYAL PAVILION
ON
MONDAY, 28th DECEMBER, 1931.

The Luncheon that never happened

In 1931 the Mayor of Brighton and the President of Brighton Football Club succeeded in enticing the South African Touring Side to spend a weekend in Brighton, culminating in a Luncheon at the Royal Pavilion on Monday 28th December. The team was due to be accommodated at the Royal Albion Hotel, owned by Sir Harry Preston (Brighton Football Club, President 1929-30), however, due to a Christmas "Overbooking" Sir Harry told the touring side he would have to split them up, sending a small group along to the Queens Hotel. This was not appreciated and the touring side immediately cancelled their trip to Brighton and headed to a hotel in South Wales. That particular weekend, the weather in Wales was atrocious, two days of wind and rain. It was reported that a number of players wished they had stayed in Brighton.

The article below found in the Brighton & Hove Herald, September 1934 is worth reporting in its entirety as it is very informative and tells the story of the Club, including some hitherto unknown facts (maybe) and figures.

BRIGHTON RUGBY CLUB
One of the Oldest in England

Started in 1868
And still without a Ground

Though the Brighton (Rugby) Football Club is one of the oldest in the Country it is still more or less struggling for recognition.

It has never received the support locally that it deserves. The result is that the Club has never taken its place among the first class clubs.

Imagine a club sixty-six years old without its own ground! That is the position of the Brighton (Rugby) Football Club. Ever since 1868 it has had to play on various hired pitches and has tried in vain to secure its own enclosure.

It is doubtful if the people of Brighton realize what an asset the club could be to the town. If Brighton had its own ground, properly equipped. the most famous teams in the Country would be glad to come and play here, while the club would be able to stage international trials and matches with touring sides such as the All-Blacks.

Think of the publicity value this would be for the town, without mentioning the money that would be spent in the town by an influx of rugger spectators.

THE CLUB AND ITS GROUND PROBLEM

In the early days the club played on Wish Meadow, Hove, and the Sussex County Cricket Ground. It has used the pitches in Preston Park for fifty-two years, starting three years before the park became the property of Brighton Corporation.

Since the War, matches have been played at the Brighton & Hove Greyhound Stadium and Preston Park Cricket Ground with junior matches played at Hollingbury.

The centre of the Stadium was turfed, and made an ideal pitch, on which an International match could have been staged. Unfortunately, an agreement could not be reached over the lease, and the ground has not be used for the past two seasons.

The Club has also tried to acquire two other sites for grounds in the last few years.

These were Hampton's Farm (Off Preston Road), and an estate at Hangleton. On neither case was the Club successful.

THE ORIGIN OF THE CLUB
The "Shooflies" and the "Wasps"

The first local Rugby club came into existence in 1868 and was known as the "Shooflies". Another club called "The Wasps" was formed about the same time. In the early seventies the clubs appear to have amalgamated, and the result of the union was designated as the "Brighton (Rugby) Football Club".

In those days Rugby Football differed considerably from the present day game. Rules varied in different parts of the country, and even the number of players per side was not constant. One thing, however, is certain and that is that some of the methods and tactics which were then legal must have made the game even more murderous than American Football.

It is a remarkable fact that Mr John G. Raven K.C. the first Captain of the club, and Lieut-Colonel Cecil Parsons, one of the first secretaries, and some of their colleagues, still take an interest in the Club. The early records, however, are not too informative. It is apparent that the Club gradually built up a reputation, and at all stages in its history it included among its players men who were, or became, some of the distinguished citizens of Brighton and Hove.

SOME NOTEABLE MEMBERS

Some of the most distinguished citizens of Brighton and Hove have played for the Club.

Mr G.S. Godfree, Clerk of the Peace, has played in every position on the field, and filled every office in the Club during an association of 45 years.

Mr A.C. Borlase, Secretary of the Chamber of Commerce, runs this record close. He has held every office in the club except that of Captain.

Among other distinguished players have been Lieut-Colonel Cecil Parsons, T.D, Mr John E. Raven, K.C., Colonel Sir Charles Boxall, K.C.B., Colonel E. Leslie Beves, V.D., J.P., and the late Mr Graham Hooper.

Among recent Presidents of the Club have been Mr Godfree, Mr Borlase, Sir Harry Preston and Mr Charles Griffin (formally Chief Constable of Brighton).

Sir Harry has been a member of the club for over thirty years and has always been one of its most valued supporters.

Mr W.A. Gibbs, Hon Secretary and Treasurer

The man who is chiefly responsible for the prominence the club has gained since the War. At every annual meeting he asks when he is going to be allowed to resign, and the answer is "Not Yet"

A first-class full back in his time, played for Northampton. Came to Brighton in 1911, and played regularly for the club until the outbreak of the War. Served abroad and helped to form an Army Rugby fifteen.

Helped to reform and reorganised the Brighton Football Club after the war. Vice Captain 1919-20. captain 1920-21. Concluded his playing career at the end of 1922-23 season, when he accepted office as secretary and treasurer.

Profession ; School Master. Teaches art at Vardean School (where incidentally, the boys play "soccer")

Mr W.F. Moir

"Gunner" Moir has the interest of the Club completely at heart. Formerly played for Catford Bridge. Hence the cordial relations between the two clubs.

Is a keen Golfer. President of West Hove Golf Club, two seasons ago.

First to Tour France

The enterprise of the club officials is shown by the fact that Brighton was the first English club to tour France under the regulations drawn up by the Rugby Union. In 1902 on December 21st Brighton met Stade Francais at the Parc des Princes, and lost by 9 points to 3.

The most famous player who has appeared for the club is J.G.G. Birkett (centre-threequarter). He was awarded his Cap for Brighton in 1905, he played for England 17 times, before and after the war. After a spell with Harlequins he returned to Brighton...

Another Brighton player to gain international honours was Dr E. Fitzgerald Frazer, who was capped for Ireland.

The club had gained considerable repute by the time the war broke out. Its activities came to an end, of course , during hostilities. After the war the cub went on from strength to strength, for the influence and ability of Mr W.A. Gibbs, who became hon, secretary and treasurer in 1923, began to make itself felt.

The Club's peak years were reached in 1926-27 and 1927-28. In those two seasons the first fifteen played fifty-four matches, won forty-nine, drew one, and lost only four. The huge total of 1,033 points were scored for the team, and only 226 against. The fixture list then included a number of first class clubs, but Brighton in those seasons had a side that would match any in the Country.

The club officials have also helped to increase the repute of the club by arranging tours, of these the most successful were the visits to Wales.

Efforts have also been made to arrange fixtures abroad. The Brighton-Biarritz Entente gave Mr Gibbs an opportunity, and he made arrangements for annual matches alternately in Brighton and Biarritz for six years.

Unfortunately, the rupture between the Rugby Union and the French governing body prevented these fixtures from being fulfilled. If the rupture is ever healed--- there does not seem much hope at the moment--- Brighton may have fixtures with a number of French Clubs.

Decline in the Club's Fortune

During the past few years there has been a decline in the club's fortunes, This has been due to the lack of local support, and the failure to secure a club ground. Mr Gibbs has managed to get such famous clubs as Neath, Abervon, Blackheath and Harlequins to play here and the "gates" have only been about a thousand at each match. The fact that the club has no ground means that the club has had to give up some attractive fixtures. The result being is that the star players have left the club and others who would have joined have not done so.

The Brighton (Rugby) Football Club wants more support in its own town.

Reminiscences by Dick Braybon

In 1936, I was in Brighton College First Fifteen and played against "The Brighton Football Club" First Fifteen and I have a happy photograph of the time.

Reggie Turner, who was one of my mentors of my rugby with the club told me that I was playing in the "A" or "B" sides as he thought that the first fifteen rugby would be too hard for a young schoolboy.

Ronnie Malby, David's father, was Captain of the School Rugby Team at Brighton College and eventually went to play for Blackheath.

Two years later when I had left College and played occasionally for the first fifteen it was a surprise to find that the "B" XV rugby was a harder physical game.

I enjoyed playing in the early 30's and have happy memories of Copers Cope Lane, where many of the Banks had their Clubs.

Brighton Football Club v Harlequins Football Club

1936, at Preston Park, The Villas that lined London Road, unfortunately have all disappeared and spectators at games would average 1200.

Playing at Preston Park near to the main London Road with a canvas screen to protect the few spectators. Changing during Pre-War was in the gymnasium at the back of the "Crown & Anchor" in Preston Village and we had to walk through the corridor to the Gents toilet where there was one cold shower.

Coming back in 1946 as Captain, the report of the Brighton v Worthing match was that 14 of the Brighton had played a 14 of Worthing and that Gerry Saunders (Worthing capt) had played George Hampton. an ex Brighton player (I believe at the time there was a lot of ill feeling between Brighton and Worthing. Worthing had started to use Brighton Hotels for their Annual Banquets, because they had been barred from Hotels in Worthing for "Bad Behaviour". This bad behaviour continued in Brighton, which upset a few Brighton players, and I believe that George Hampton (Brighton) was excluded and barred from Brighton Football Club. (for fighting) hence the animosity.

We played at the County Cricket Ground at Hove in front of the Old South Stand for several seasons and then again back to Preston Park, although by now we changed in the new pavilion on the Cricket Ground. In latter years I enjoyed playing in an "A" or "B" fifteen, particularly at Tonbridge where a building friend John Children, who was the same height and weight, used to mark each other in the line out and jointly trot together from scrum to scrum. Next was playing at Withdean Stadium and being able to have a drink in the minor clubhouse.

I can remember difficult times driving back from London after a game one particular foggy night trying to follow a Southdown Coach, but the fog was too dense for me and in the end I had to amble back at a very slow pace.

Brighton & Hove Herald, Saturday, March 11th 1939

RUGBY CLUB CELEBRATE 70th Season

Jubilee Match, Banquet and Ball

The Seventy year's history of the Brighton (Rugby) Football Club were celebrated on Wednesday by a jubilee commemoration match, followed by Banquet and Ball

The match, which was between the Club and Rosslyn Park, was played in Preston Park in the afternoon and proved a great attraction, although Prince Alexander Obolensky was unable to play as had been hoped.

Brighton put up a very good performance against the strong London side..

The Banquet, held at the Royal Pavilion, was a fitting Climax to the Jubilee celebrations. The Rosslyn Park team attended as guests of Mr W.F. Moir, the Brighton President, and many other well know personalities in the Rugby World were present.

In one respect the function made history, as many Ladies were present.

The only previous occasion during the past seventy years on which a Lady has attended the annual dinner of Brighton Football Club was when an invitation was extended to Alderman Miss Margaret Hardy, MBE, JP. during her year of office as Mayor of Brighton.

Firm Control

The speech-making was started in eloquent style by Mr J.G. Simpson Lee, the Club's hon team Secretary, who proposed the toast of "The Rugby Football Union".

"The game of rugby football" he said "played as it is by tens of thousands of vigorous young men needs to be under a firm impartial control. That control is in the capable hands of the R.F.U. The union is a typical British institution. It combines the democratic forms so dear to the heart of the English men with the truncheon of the dictators.

Mr Lee went on to suggest that there might be close association between the Clubs of the country, and he criticised the system whereby the smallest preparatory school enjoys the same voting powers as the largest club as "repugnant alike to common sense and justice."

"The achievements of the R.F.U." he said in conclusion are remarkable, and I attribute this to the fact that the officers of the

THE BRIGHTON FOOTBALL CLUB
(R.F.U.)

1868-69 1938-39

70th SEASON
COMMEMORATIVE
BANQUET AND BALL
— AT —
THE ROYAL PAVILION
BRIGHTON

WEDNESDAY, 8th MARCH
1939

PRESIDENT (in the Chair) - - W. F. MOIR
Hon. Secretary and Hon. Treasurer - W. A. GIBBS

Union are old players. When we survey the World of Sport as a whole, when we see games which were once free expression of our national spirit and courage now being degraded under the heel of finance, when modern Gladiators are bought and sold in the market

The President, who. with Mrs Moir received the guests, presided at the banquet. Among the civic guests were the deputy Mayor and Mayoress of Brighton, Alderman H. Hone, and Mrs Ralph Hone and the Mayor and Mayoress of Hove, Councillor and Mrs A.W. Hillman.

place, when the very name of sportsman denotes a spectator or a gambler, then do we realise what an incalculable debt we owe to the R.F.U., the union which has preserved for us unsullied, as noble as it was in the days of our fathers, this greatest game of all.

Responding to the toast. Mr H.E.B. Wilkins, who represents Kent on the R.F.U., congratulated Mr Lee on his smoothly worded compliments, in which he had managed to wrap up a note of criticism. He pointed out, however, that the clubs of the country have their remedy at their annual meeting if they dislike the decisions of the union.

"The Brighton Football Club" said Mr Gadney, proposing the toast of "The Club" is the tenth oldest in England, having been founded in 1869. "It seems to be very appropriate that you should ask Rosslyn Park, a Club who have just celebrated their sixtieth season, to help you celebrate your seventieth season." He referred to some of the famous players the Brighton Club have produced.

Move to Hove!

"It seems amazing to me" he went on "that a Club of the standing of Brighton should not have a better following.

It may be, as the Mayoress of Hove has suggested to me, that the club should move to Hove and get a ground there. And it is also amazing to me after seeing the way the team played this afternoon.

----- the hooking was as good as I have seen.

-----that Brighton have not won more matches this season"

Responding to the toast. Mr W.W. Sayers, the captain, said he felt confident that with men such as the president, Mr W.A. Gibbs (the Hon. Secretary), and Mr J.G. Simpson Lee, looking after the club, they had no need to fear for its future welfare.

70th Season Commemorative Banquet and Ball at The Royal Pavilion

Mr Gibbs, who also responded, looked back over the history of the club and recalled that the "Shooflies" played the "Wasps" in the sixties for the right to call themselves the Town club and won. They then took the name of the "Brighton Football Club" some of their matches being played under soccer rules.

The club was existence before the Rugby Union, and in 1871, when the Union was formed, Brighton was among the first clubs to affiliate.

Past Achievements

Mr Gibbs remarked that the records of the club were far from complete. They showed however, that the club had many fine achievements in the past and he had every confidence that there would be many more in the future.

Councillor P. Friend James, who until last season was the oldest playing member of the club, proposed "The Guests", Alderman Hone, the deputy Mayor, who responded, expressed his regret that the negotiations between the Club and the Town Council with regard to a pitch at Braypool Barn had broken down "It would have been a good thing for the Club and for the town if it had gone through" he said.

Mr K.H. Smith, captain of Rosslyn Park, who also responded, said that he was amazed, in view of Brighton's form that afternoon, that they had not a better playing record this season, "You have a big bustling pack who would give any team something to think about" he said, adding that hoped further fixtures would be arranged in the near future between Brighton and Rosslyn Park.

Tribute to President

Mr G.S. Godfree, who has been a member of the club for more than half a century, proposed a toast of "The President". In all his experience, he said, he had not known a better man for the office than Mr Moir.

Mr Moir, who was accorded musical honours, said that the clubs chief trouble appears to be that although the district in which they play has a population of a quarter of a million, only a small percentage appears to be Rugby minded. "On the other hand the Club gets the most loyal support from the Vice-Presidents and Offices" said the president.

"I commend their example to the present playing members. I hope when their playing days are over that they will continue to take an interest in the club and do their best to support it."

After dinner there was dancing in the Music Room. The Trowell Trio played selections during the dinner, and the toasts were interspersed by entertainment items from Vernon Lee, Mr R.R. Turner was Toastmaster.

From L. to R.

Stood, Reginald Turner, Ced Styer, John Lee, "Woofy" Ravenscroft, Richard "Dick" Braybon, Jock Cook, Mr Styer, Johnny Lord, William Gibbs, Michael Barron, Basil Pett, Phil Myers.

Sitting, Clifford Curtiss-Williams, Stuart Hamer, "McIntyre", Warrick Sayers, "Gunner" Moir (President), Mr Jeffries, Hughie Sayers, Gary Allen, Jimmy Atkins.

On Ground, "McNair", Doug Wilson, George Hampton.

The above named photograph was taken before the Rosslyn Park match, and is the only photograph I have found with christian names on the reverse.

"70th Anniversary, 8th March 1939, Brighton v Rosslyn Park"

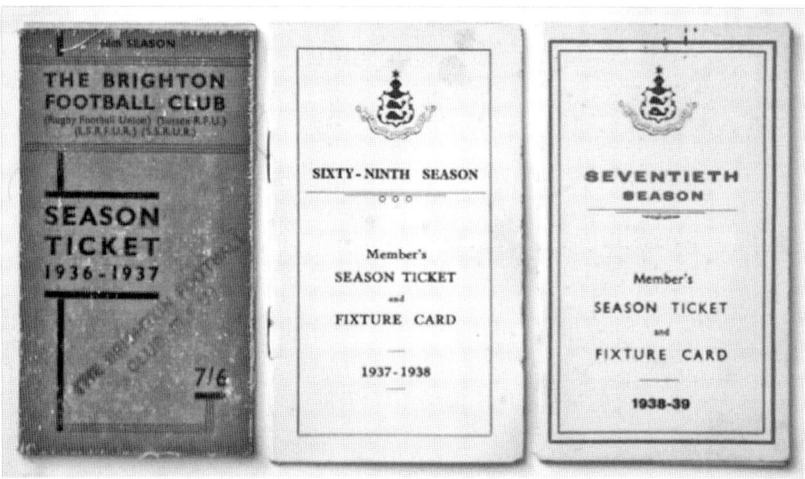

The 1930's were obviously experimentation time with fixture cards

70th Anniversary
1st XV & Committee.
8th March 1939 v Rosslyn Park

The Match
BRIGHTON'S FINE FORM AGAINST ROSSLYN PARK

The commemoration match at Preston Park during the afternoon between Brighton and Rosslyn Park resulted in a win by the visitors by 16 points to nil, which from Brighton's point of view was not a bad result, even allowing for the fact that the winners were one short.

For the greater part of the game Brighton had a fair share of the play and in the first half, when they had the assistance of the wind, they were pressing continuously. The forwards packed solidly and Curtis-Williams hooked so well that Brighton got the ball from almost every scrum. In the loose the Brighton pack also showed splendid form, and with Lord, Cook, Ravenscroft Barron and W. Sayers always prominent, they surprised the visitors with a number of great forward rushes.

Passing Faults

Behind the scrum it was a different story. McNair and Wilson both took some time to settle down. McNair's passing was slow and inaccurate at the start, while Wilson spoiled one or two chances by holding on too long. Even when they did get going the threequarters line did not work smoothly, McIntyre's handling and passing being very much at fault.

On the other hand , whenever the visiting outsides got away they were both polished and thrustful, and but for the close and determined marking they would have considerably increased their score.

Rosslyn Park started one short, and when Bassett, scrum half, injured his ankle ten minutes from the start. P.F. Cooper, the reserve, went on as centre threequarter, so that Deere was able to take Bassett's place.

Rosslyn Park And Brighton, Struggle For The Ball

First Half Score

The scoring in the first half was limited to one try by the visitors, and even this was against the run of play. The Brighton pack heeled under the visitors posts, but Wilson held on too long, and from the resultant loose maul the visitors broke away. Craven sprinted down the wing, punted over Hampton's head and though the bounce of the ball beat him, Deere who followed up, was able to get a touch down.

After this Brighton put in some prolonged attacking without success, the nearest they came to scoring being when Hammer cut through and was tackled on the line.

The Park made one dangerous breakaway when Huxley intercepted a pass from the base of the scrum, but after he had side-stepped Hampton he was overtaken a brought down by Allen.

Play was more even in the second half and the visitors began to get the ball from the scrums. In attack their three-quarters were always menacing and Brighton had to rely on loose forward rushes and determined tackling to hold their own. A golden opportunity of equalising was lost when, with a clear route to the visitors' touchline, Allen dropped a long and rather inaccurate pass from McIntyre.

In spite of the speed and precision with which the visiting outsides launched their attacks, Brighton held out until about half way through the second half, when Hampton was penalised for holding on to the ball, and Huxley made no mistake with the kick.

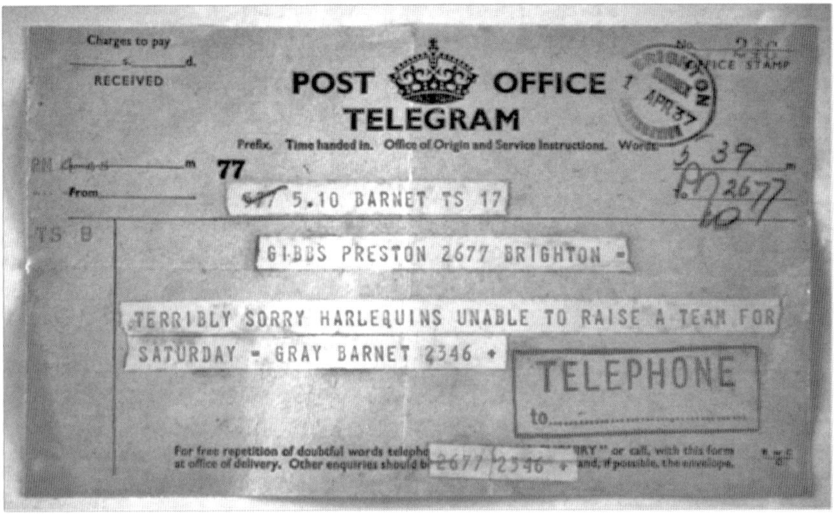
Charges to pay
s. d.
RECEIVED
POST OFFICE
TELEGRAM
Prefix. Time handed in. Office of Origin and Service Instructions. Words.
77
5.10 BARNET TS 17
GIBBS PRESTON 2677 BRIGHTON =
TERRIBLY SORRY HARLEQUINS UNABLE TO RAISE A TEAM FOR
SATURDAY = GRAY BARNET 2346 +
TELEPHONE
to

I found this Telegram dated 1939, addressed to W. Gibbs (Hon Secretary) Brighton F.C., from the "Harlequins F.C., I thought it quite amusing

70th SEASON — COMMEMORATIVE
RUGBY FOOTBALL MATCH
BRIGHTON v.
ROSSLYN PARK
Wednesday, 8th Mar., 1939. Kick-off 3 p.m.
At PRESTON PARK
ENCLOSURE SEATS 6d.

Chapter X

WORLD WAR II
and subsequent years
1939-1949

The last Seven years is best summed up by William Gibb, Hon Secretary report at the ;

77th Season
Annual General Meeting
held at "The Clarence Hotel" North St, Brighton
at 6pm on 16th May 1946

Mr President, and Gentleman

It is not an easy task bridging a lapse of time from six to seven years such as this Country has passed through and restarting a Club as if nothing had happened. I will, however, be as brief as possible in this report and statement.

The Club closed down officially, immediately on the outbreak of War, but I was able to arrange a few games locally up to Easter 1940. From then until January 1946 no further playing activity took place. Practically all our playing members and a number of non playing members joined up in one or the other of the Services.

I regret to have to say that the following former players made the great sacrifice ;

E. ALEXANDER: M. BARDOLPH: W.F. BARTON: M. BAXTER-PHILLIPS: T.V.C. CROSS: C.L. CURTIS-WILSON: P.E. GIBBS: J. HARRISON: J.M. PHILLIPS: F.P. SKELLY: P. KEECH: D. NOLAN: M. NOLAN: J.PLUNKETT: O.P. PLUNKETT: R. PRICE: G.R. THYER:

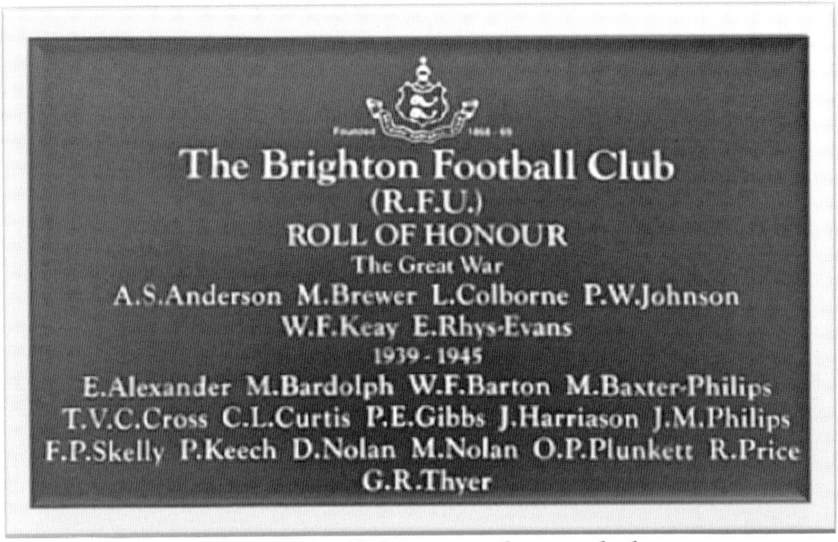

A recent acquisition to the Clubhouse, unfortunately the names were transcribed from our Handbook and over the years mistakes have been made, this has been highlighted on the rediscovery of the 1946 A.G.M. minutes. This will be amended.

May I ask all present to stand in silence for a few moments in memory of these gallant men who gave their to-morrow that we might have our to-day.

To the injured; who through their wounds cannot play again have our sympathy at being deprived of their active spirit.

Unfortunately, in addition to these war casualties the Club has lost by death A.C. Borlase, a life member, who was Hon Secretary as far back as 1883 and also J.E. Raven K.C., Club captain from 1870 to 1873. Further. Lt. Col. Beves and his brother M.H. Beves, the latter Club captain from 1893 to 1897, together with E.M. Taylor who was Hon. Treasurer from 1913 to 1921 and H.J. Green from our Vice Presidents list.

Among our valued supporters also T. Cooper Rogerson and S.N. Neild have passed away. You see, therefore, the Club has suffered considerably; it could ill afford to lose any of them and their places will be hard to fill.

We are very glad to welcome home a number of our members from P.O.W. Camp privations and monotony and hope by now they are feeling fit and well and will be able to forget their unpleasant experiences.

We are also very glad to welcome home from Services all other members and congratulate those whose gallantry and services have brought them distinctions and honours.

The finances of the club, when they were finally audited by the staff of P.V. Friend-James, saw us clear of all debts and a small balance of £6 odd. With this sum the club started active operations in December of last year and from then on seven matches have been played, six of which was won, 98 points being scored for, to 42 against. No subscriptions have been asked for and but for the generosity of a number of you and our non-playing members we could not have carried on and finish up with a balance £21 s. 0 d. 0.

The Club, during the War years, supplied goal posts, balls and jerseys to different Services and Units, all of which are difficult to get now - and costly at that. Further, we should not have been able to play at all until next September had not the Brighton Students' Association granted us the use of their admirable ground and changing facilities at Patchdean ; our very best thanks are due to them. After a quite a struggle in which our councillor P.V. Friend-James took a leading part I am very glad to report that we shall be playing once again on our former pitch in Preston Park and changing in the the rooms under the stand in the adjacent Cricket Ground. I understand that our former additional changing quarters at the Old Crown & Anchor Hotel are no longer suitable, being without bathing facilities. I attended the Annual General Meeting of the Rugby Union last year and have been present at the Sussex County Union Meeting and two meetings of the Sussex Fixture Bureau as your representative during the past few weeks. I have arranged fixtures for two XV's for 1946-47 and a few for 1947-48. In this connection, I have hopes for of a match next Easter with Oxford University in Brighton. I think, Mr President and Gentlemen. I have covered most of the points - if not all - and now present this report and statement for your approval and adoption.

W.A. Gibbs
Hon Sec. Hon Treasurer

G.S. Godfree

I have previously mentioned Mr G.S. Godfree and the sterling work he did for the Club, unfortunately, he passed away on April 4th 1947.

A.G.M. minutes, 78th Season, 1946-47, and I quote, W.A. Gibbs ;

"My first remarks however are of regret - very sincere regret, that in it we have to record the loss by death of our oldest and very valued member G.S. Godfree, Esq who passed away rather unexpectedly. He had the unique distinction of having held every office in the Club, both on and off the field, and I have heard him say, "Played in every position" he had been a member of the Club upwards of 50 years, and was President from 1925 to 1928. He was at the time of his death. Hon: Treasurer of the Sussex R.F.U.

The serene manner and quiet dignity which he always displayed in carrying out his offices in the rugby councils of this Town and County endeared him to all with whom he worked.

His name will long be remembered by Rugby men and Cricketers in Brighton and Sussex.

November 1st 1947, the "Dome" The Mayor of Brighton, (P.Friend-James President of "Brighton Football Club") gives the "Freedom" of the town to Sir Winston Churchill

The photograph (below) was taken October 1947, prior to the match against "Kings College Hospital" and the first to be played on the Sussex County Cricket Ground, Hove, following negotiations with the Sx. C.C.C. for its use.

Reading from L to R

D. Glover, "Squeaky" Harris, F. Thomas D. Benjamin
Costa Halamandres,
D.N. Sence, A.Gough, J.A. Harrison, G.Sibrey, J. Hale,
G. Burt, Winkworth,
T. Wilson, R.C. Malby, R.H.Braybon (M.B.E.)
Capt J. Moseby
W.A.Gibbs, P.Friend-James,
(Hon Sec) President
Mayor of Brighton

I came across the Annual Dinner Menu Card for April 3rd 1948, our 79th season, and thought it was worth mention because of two of the speakers.

The response to the toast to the "Rugby Football Union" was by Colonel B.C. Hartley C.B., O.B.E. who received his Brighton Football Club honours cap in 1896-97 and was The President of the "R.F.U." in 1946-47, only a year before this dinner.

The second gentleman, who proposed the toast to "Brighton Football Club" was Adrian D. Stoop Esq, who over the years became a very good friend of Brighton. The last game of the season was always played against the 'Harlequins' which was followed by a "Smoking" concert which was always supported by the Harlequin members.

If you are visiting the Harlequins ground today, the 'Stoop' memorial ground, spare a thought for a good friend of the Brighton Football Club (RFU), even though 43 years earlier he came down and "stole" John Guy Giberne Birkett (our Vice Captain).

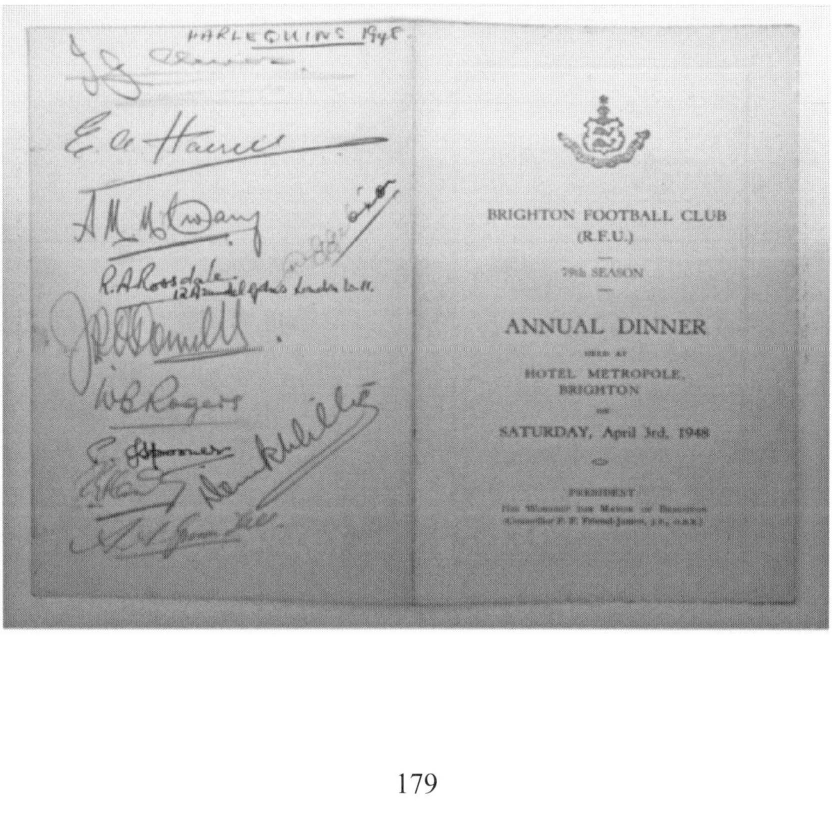

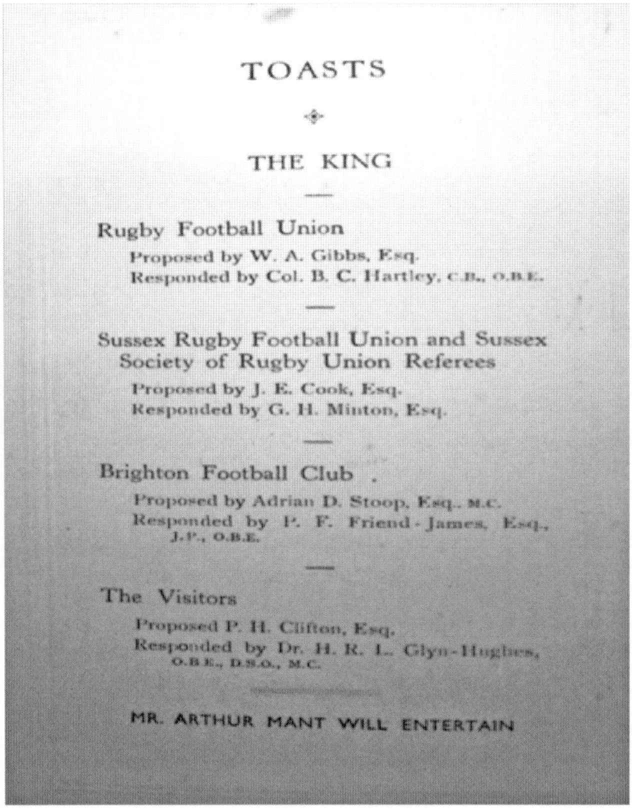
TOASTS

THE KING

Rugby Football Union

Proposed by W. A. Gibbs, Esq.

Responded by Col. B. C. Hartley, C.B., O.B.E.

Sussex Rugby Football Union and Sussex Society of Rugby Union Referees

Proposed by J. E. Cook, Esq.

Responded by G. H. Minton, Esq.

Brighton Football Club .

Proposed by Adrian D. Stoop, Esq., M.C.

Responded by P. F. Friend-James, Esq., J.P., O.B.E.

The Visitors

Proposed P. H. Clifton, Esq.

Responded by Dr. H. R. L. Glyn-Hughes, O.B.E., D.S.O., M.C.

MR. ARTHUR MANT WILL ENTERTAIN

May 1948 Sussex Daily News

FUND STARTED FOR NEW RUGBY GROUND

MR W.A.GIBBS, who has played in every position and held every Office of the Brighton Rugby Football Club since he joined it in 1919, would not allow a five-hour operation on a serious knee injury yesterday to prevent him from attending the evening's annual meeting. He had previously only missed one such meeting.

He was elected President, ending 24 years as Hon: Secretary, and the retiring President Councillor P.F. Friend-James O.B.E. (Mayor of Brighton), a former playing colleague from 1919, described him as one who had done more than any other for the Club and who had endeared himself to them all.

Mr Gibbs, after referring to the Club's happy position in having pitches on the Sussex County Cricket Ground, Hove, and Preston

Park for next season, said that they were still searching for a site where there could make their own home.

"IMPORTANT PLACE"

"This Club should occupy quite as important a place in the town as Brighton & Hove Albion F.C." he declared.

It was agreed to place £100 to a sinking fund for a new ground and to make a drive to secure at least 500 non-playing members at a guinea each to swell that fund.

Mr R. Braybon lamented that there seemed no possibility of acquiring a suitable ground within eight miles of Brighton.

The accounts revealed a credit of balance of £142 subscriptions and donations totalling £265 and gate receipts of £52.

NEW "EXTRAS"

Mr P.G. Myers was elected Hon. Secretary and Mr Gibbs was re-elected Hon Treasurer, Mr J. Harrison became captain of the first XV, with Frank Thomas as his deputy and Mr J. Cook captain of the newly conceived Extra First XV, with Mr G.H. Copes as Vice Captain.

New fixtures for the first fifteen include Old Leysians, Harrow, Sutton, Old Emanuel. Old Citizens, Portsmouth and Sidcup, while the Easter touring side will meet Chiltern, Oxford Exiles and Aylesbury.

I have many extracts and team reports from local newspapers, too many to publish, but, the game against Blackheath is worth a mention.

Sussex Daily Sports News, Monday 7th March 1949

WON AGAINST ODDS

Brighton 9pts, Blackheath "A" 3pts

An extraordinary match was that between Brighton and Blackheath "A" on the County Ground, Hove, on Saturday.

To begin with, winger D. Benjamin broke a leg within the first 20 minutes. In spite of this Brighton maintained an undoubted superiority and won by nine points to three (writes Leslie North). Brighton might have had at least another three points; a lineman gave a verdict against Burt after the winger had scored what appeared like a legitimate try, although his foot had gone over the touchline before he gathered the ball. Then when a Blackheath man attempted to convert their solitary try the ball hit the near post and bounced twice on the cross-bar before falling the wrong side ----a remarkable happening. And in the second half Weedall struck the same post with his kick! Also unusual was that Brighton had all the style and really showed the London side how to play.

Toye Excels

So for their last fixture this season on the County Ground, Brighton's 1st XV did everything conceivable to earn honour. We saw Pat Toye behind the scrum in form that even from this sterling worker I had never dreamt possible. He had been criticised for the lack of enterprise: here he was cutting through like lightning and his service from a splendid scrum---with W. R. B. Holt hooking so well that even one short they had far more of the ball--gave Tony Wilson full opportunity for his own particular brilliance and for the threes to thrust in a manner that made the Blackheath line look clumsy.

When Benjamin was carried off---- and what a hand the spectators gave this most popular player!----Killwick filled his place and showed himself to be even better three quarter than forward.

Full Back Thomas off form almost let Blackheath through three or four times with fumbles although he did much good work otherwise.

Easy for Burt

Rosen was the first Brighton man to get over, but could not touch down. Ten minutes after Benjamin's accident a beautiful three quarter movement saw Weedall cut through and give to Burt who romped over.

Rosen obtained a forceful try wide out. Weedall's kick narrowly going wide. Blackheath responded strongly and after a drop had gone near their try followed. Brighton's second half try came from Killwick who proceeded it by very clever play. Pratt always well up, almost scored and in the closing stages Blackheath lost an otherwise certain try by passing forward. One of their players alone put a drop-kick just under the bar.

I am writing this on Sunday 14th January 2018, the day after I went to the Rugby Club to watch 1st team game against Cobham, which unfortunately, we lost in the last play of the game. I was introduced to Mr David Benjamin, the gentleman named in the above article for breaking his leg. He told me "I remember the incident very well, it was when I was kicking the ball, I was tackled on my weight bearing leg, and bang, it was very painful". David went on to say he joined the Club in 1946 aged 19.

David Benjamin at the "Old Farts" Luncheon April 14th 2018

I have seen a few of these "Cartoons" but after a general email to all our members, I was still no wiser to who drew them or who they were for. This one is dated 1949.

"Stop Press", these were actually drawn by W.A. Gibbs, Art teacher at Varndean, who penned his commercial cartoons (The Argus), with the name "Howens". It was obvious really!

Chapter XI

1950 -1959

May 1950 Brighton Guardian

BRIGHTON BIDS TO END RUGBY "GRAB"

Brighton Rugby Club ----- claimed to be one of the oldest clubs in the world----is concerned at what was described at the annual meeting as the "grabbing and pinching" of Brighton schoolboy players by London Clubs.

One member stated that Blackheath invited members of Brighton College first fifteen to become honorary members each year, and that the youngsters were taken by such clubs as Blackheath and Harlequins if they went to school in the London area.

To build up the clubs future playing strength, it was agreed to invite Brighton school boys to become honorary members at the clubs discretion.

Ground still needed

The first home of the club of the club in the 1870's was the Hove Cricket Ground and Mr P.G. Myers, honorary secretary, said that if the new committee of the Sussex County Cricket Club did not allow them to use the ground it would prove a severe blow, and mean that the four teams would only have one pitch.

The Burt Trophy was won by Robin Slater, one of the best young players, and honours caps had gone to Weedle, Pratt, Barnett, Burt, Osbourne, Cook, Whiting, Mason, Elliot and Chamberlain.

The fact is, throughout the history of Brighton Football Club, we have always been a stepping stone to the London Clubs:- Bernard C. Hartley to Blackheath in 1897, John G.G. Birkett to Harlequins in 1905.. and to date, Marcus Smith, Harry Lenard, Jon Searle,

Fixture Posters were distributed in the Brighton area

Frank Taggart, Sam Morley et al, who may not have left Brighton Football Club, (RFU)if we were able to offer the equivalent of any of the senior clubs in London.

This will continue to happen, all the time we are a junior club, and it must be accepted that we are a feeder Club. However, the 1950's idea of offering Club membership or an incentive to outstanding school boys is certainly worth considering.

In my search for memorabilia, I have been given numerous large plastic bags containing invoices, bills, weekly bar takes, and other such like, and then once in a while I come across a gem like this.

I must admit I had to explain De-bagging to my wife which I will repeat here courtesy of Wikipedia.

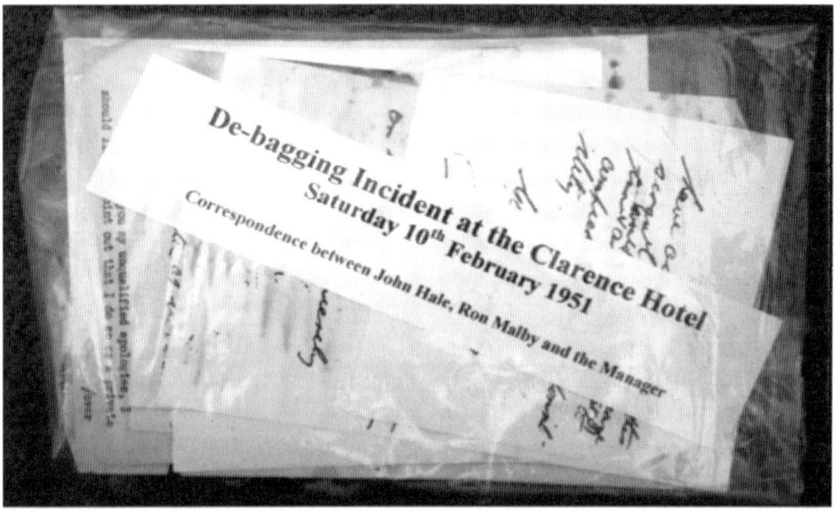

Debagging, also known as depantsing and just known as pantsing in the United States, is the pulling down of a person's trousers or underwear mostly against their wishes, typically as a practical joke.

It was reported that a group of four "gentlemen" de-bagged another gentleman in the foyer of the Clarence Hotel, unfortunately, in front of some elderly women, two fainted and one had a stroke! Sorry old joke but seriously it was in front of some Hotel residents, who consequently complained to the Manager who in turn wrote to the Club. John Hale took full responsibility and wrote to the people concerned offering his apologies which were accepted. Case closed.

And as far as we know none have admitted to turning on the fire hydrants in the corridors of the Grand Hotel during an Annual Rugby Ball, providing the assembly with the perfect aquarium setting as water gushed down the stairs and over the balcony and onto the gathering. I am told that some fairly respectable and successful local citizens still pale at the memory which was fully reported in the national papers. However, the culprit to this day has never been named, have they Mr Mike Buckingham?.

While we are on the subject of 'Shenanigans' I must include the story of the 'Harrow Dish Cover'. I have read three slightly differing stories regarding a trip to Harrow RFC. However I will combine all three for your amusement.

Apparently in the good old days, now almost beyond recall, Brighton used to have a regular fixture against Harrow. One such encounter took place on the 1st November 1952. Yes, 1952 the year George VI died and when most of our current players were not even a glint in our eyes (This was written in 1985).

Ronnie Malby was Club Captain at the time and I quote "On our way to Harrow RFC we went armed to the teeth with "Bangers". My passengers became adept at timing explosions immediately beneath the following car by the simple expedient of using a ball of string and playing it out judiciously. Reigate tunnel was a natural sound chamber and I well remember seeing an elderly couple in their early eighties jump two feet perpendicularly on the pavement. Not much is remembered about the game but it seems that Brighton might have done well as Eric Womersley, Reggie Pratt and Ronnie Malby (who played that day) recall.

Much ale was consumed and it being close to November 5th, fireworks (including rockets) were set off. As it was probably raining it's easy to understand why these were lit inside the clubhouse and perhaps the volume of ale about is a pointer to why the club house did not go up in flames. One Gerry Carr was so taken with events, that he took all his clothes off and rode around on a team mate's shoulders, declaring himself to be Lady Godiva. It seems to me that Gerry might have been confused about the historical character associated with the events of November 5th and was lucky not to have been given the treatment meted out to old Guido (Guy Fawkes) in 1606. It transpires that the squibs (bangers) worked under water as we found out in the communal Baths. Rumour has it that our Ronnie Malby himself may have had an active role in the shattering by mega squib, of an enamel jug hanging over the Harrow bar on a hook, thus scattering the membership and severely singeing a perched duck adjacent which later had to be repatriated to Brighton for convalescence.

When the Brighton lads had had their full of Harrow, they set off back to the South coast. Being a playful lot they took the odd trophy, including part of the post match dinner service. Now, those of us who are used to our pie and beans off paper plates might wonder why our heros would do such a thing. There's the rub, as he says, at Harrow, in '52 they had full silver service and what the Brighton team had half-inched was a solid silver dish cover. A stern letter to the secretary followed and a crawling and apologetic Brighton FC returned the precious item, suitably engraved thus, "All dangers passed - home safe at last. Captured from Harrow by Brighton 1.11.52 repatriated 10.1.53".

All this came to light recently when the dish cover was repatriated from Singapore where it had been taken by a touring cricket side. Now Harrow, who plainly have reverted to paper plates like the rest of us are suggesting that the dish cover become a trophy to be played for each year by our veterans XV's. Wouldn't it be fine if Eric Womersley was to play in the next match to capture the Harrow Silver.!

Another year or maybe it was the same one, we decided to visit Battersea Gardens to watch the ' Grand Firework Display', the 'swan song' of the 'Festival of Britain'. We left early, as the display never materialised. Next day the Sunday Express reported sabotage of the entire collection of fireworks citing someone was seen dropping a match in it, which was surprising as John Hale didn't smoke!

On our way back to Brighton, we stopped at the 'The Angel' at Cockshot Hill near Reigate which was a frequent stop because it was a nice pub with a nice gentile regular attendance and a large fish tank in the main bar. Relations with the publican and the clientele deteriorated sharply after a large squib (firework) of the water type mentioned by Ronnie Malby detonated inside the fish tank, creating a depth charge effect and destroying all illusion of unsullied tranquillity.

The next stop was the George in Crawley, and I understand, Alistair McKechnie's M.G.T.F. (a beautiful English sports car, very popular with WW2 pilots) which he drove to away matches was involved in an incident with a fence. No one could remember exactly who it was who chained this car to the fence, outside the George in Crawley, on the way back home from a game, but the fence left with the car and Ann Holt said she never did hear where the twain finally parted. " it was a case of self de-fence your honour".

The 8ft bench we 'borrowed' from Harrow changing room was very advantages as it allowed us to sit together in the pubs on our way home. Oh, I've just remembered--The Harrow Clubhouse did eventually go up in flames, but definitely after our fixture dates were changed.

Last but not least, Peter Clifton and Gerry Carr are linked to a story of a donkey found tethered near some club house. They led the animal inside allegedly to meet his mates from the scrum and fed it pints till it disgraced itself on the carpet.

The standard programme format of the 1950's, I always thought that was a caricature of "Gibby" but have now realised that "Gibby" was the artist, and the gentleman... "Tony Wilson"

Evening Argus Sept 1952

BRIGHTON'S NEW TEAM CRUSH HOVE IN FIRST GAME

Brighton's new Scottish International, Charlie McDonald, was the inspiration behind his sides crushing defeat of newly formed Hove in the first game of the season by 32 points (four goals, three tries, one penalty goal) to 3 (one penalty goal). The Scot, who scored 15 points himself, was too much of a handful for the Hove defence, who spent a large part of the afternoon unsuccessfully chasing his elusive shadow. Fast and quick off the mark, he showed glimpses of brilliant football, and a baffling sidestep which he used often enough to open up the game and got Hove into a tangle.

McDonald also revealed himself as a sound kicker, and when the other Brighton place kickers muffed easy and difficult chances alike he took over the role with points winning accuracy. After a slow start, Brighton's superiority stemmed from a fit and formidable pack which increasingly subdued the lively spirit of the Hove scrum and finally planted it into the ground.

The Hove backs were sadly outclassed by the Brighton three's who were competent without being outstanding and some of their work was spoiled by holding the ball too long and by careless passing. Once they had settled down, the Brighton scrum set a gruelling pace. There was no apparent weakness and it worked with unrelenting fire and energy until the end. Hove played with dogged courage, but soon enough in the first half when Brighton kept up the pressur, it was obvious that they did not have the experience, skill or class to hold either the Brighton forwards or backs. They gave everything they possessed and kept the score down to a Hunnisett try, converted by Barnet, and a typical dash by McDonald which was successful on the blind side. From then on their resistances was weakened and in one black period they went to pieces ; poor half-hearted tackling let in the hard running Brighton backs and forwards at regular intervals.

Hunnisett well covered by his back row combined effectively with McDonald, but unfortunately for Brighton, this promising partnership looks like breaking up shortly when the scrum half returns to Cambridge. A. McDonald made a good impression in the centre with his namesake may well be the answer to a weakness that has not been adequately cured since Tony Wilson's day.

Skipper Johnny Boreham with as sound support from Ian Ross and Winckworth as anyone else led the Hove pack with untiring dash, and it was fitting that they should score their only penalty goal. Brighton need better opposition before their real value can be assessed, but they showed sufficient to become a threat to other Sussex Clubs as well as those further afield.

C. McDonald (2) Burt, Farrar, P. Ross and Anthony crossed for Brighton's second half tries. McDonald also kicked a penalty and converted two and Barnet one.

Hove -- J.A. Hodgkinson, R.E. Smith, J. Wilkinson, J.E. Stanley, S. L. Jackson, D.L. Shepard, E.P. Griffin, B. Smith, W.K. Wiseman, T.R.C. Brodie, T.G. Winckworth, D.R. Lawes, M.G. Gummer, I.G. Ross, J.H.R. Boreham (Captain).

Brighton -- E.H. Barnet, G.C. Burt, R.F. Weedall, A. McDonald, A.H. Farrar, C. McDonald, D.R. Hunnisett, D. Smith, J.G. Hale, R.O. Pratt (Captain) M. Coombes, P. Maurice, M. Anthony, P. Ross, D.F. Brown.

This was the first ever game against our local rivals and unfortunately since the days of the league tables we don't play each other as often as we would like. The rivalry between the two Clubs has been intense and hopefully we will get to play each other next season. Brighton are sitting in London South 1, and Hove are hoping to get promotion to that league, so fingers crossed.

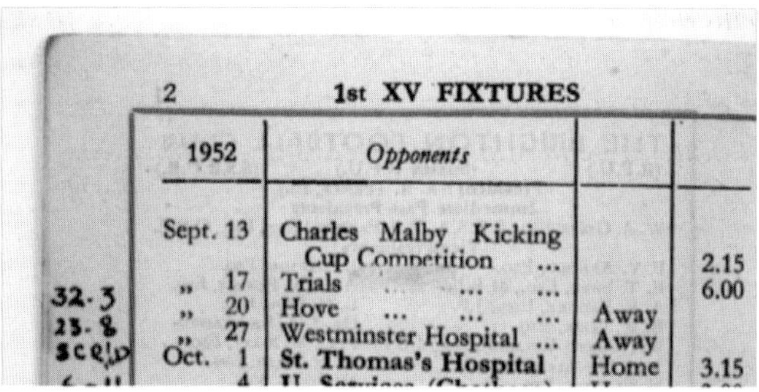
2 **1st XV FIXTURES**

	1952	*Opponents*		
	Sept. 13	Charles Malby Kicking Cup Competition ...		2.15
	,, 17	Trials		6.00
32-3	,, 20	Hove	Away	
23-8	,, 27	Westminster Hospital ...	Away	
	Oct. 1	St. Thomas's Hospital	Home	3.15

This game was played at the 'Greyhound Stadium' unfortunately, there was no representation from the Brighton Football Club but its worth a mention, as it is not every day the 'All Blacks' play on your doorstep.

Sussex Daily News March 17th 1953

BRIGHTON'S GREAT GAME WITH THE "QUINS"

One of the finest and most exciting exhibitions of Rugby Football ever seen at Preston Park was staged on Saturday by Brighton and Harlequin Wanderers, a powerful side sent down by the famous London Club. At half-time the young and heavy visiting team, playing traditional attractive "Quins" attacking game, had a lead of 14 - 3 and seemed bound to run up a cricket score. But by sheer determination Brighton made the final score 19 - 19.

Buckingham opened the score for Brighton with a try which they were fortunate to have allowed. For the rest of the first half the massive and elegant Quins took charge of the game. Brighton seemed to have no answer to the pace of Anderson on the right wing and were fortunate to be no more in arrears at the interval.

But afterwards Brighton transformed the game by sheer fury and will to win, "Mush" Holt got more than his fare share of the ball against a massive Harlequins pack in the set scrums. In the lineout relentless and drastic marking nullified the advantage of the Harlequins giants and their clever tactics.

Brighton could still not match the visitors for polish, but their enthusiasm was unconquerable. Charlie McDonald gave them a fighting chance by dropping a goal at short range when everone expected him to try and cut through.

Then Father Grogan tucked the ball firmly under his arm, put his head down, and gave an imitation of a man running through a brick wall---the only difference being that he got through.

Quins Composure Shaken

This really roused Brighton and they swarmed round the Harlequin line like angry Hornets. The composure of the Quins was shaken, but to their credit in face of a terrific hammering, they never abandoned their traditional open game, starting attacking movements behind their own posts. This policy paid, for they scored a converted try in a breakaway.

Even this reverse could not check Brighton. Back they came again. A long-range wide-angle penalty kick by Thomas caused a difference of opinion by the touch judges and was disallowed. Then Father Grogan went over for another neck or nothing try and close on time Mike Buckingham got another which levelled the scores. With practically the last kick of the game McDonald's conversion effort was carried by the wind during it's last few feet just outside the post. But a draw was a grand result for a grand game.

Brighton v Storrington College, statutory half-time refreshments 'Oranges'

The Brighton F.C. XV who played so magnificently to draw 19 points all with a powerful Harlequin Wanderers XV at Preston Park on Saturday. Left to Right (back row) ; Mr P. G. Myers (Hon Sec), Mr J. A. Harrison (referee), Father J. Grogan, W.R.B. Holt, D. Smith, P. Ross, Mr W.A. Gibbs (President Sussex R.F.U.). M. Anthony, R.M. Davis, F. Thomas, P. Maurice, C. Wilkinson, R.F. Weedall. (middle row) ; E. Womersley, P.S. Marson, R.O. Pratt (Capt) Mr R.R. Turner (President Brighton F.C.), D.F. Brown, C. McDonald, T.R.B. Scruby. (front row) : M. Buckingham, K. Wood

The Club News in the Mid season Report of 1953 caught my eye. “Some will remember "Tubby Marshall", who is with the Army in Korea, and is getting some notoriety in connection with his piano and entertaining. He has been carrying that piano around since he obtained it in Italy in 1943"

A club member Jon Orrel has recently published a book "The Regimental Piano" the story about his father who liberated a piano when he landed on the D-Day beaches, and it followed him to Germany. Definitely worth a read.

January 1954

'LEADER FOR RUGGER'

In spite of having five ribs broken at the age of 35 in a car crash, rugged John Hale, new Captain of the Brighton Rugby Football Club, is determined to make this season a victorious one.

Peter Ross, who had been elected Vice Captain, was injured in the same crash, and is still in plaster. But it is possible that Michael Anthony, Derek Hunnisett and "Mush" Holt, who were kept out of the game due to injuries last season, will be back in action.

The club have also gained two useful newcomers, One is Leslie Griffith-Slater, a 6ft 2ins guardsman, who plays wing three-quarters, and bob McPherson, a Welshman, with an Irish name, a scrum-half or fly-half, he has played for Swansea Athletic, Newport High School Old Boys, Chatham and Aldershot services.

Griffith-Slater weighs 16 stone, so he seems to be built on the lines of Vic Woodrow the International.

The Club hold their first public trials in Preston Park this afternoon. Anyone thinking of joining the Club would be welcome. The same applies to anyone thinking of joining Hove, who are holding a trial in Hove Park at 2:30.

This article caught my eye, as it mentions John Hale the new captain who was classed as "rugged", a slight understatement as the gentleman had a reputation of causing mayhem on and off the pitch, especially at the Annual Dinner Dances and in fact, he was very close to being expelled from the club, captain or not.

Another name to stand out was "Mush" Holt, who went on to be in my opinion, one of the best Presidents this Club has ever seen. I remember he would offer boiled sweets from his jacket pocket, complete with "Pocket Fur"! Last but not least, I had no idea that Derek Hunnisett played for Brighton Football Club, before he joined Hove. When I joined the Club in 1976 I was constantly asked if I was any relation to Derek Hunnisett.... No, but our ancestors arrived in East Sussex in 1542, but that's as far as the connection goes.

On the 14th May 1955 Brighton Corporation opened its long awaited 'Sports Arena' at Withdean and I quote from the "Official Programme"

Souvenir Programme for the "Official Opening"

"The Arena includes a first-class athletic ground with a running track of four laps to the mile and a straight of six lanes 520 yards in length. There are also two rugger pitches, basketball and netball pitches, squash courts and other facilities for all kinds of special sport events, displays and shows. There is a grandstand accommodation for 2,000 and open terraced seating for 2,600.

The first game Brighton played at the Stadium was on 1st October 1954 against the R.A.F.

W.A Gibbs "Sliced" the kick, when he kicked off the first game at "Withdean"

This Stadium became our home, on and off for more than a few years, and talking to Dick Thoms we agreed they were probably the worse changing rooms ever, cold, bleak dark concrete boxes but, in the 50's and 60's a showcase of a rugby stadium.

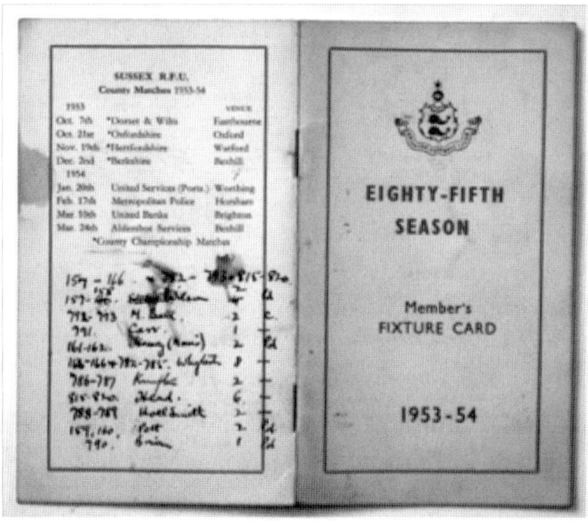

The "Sportsman" pub, and Clubhouse, Unfortunately, all bar profits went straight into Brighton Corporation coffers.

Brighton and Hove Herald 26th October 1957

RUGBY STARS AT BRIGHTON NEXT WEEK

Biggest local sporting attraction next week is the Brighton Invitation XV versus C.E.M. Lowes's International XV rugby clash under floodlights at the Brighton Sports Arena, Withdean, on Wednesday (kick off 7:30p.m.)

Introducing the largest batch of big-name players to ever visit the town for such an event, the game is being promoted by Brighton Rugby Football Club who are hoping for the same support as given to their ventures last season.

The International XV will be lead by the renown England and Rosslyn Park player, C.E. Winn, and will include, J.E. Williams, (Old Millhilians and England), D.A. Sloane (London Scottish and

Scotland), W. Kerr (London Scottish and Scotland), G. Bendon (Wasps and England), G. McKenzie-Wylie (London Scottish and Scotland trialist) J.L.A. Brown (London Irish and Surrey) and R.T. Hawley (Guy's Hospital and Surrey).

Star player of the Brighton team will be Dirk Visser, whose experience was gained with Wasps and Northern Transvaal. Others are C. McDonald (Brighton and Scotland), K. Jones (Esher and Sussex), Vernon Davis (Eastbourne and Sussex), John Taylor, (Sussex), D. Jolliffe (Wasps and Middlesex), P. Fuller (Harlequins and Sussex), J. Porter (Brighton), L. Western-Kaye (Wasps and Sussex), W. Laws (Rosslyn Park and Sussex), D. Smith (Brighton), J. Hale (Brighton and Sussex) A. Valentine (Brighton and Scotland), M. Buckingham (Brighton and Sussex).

Unfortunately, I have yet to find any information regarding the above game.

Chapter XII

'A Bitter Sweet Decade'
1960 -1969

"The Brighton Belles"

OUR LADIES LAUNCHED THE SWINGING SIXTIES!

Think back to 1960 - the start of the dazzling decade which celebrated flower-power, love, laughter, Mary Quant, the Beatles, Babycham, outrageous fashion and minis: skirts and motors!

If you can remember it (maybe not?) you will know that, although life was tough and money was short, we were optimistic and determined to have fun. The austere fifties behind us, we lived in a beautiful town, were good-looking, ambitious and, above all, young!

The Brighton Football Club (RFU) belles were the most glamorous rugby supporters in the country. Sweethearts (a very “sixties” word!), wives and friends of the players, they dressed to thrill and were, without exception, the most intelligent, articulate and charming members of the Club. The players were proud of their beautiful partners, and the girls were proud of their rugger blokes!

As poised and elegant as any of today’s celebrity models, they were often asked to appear in the press: in local papers and in national magazines. This picture was taken for a magazine feature; hair, makeup and clothes organised by the ladies and the sultry expressions of the day adopted for the shot – although I do remember that it was very difficult not to laugh.

Check out their names: you may find yourself standing next to one of these exceptional women at the Club bar!

Sally Ward-Lee,

Hon Vice President.

Back row, left to right: Marion Wyre, Janet Veasey, Mercedes Sewell, Dee Pickering, Pat Ashby, Sue Fokes, Val Boyd-Paine, Sally Ward-Lee

Middle: Fran Wallace

Front Row: Mary Corbin, Yvonne Shorland, Jill Burt.

The French poster opposite advertising, I believe, one of the first matches between Lille and Brighton. These exchange tours continued for approx 25years (Rugby) and resumed on the Golf course post "able bodied" but more on "Lille" later.

This was probably the most significant decade of our history, not necessary in terms of Rugby, but definitely regarding turning Brighton Football Club (RFU) around. From its nomadic existence in the "Drill Hall" in Gloucester Road, to the "Sportsman" at the 'Withdean Stadium' into a Rugby Club, they after 100 years can boast of having a "Clubhouse" they can call their own.

During the writing of this history, I have encountered many gentlemen. "Coster", "Moir", "Friend-James" and of course "Gibby", W.A. Gibbs, who have strived from the early days to establish a 'Home' for the Club. Gibby especially was at the forefront of establishing a 'Ground Fund' in 1948, without which we would not

be where we are now and yet he never saw the fruits of his hard work. Unfortunately William Gibbs died in 1962 so close to seeing a dream come to light, and the Clubhouse at Waterhall, well... he just would not believe it.

His death was reported at the Brighton F.C. committee meeting Monday 8th January and after communication with the Sussex R.F.U. it was agreed that an annual memorial match would be played to honour the name of the late W.A. Gibbs.

"THE BRIGHTON FOOTBALL CLUB (RFU) are very happy to arrange this Rugby Match as a tribute to the late W.A. GIBBS. He revitalised the Brighton Club after two World Wars and in his time was everything for the club from baggage boy to President, and guide mentor and friend to thousands who played in this district.

"Gibby" loved the game for the game's sake and that is why the Sussex and Brighton committees decided that a game of Rugby would be a fitting memorial, though we know "Gibby" would loved to have seen Brighton playing on its own ground. With this in mind a small plaque is being commissioned and will be affixed in a predominant place on the Brighton Clubs own Pavilion."

An Appreciation
by
R.R. Turner, Esq
President, Sussex Rugby Football Union

On the cessation of hostilities in 1918 of what we now know as World War 1, a young art master at a Brighton School returned home after serving overseas as an Officer in the Machine Gun Corps.

That young Officer was W.A. Gibbs a man dedicated to Rugby Football.

He soon entered into the task of reviving the fortunes of the game in Brighton and Sussex and thus started his career with the Sussex Rugby Football Union. This service was continuous throughout the rest of his life. He was forthright in his opinions but sincere in recognising the ideas and decisions of others. The County Union honoured him by election to the office of President for the years 1950/53 and for a term he was representative on the Rugby Football Union Committee. Both of these appointments he accepted with pride.

He was a man of varied interests. His other activities included a keen interest in philately and as a painter he had considerable ability and charm but it is as a Rugby Football administrator that he will be remembered.

When the Brighton Club conceived the idea of perpetuating his memory by suggesting a match against a side comprising of players who regularly play in Sussex, the County Union readily agreed to participate by raising the Sussex Clubs XV as their tribute to a past colleague and friend.

Our game has produced many distinguished servants but none more sincere and zealous than he whom we honour tonight and who was affectionately known in Rugby circles in Sussex and beyond as "Gibby".

"Gibby"

A note by E. Hamilton Pope, Esq

President of the Brighton Football Club (RFU) 1956-57

"Gibby" joined the Club in 1911. I joined in 1912 and we played together in the 1912-13 and 1913-14 Seasons. "Gibby" used to say that we played together in the first match after the 1914-18 War. All homes Matches were played in Preston Park in those days and we changed at the "Crown & Anchor", Preston. One of the post war photographs of the-one-and only Club Team was taken outside the Crown & Anchor and "Gibby" and I appear in this photograph. As far as I can remember, "Gibby" played in the forwards before the 1914-18 War, and full back after the War. For many years "Gibby" was Secretary and treasurer of the Club and he spent many years searching for a ground and Clubhouse. We went out to Hangleton and Braypool searching for a ground. If it had not been for "Gibby's" efforts the Club might well have closed down.

The Club played at one time at the Greyhound Racing Association Stadium and also in the Sussex County Cricket Club Ground, and then came back to Preston Park.

"Gibby was very pleased when the Club was finally established at Withdean. "Gibby" was Art Master at Varndean, and we are indebted to him for many sketches he made for programmes of Club Functions.

"Gibby" was a most loyal and hardworking member and supporter of the Club. Mr Philip Myers, who took over the secretaryship from "Gibby" said "He really WAS the Brighton Club.

Alderman Percy Friend-James (President 1946-48) said "He was a very good full back and also a hard working secretary. He was the man that put Brighton on the map and I think that's the greatest tribute one can pay him".

The Game

A classic last minute rush by the forwards, with the left wing collecting the loose ball to touch down within inches of the dead-ball line, was a suitable end to a sparkling game played at Withdean on Wednesday night, when Brighton Football Club (RFU) beat a Sussex Clubs Xv by 11pts to 3pts.

The game was a fitting tribute to one of the great personalities of Sussex rugger, the late W.A. Gibbs. It was "Gibby" who brought the Brighton Club back to life twice when World War I and II had almost destroyed it.

An art master at Varndean, his sketches were often a delightful feature of the "Evening Argus", Programmes and Club functions.

He was secretary, treasurer and president of the Brighton Club, and was a distinguished member of the Sussex Rugby Football Union, serving as its representative on the R.F.U. committee.

From 1950 to 1953 he was president of the Sussex Union, and would have watched with pleasure, this game of open, exciting rugby, held in his memory.

Brighton pushed the Sussex Clubs XV hard during the first half. After only eight minutes they were awarded that was neatly kicked by Pickering to start the scoring. Six minutes later wing forward Boddenham touched down to increase the score to 6-0.

The County team looked up, and within a minutes of the start of the second half were pressing hard on the Brighton line. There was very close marking on both sides, and on several occasions Sussex looked very much like scoring.

Then M. Herbert (Eastbourne), the Sussex left wing, ran through in the 25th minute to make the score 6-3 but the try was not converted. From then on the county players really turned on the heat. Good kicking and even better catching by full back Trott were the only thing that saved the home team on several occasions.

It was left to D. Sherwood to complete the scoring with a magnificent try in the last moments, and the Captain Derek Pickering converted, although it was within ten yards of the touch-line.

On the April 10th 2018, I purchased this rugby "Honours Cap" presented by "Brighton College Football Club"

The cap was advertised for sale with the name W.A. Gibbs!

The local Sussex Daily News regularly produced a "Rugby Personality" article and would seem a good time to embarrass two Captains from the 60s.

"Local Rugby Personalities"
'Derek Pickering'

Derek Pickering, A great all round sportsman, now in his tenth year with the Club. Was Skipper of the Brighton Football Club (R.F.U.) from 1961 to 1964. Has played for Sussex and Martlets. Really a full-back, but often plays at fly-half or in the centre.

An excellent batsman, he plays for St James's Cricket Club and occasionally turns out for Sussex Second XI.

Played for English Schools' Cricket team against Combined Services when he was at Brighton College.

So, as you can see, Derek's daughter, Karen Pickering M.B.E. had little chance at any success in the Sporting World..! Sic, (British Swimming Squad, 8 World Championship medals (4 gold), 14 European Championship medals, 38 National Championship titles, and a Commonwealth Games medal haul of 13 including 4 gold.

'Peter Harbidge'

Peter Harbidge, who is skippering Brighton this season 1967 (I may add until 1970, and then again in 1979-80), is an all-round sportsman.

He was formally a soccer professional with Gillingham. He plays cricket for St James's, and is a fine squash player, belonging to Hove Squash Club.

Peter joined Brighton at the start of the 1965-66 season. He is a most versatile rugger man, playing ably in the centre although he is naturally a back row forward. He came to Brighton from the well-known London Club, Old Anchorians. He has proved a most popular member of the Brighton Club.

Sussex Daily News, Sept 31st 1963

THREE PLAYERS GO OFF

Brighton continued their good start to the season with a fine win over the touring side Llanelly Wanderers at Withdean, although due to three unfortunate injuries the margin of victory ; 27pts to 3, was somewhat flattering.

Brighton included John Moffatt, who played for Ireland two seasons ago, as a replacement for Bell at fly-half and he played a major part in proceedings, initiating three try scoring movements from inside his own half and contributing 10pts, to the score in penalty goals and conversions.

Two early penalty goals by Moffatt for Brighton in a slow opening period gave little indication of the action to come. Llanelly lost three players with leg injuries in the space of 20 minutes--two of them permanently---including their fly-half Eifion Thomas, in the act of scoring a splendid unconverted try.

Platt restored the margin of Brighton's lead with a try before half-time. In the second half the handicapped Llanelly side fought back courageously and their six remaining forwards almost contained the Brighton Pack.

But superiority in numbers eventually told and Brighton further increased their lead with tries from Dayson (2) and Watts, two of which were converted by Moffatt and one by Trott.

Jonathan Moffatt, who was born in Belfast on 30th April 1937 won two caps for Ireland in the 1961 5 nations tournament against England and Scotland

Brighton & Hove Herald, Dec 1965

BRIGHTON WIN THE CLASH WITH HOVE

Brighton entertained Hove in the local derby, and won convincingly by 17points (one goal, one try, one dropped goal, and two penalties) to 3 points, (one penalty).

The superiority was in the Brighton front row in the set pieces, where Holt and the new prop forward Powell combined well.

Hove opened the scoring after 25 minutes with a penalty well taken by JACKSON, their full-back, after the Brighton pack had been penalised for a scrum infringement. Five minutes later Brighton were awarded when a Hove player was pulled up for lying on the ball and PICKERING made no mistake with the kick

Shortly afterwards the Brighton three-quarters made a fine run for the line, only falling short when Watt's pass was adjudged forward to Harbidge on the wing, so the sides turned around with the score at three all.

After resumption of play the Brighton pack pushed Hove on to the defensive and from a quick heel on the Hove 10-yard line, the ball went out to NICHOLLS who dropped a magnificent drop goal from 45 yards. From this moment the Hove side became somewhat demoralised which enabled the Brighton three-quarters to capitalise on any mistakes that were made.

Midway through the second half, Brighton were again awarded a penalty for another scrum infringement which PICKERING converted.

The best movement of the afternoon developed from a set scrummage near the Hove line, when Brighton gained quick possession and the half back pair worked a dummy movement resulting in WATTS going over in the corner.

The final score of the afternoon was made by county centre WATTS who, from just inside the Hove half, kicked the ball forward, took the ball on with his feet, finally outran all the Hove defenders and scored near the posts. PICKERING made an easy conversion.

While the final score might suggest an easy win for Brighton this was by no means true.

The appeal leaflet showing the "artist impression" of the "New" Clubhouse at Horsdean

Brighton "A" were narrowly defeated by Hove Yeomen by 8 points to 6 points. Hove scored twice in the first half, by means of a try and a goal, but Brighton fought back with tries by STRATTON and REDBOURNE ; unfortunately the conversions failed.

Extracted from the "Appeal Leaflet"

In June 1967, an appeal was launched to raise funds.

This is an appeal for funds to help the Brighton Football Club (Rugby Football Union) finance the building of their first ever Clubhouse in almost 100 years. The Club will celebrate its centenary in 1968 and has a wonderful opportunity of establishing its own headquarters at Horsdean, if friends, old and new, will give a little help.

As the result of negotiations with Brighton Corporation, the Club will have two fine new additional pitches at Horsdean and the opportunity to build its own clubhouse on adjoining land. An artist's impression of the project is shown on the front of this leaflet. Building costs being what they are today, the club needs substantial additional funds to fulfil the dream of many generations of Brighton and Sussex players.

This is why we are asking for your help.

We would not be making this appeal if the club had not already done a great deal to help itself. Due to the investment of members' generous donations and amounts set aside from the general fund, the club has accumulated approximately £2,000 in its Ground Fund, for the express purpose of financing its own ground and clubhouse.

We believe that the establishment of real headquarters will greatly assist the attainment of a higher standard of play, which will help one of the country's oldest rugger clubs to take its rightful place amongst the top clubs in this fine sport and will, therefore, also be of benefit to Sussex County Rugby.

We hope you agree with us and will join in helping make this hundred-year-old dream come true. We ask you to choose one or more of the alternative methods set out below. This is a "once only" appeal, made in the sincere belief that, given the means of seizing this opportunity, the club will become fully self-supporting for its second hundred years."

In 1961, Brighton F.C. were aware that there was a possibility of establishing a Clubhouse and pitches at Horsdean. This had been negotiated by the Club and Brighton Corporation. The Licence at Withdean Sports Stadium was running out and more matches were being cancelled due to the pitches being "Unfit" to play on.

Tom Wing and Derek Pickering were the Club members who had the initial liaison with Brighton Corporation and along with David Benjamin formed part of the new "Ground and Centenary Committee"

Mr W. Gibbs 1948 "Ground Fund" was finally coming to fruition. It was reported in February 1964 that £8,000 had been allocated, by Brighton Corporation, for work on the new ground and Clubhouse, it was anticipated that operations would start in April 1964. The earliest possible time for the Club to move in would be September 1966.

It was January 1965 that Derek Pickering reported to the "Ground Committee" that he had prepared a layout, the estimated cost of which was £6,000, probably excluding the cost of the main services. The next step was to get out drawings, specification and cost in detail so that the Club could apply for planning permission, loans etc.

It wasn't until April 1965 that Plans for the proposed Clubhouse had been lodged with the Corporation for planning permission.

Brighton and Hove Herald, Friday November 15th 1968

BRIGHTON CELEBRATE THEIR CENENARY
Romance behind 100 years of rugby

Brighton Rugby Football Club celebrates its 100th anniversary this season, and in doing so, the Club attains the seniority only shared by a handful of Clubs which include Blackheath, Harlequins, Richmond and Wasps.

That the Club has stood the test of time is itself, of course, a matter of congratulation. And the club knows that on this memorable occasion it carries the sincere best wishes of all its associates for its future.

On such occasion, it is only natural to reflect on the Club's past fortunes and to attempt to measure its progress by the yardstick of the years. Over a span of years, every institution reaps its poor, as well as rich harvests, and Brighton bears out this historical truism with remarkable regularity, since the 1920's, it has followed a pattern of rise and decline which can be measured, to a fair degree, in terms of decades.

Unfortunately, very early records of this Club --- apart from the odd, anonymous photograph--- are not available. But we do know that after the first World War, they went rapidly from strength to strength. If one was to ask which period was Brighton's "Golden Age" one would point to the late "twenties"

The Club's fixture list was the strongest it has ever been, including the first teams of clubs like Saracens and Sutton.

In the 1927-28 season, Brighton reached peak form---the club won 24 of the their 27 fixtures drawing one and losing two.

In the early "thirties", however, in keeping with the social depressions, the Club begins to slump. Other local clubs were being formed---the Coldean Club, the Sussex Yeomanry club---even the Brighton Cruising Club started a rugger section---which tended to dilute the local talent.

The club experienced long losing sequences, the press reports became more and more despairing and the fixture list was gradually weakened.

In the 1936-37 season, when Brighton only won three of its 24 games, the Herald blamed "the departure of regular players to other districts, injuries and bad luck.

The situation got so bad that in 1937, this rather desperate notice appeared. "Brighton Rugby Football Club" have been so heavily hit by injuries recently that they are finding it very difficult to field three fifteens. Any visitors to the town who would like a game will therefore, be welcomed if they get in touch with W.A. Gibbs.

"Dramatic"

The only highlight of this period was when Brighton routed the Surrey side Wallington, 61-0 in 1938, thus establishing a Post War record. The 1903 record when Brighton beat Eastbourne College 65-nil

Against this however, Brighton had been thrashed 64-8 by the 1907 Harlequin side which included four Internationals.

Matters didn't really improve until after the second World War, but when they did, the change was dramatic.

After a few promising seasons Brighton created a new club record in 1949-50 season when they scattered all before them. They dropped only one game the whole season and that was against the Old Citizens over a Easter weekend, when many regular players were absent.

Current President, "Mush" Holt, played in the team as hooker during that season. He recalls:

"We had an incredibly strong side which contained eight County players. We played over thirty fixtures and nothing could go wrong. But it did become a tremendous strain as the season wore on with every club anxious to be the first to crack our record".

But, even during this period, one foreboding note was sounded by a local correspondent who said, "No other Sussex Club has such a good record, Never the less, it is nowhere near enough if Brighton are to become a truly first-class club. I would rather next season that they lost most of their games, as long as they did so against better teams. Only by playing sides better than themselves can they improve their standard.

That voice of reason can still be heard today. The Club experienced another decline during the fifties culminating in a disastrous 1959-60 season from which only a handfull of victories were salvaged.

But, in the early sixties, the club began to expand its membership and deepen its reserve strength, it has been making steady progress ever since and this season, appropriately, promise to be the best so far.

In the "Gibbs" Memorial game at Withdean, they even took on--- and beat---the Rest of Sussex team by nine points to five!

If Brighton can get four or five top London Clubs on their fixture list---even five or six years hence, it could herald a new era for them.

A letter to all members, 24th September 1968

NEW CLUB HOUSE ARCHES 214, 215 KINGS ROAD (BY THE FISH MARKET)

Centenary year - no Clubhouse - no loans likely for the next two/three years - no Clubhouse likely for the next two/three years.

The above summarises our plight at the last A.G.M. and in order to rectify the position certain club members have put in a great deal of effort with the result that the position at the moment is as follows ;

a) Negotiations are in progress to lease the above adjoining Arch premises from Brighton Corporation with security of tenure for the next three to five years.

b) Applications have been made for licensing, planning and bye law approval, the intention being to provide two new arch fronts, together with toilets, cloakroom, storage and bar facilities in one arch and recreation facilities in the other.

c) The various committees considering the application all sit during the first week of October and, if approvals are forthcoming, we hope to start work immediately and have a Clubhouse running before the end of November.

This is your Club - the results of the last two weeks have proved that there is a great rugby potential in depth in the club and there is no reason why in addition we shouldn't be the best social club in Sussex.

To this end it is not in our best interests to produce a makeshift "spit'n sawdust" headquarters when, with a certain amount of effort from all members we could easily produce a sophisticated, comfortable and unusual meeting place for after match entertainment, dances, evening drinking, summer sailing, rowing and the like.

With the above facilities we should then have something with which to attract ex-members and past players living in the district as well as enabling a greater club spirit to be developed with the club.

All this can be achieved but only if you make it - we are already counting on assistance labour wise, however, the more materials that are provided by you the more we will have to spend on furnishings and fittings, and to start the ball rolling, Bill Holt (El Presidente) has offered to supply the labour and materials for the arch fronts - £120 plus. Attached is a list of the materials required at this present moment - let Bill know at Peacehaven 2215. If anyone wants to see the arches please contact John Wallace and he will endeavour to show you around at lunchtimes. Remember, it's not the other member that is going the achieve this - IT'S YOU.

I'm glad to say, that eventually, with the help of Pickering, Laing, Wallace and "Mush" Holt and many others, Brighton Football Club (RFU). received the planning permission to build our New and "first" Clubhouse. Meanwhile, on the 14th October 1968 we were granted a tenancy of "The Arches" 214/215 King's Road, Brighton. at a rental of £312 per annum. I must mention a note attached to the Agenda of the Annual General Meeting 1969, that was held at the Royal Pavilion Hotel.

Note; In view of the increase in the price of a basic mini car since the inauguration of the 100 Club, your committee recommend that, for this year, there should be an added bonus of £50 cash, if the winner decides to take the money. This brings the cash prize up to £450 which more than fairly represents what the car would realize second hand if taken as an investment. It should also be noted, in order that there is no disillusion afterwards, that approximately £50 in the way of seat belts, Road Fund Licence, delivery charge etc, needs to be found by the winner to put the car on the road. Your committee also recommend that for the future, the annual prize be fixed at £400 in order to avoid any embarrassment due to tax and price fluctuations.

And I quote Roger Lowrie "It was either a mini or £400. I took the money and bought a second hand MGB. Being the second or third time I had consecutively won I was dragged upstairs at the Pavilion Hotel and thrown fully clothed into a bath of cold water by John Jennings and his cohorts, Bastards!! I still put £20 behind the bar for post dinner Port".

1970 - 1978

Brighton and Hove Herald, Friday, January 31st 1969

Brighton Rugby Club look like hitting the jackpot in this, their Centenary Season. At the beginning of the season the club was in an embarrassing position of being one of the oldest clubs in the Country, but without either a Clubhouse or Pitch.

Now they have their Clubhouse and are on their way to getting permanent grounds. Their lease at Withdean Stadium has been extended for another year and a working party of the local Sports Advisory Council are to meet members of Brighton Corporation to discuss using Withdean at least until the pitches at Horsdean have been tried and proven

And just after the New Year, The Arches Clubhouse was opened with all the boisterous proceedings which usually flavour rugby gatherings. The Club has negotiated the lease on two Arches on Brighton's Sea Front on a six-monthly basis.

The main social room-a huge purple-and concrete version of a Nissan hut-- is open daily and the other arch serves as a dance-hall.

Talents

All the conversion work, both interior and exterior, has been done by Club members. Under the efficient general ship of John Wallace, talents other than rucking and covering have been uncovered to put to good use.

Club President, "Mush" Holt, provided and installed the brickwork, Mike Buckingham was responsible for the painting and Kerry Nind and John Hindmarsh have shown themselves to be expert carpenters. A tremendous amount of work has been done by Chris Smith, skipper Peter Harbridge and others too numerous to mention.

Earlier this season the Club raised £250 on a sponsored walk and the executive committee allocated a further £300 to be spent on the new premises, £400 of this has already been spent and the remaining £150 will be used to provide heating and other amenities.

Members of the Brighton Club do not have to pay any subscription to join, but for anyone else wishing to join there is an initial entrance fee of 2/6d and then an annual subscription of 10s. Those wishing to do so should contact the Club secretary.

New Clubhouse

The big question which now hangs over the Arches is--- will the clubhouse be temporary or permanent? Initially, it was planned to use the Arches as a temporary base before social premises were ready at Horsden..

But the club is providing such a money spinning success that many members are now having second thoughts. Personally, I think it would be disastrous to move the clubhouse out to Horsdean, when, if ever, the new pitches are ready.

Gatherings at the Withdean annex bar after rugby matches always used to fizzle out pretty quickly because players wanted to get home for dinner.

Central

But at the Arches---mainly because of its central position--- the numbers swell rapidly after the game and the proceedings become more convivial as the evening wears on.

More than that, the Arches are providing a great success on weekdays and Sunday afternoons.

It is proposed to continue running the Arches during the Summer and this of course will be the crucial testing time.

Most important of all is that the Arches could prove an enormous financial, as well as a social asset. We will have to wait another few weeks before the profit-margin over a period of time can be assessed with an degree of accuracy.

But at the first Saturday Hop, the Club took £50 at the door and over £150 over the bar---so they can't be doing badly.

So, at the moment, the future looks bright. As they say up North, where there's muck there's brass---so here's mud in your eye!

The Arches were a roaring success to the extent that the Club tried to extend the tenancy of the 'Arches', even though the clubhouse at 'Horsdean' would soon be under construction.

However it would seem that Brighton Corporation had other ideas, a glimpse into the correspondence of the time might show some light on their unwillingness to oblige.

From the "Town Clerk" 21st November 1969

"I wish to refer to your letter of the 11th July to which no formal reply was sent in view of the action taken by the Police immediately afterwards. There is no need to remind you that the officers of the Club, including yourself, pleaded guilty at the Brighton Magistrates Court on the 31st October to a number of Summonses issued under the Licensing Act and the Betting, Gaming and Lotteries Act. From the Proceedings in the Magistrates Court it was clear that the Club had been in breach of a number of terms of its Lease from the Corporation dated 20th January 1969, and this despite the emphatic denials in your letters of the 3rd and 11th July". (The letters dated 3rd and 11th July stipulated only Club members and their guests would be allowed to enter the premise) Unfortunately, that was not the case hence the Police raid.

From "The Club" 2nd December 1969

I am in receipt of you letter of the 21st November. I cannot, however, agree that the Club is in breach of any covenant in the Lease.

The Club very much regrets the proceedings which were taken against the officers under the Licensing Act and the Betting & Gaming Act. I would point out, however, that the officers were only fined in respect of one technical offence, and stated by the Police that they were satisfied that the Club had been properly conducted before the incident in question and also since that occasion, which is some 5 months ago.

The Club considers that it has complied the terms of its lease in the past, and will certainly endeavour to continue to do so in the future.

From the "Town Hall" 8th January 1970

"I am still somewhat bemused by your insistence that the Club has not been in breach of any of its covenants in the Lease of these premises. I would have thought that at least the Club had been in

breach of Clause 2 (5) - the covenant to comply with all statutes etc, relating to the conduct and management of the Club - and clause 2 (11) - the user clause which restricts the user to "Licensed Club Premises for the Brighton Football Club.

In addition, the remarks in the second paragraph of your letter that the officers were fined only in respect of one technical offence under each act, surprises me ; according to my information, you yourself were found guilty on at least four charges under the Betting, Gaming and Lotteries Act, and at least 32 offences under the Licensing Act!"

"In the circumstances I feel that you request for a new lease is premature and cannot be considered by the committee until the future policy for the Arches as a whole is considered".

From "The Club 15th January 1970

"I note what you say with regard to a new lease of the Arches and with regard to the New Clubhouse, I would point out that this comprises merely a changing accommodation and there are no social facilities there"

From "Town Clerk" 26th January 1970

"I find it difficult to discover exactly what your Club's intentions are regarding the venue for social activities!

In June 1969 the Council as landlords approved plans for the erection of a new pavilion at Horsdean (Plan No. 69/828) and the plans included an area of the building marked "Social Area".

One assumes that it is within this part of the building that the bar and other social facilities would go?

As the Club are going to the trouble and expense of erecting a social area within the Horsdean premises, I am surprised at the implication that they will wish to maintain their actual Club facilities at the Arches when, with a comparatively small additional expense, they could complete the social area at Horsdean and so have all their facilities, and consequently their expenses, confined to one building.

Annual Dinner at the "Arches

The Mayor of Brighton, Frank Masefield-Baker Laying The Foundation Stone at "Horsdean""Brighton Football Club" on 4th March 1970. (Bill "Mush" Holt and Mike Buckingham, on the right looking on)

Brighton 1st XV 1971

The Season of 1970/71 is an historic one for Sussex Rugby in that a competition was introduced for the first time, in the form of the Knock-out Cup---although as you will see from the cover 'Trophy' would perhaps be more apt description. Thirty teams entered the competition and the interest it created was considerable, giving a clear illustration of the beneficial stimulus that "cup tie atmosphere" can bring to Rugby Football. Junior Clubs, many based on villages, were being given the opportunity of playing their more "illustrious neighbours". The results of the competition, details on the back page of this programme, reveal that the matches have been keenly contested.

The Sussex Trophy had been donated to the Sussex Football Union by the Vice-Presidents of Lewes Rugby Club.

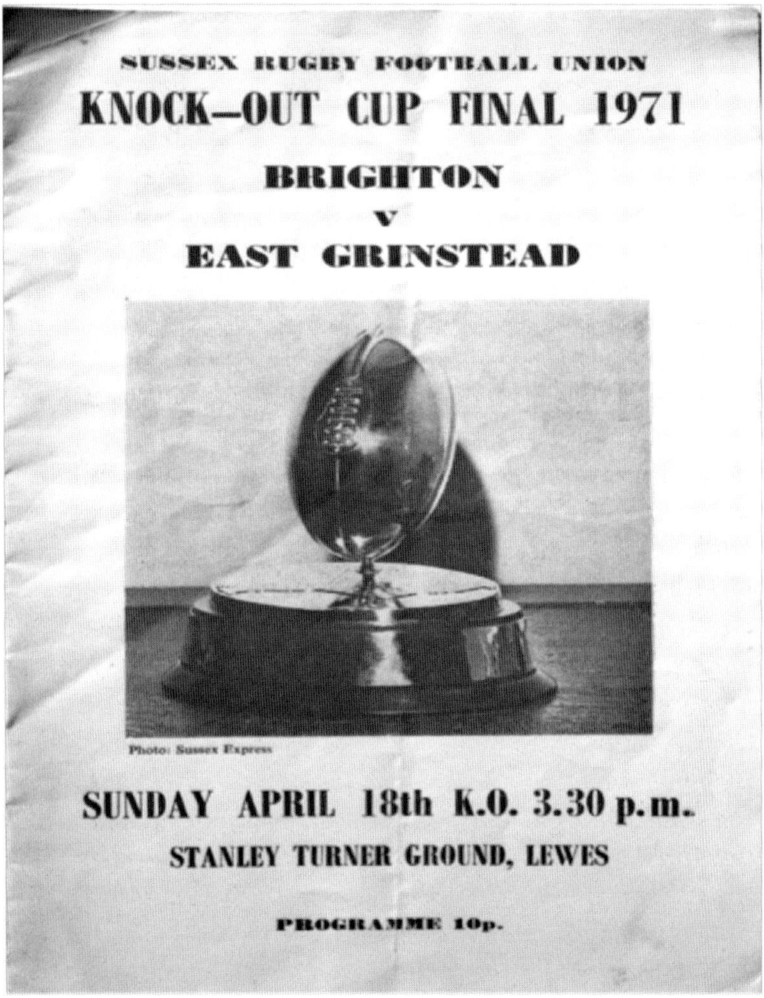

Evening Argus, Tuesday, April 20, 1971

"Brighton hang on to be the pride of the County"

Brighton are the pride of Sussex. They outclassed East Grinstead, who relied on enthusiasm, to win the Knockout Cup 11-9 at Lewes.

It was a sad end for Grinstead who have put so much into these games, Drilling, training and sheer determination haven driven them to the final.

They went straight into the attack, Centre Rick Walshaw led them in tucking the ball under his arm and charging through, Alan Plester nearly made it accelerating at the line from an inside pass from the scrum near the Brighton line.

All the tricks to make the gaps seemed to be at their finger tips, but they never quite made it. There forwards doing a fine job.

But Grinstead were getting nowhere and the experience and constant pressure of the Brighton pack was slowly dissolving their rhythm.

It was a childish gesture that gave Brighton the lead. Mike Eden Brighton's fly-half, kicked ahead and Grinstead's full-back Kirsopp had to kick backwards into touch.

Brighton were eager for a quick throw in, but a Grinstead man threw the ball away. Peter Harbidge converted the penalty from the 25 on the side after half an hour.

Grinstead were fighting hard, but making mistakes. A careless pass to Plester went astray, a desperate kick failed to make touch and Brighton put up a kick. The ball bounced awkwardly as rightwing for Brighton Ian Griffiths kicked on and went over for a try. Full-back Richard Greenaway converted from 10yrds in for the half time score.

Brighton faced a grim task with Grinstead giving all they had and the wind making any penalty in there half kickable, especially for Rick Walshaw's boot. But they excelled.

After 15 mins of the half a line out infringement gave Walshaw the chance to narrow the gap with a 35 yrd penalty. Shortly after, it was he who accidently set them up again. He attempted a drop at goal which fell short, but bounced badly for the defence and Grinstead kicked ahead and the ball looked liked it would roll easily over the dead ball line, but it curled and ran along for lock Roger Grey to drop on it.

Walshaw threw away the chance to equalise, hitting the ball slightly on one side and missing a easy conversion from a few yards outside his posts.

Then Brighton won a heel against the head, ten yards from the Grinstead Line, Jennings went blind, but could not get through. He had left wing Chris Kerin outside him, but turned as if to give it back to the forwards and the Grinstead defence forgot him and headed to the pack.

PENALTY

Jennings charged forward and got a high pass down to Kerin who dived over. The kick missed, but Brighton had kept the pressure on their line.

It still seemed to be off when a penalty was awarded near the centre spot. Walshaw hit it right in the middle for a 45 yard conversion. Time was slowly running out, but Brighton held out and can still claim to be the best side in Sussex.

The victorious Brighton Team, Champions of Sussex 1971

1971 was Brighton's turn to host the annual fixture against Lille University Club. I do not have details of the game other than it finished 15 - 15 which was the first time they drew a game.

The culmination of the weekend was the "Grand Dinner" and awards presentation on the Sunday evening. Unbeknown to the attendees, Bill "Mush" Holt our president had taken the Lille - Brighton "Cup" to his workshop and proceeded to cut it into two! which caused much hilarity when the two halves were presented to the Captains. Unfortunately, the whereabouts of the "halves" have been lost in time and a new cup was fashioned for the following years.

The "Lille" fixture continued until the early Eighties when it was deemed that both sides were getting too old to play the game of rugby, especially when all the players were now in the forties or fifties, however the "Entente Cordiale" can still be seen on an annual basis on the Golf courses of France and England.

A letter to the Magistrates Court, confirms the closure of the Arches.

19th January 1973

Brighton Football Club (RFU)

This is to advise you that the above Club has now vacated the Premises of 214/215 Kings Road, the "ARCHES", and we have moved to Horsdean, Vale Avenue, Patcham, as our new Club House is now completed.

I confirm I have sent a copy of this letter to the Police.

Yours faithfully
Robin J. Hugget

A tradition between Lille and Brighton, was the exchanging of gifts. In the past, bowls, vases, wooden plaques, flags and banners were exchanged. But in one particular year, the following photograph, with much hilarity, was given to Brighton. I believe, the photo was an insinuation on what Lille would do to Brighton on the rugby field.

Peter Harbidge, Mike Brownhill, Bill Holt, Dick Braybon, John Hale Reggie Pratt, Charlie McDonald, Frank Voak, David Benjamin, Reg Turner.

SPECIAL EVENT AT HORSDEAN

The new honours boards showing all the past Presidents and Captains of this worthy and long established Club will be unveiled at the cheese party on Sunday January 26th by Reggie Turner, past president and former Captain.

Everybody is then invited to take wine with Bill Holt to celebrate the event. Our sincere thanks are due to Frank Voak for the many hours that he spent painting the boards with meticulous care, they are a true work of art.

Thanks also to his wife for the production of the curtains that form the picturesque surround. The unveiling is scheduled for 1o'clock -- give or take a minute or two and Club members of all ages are cordially invited to attend. The boards are in the process of being updated and will be back up for our 150th season.

Evening Argus, January, 1974

TROUBLE AS LEWES FLOP IN TOP CLASH

BRIGHTON avenged their defeat in the quarter finals of the Knockout Cup, to clinch their first win over Lewes for four years by 7 - 3 at Withdean Brighton. Lewes flopped miserably, could do very little right and showed hardly a glimmer of fire, even as they struggled desperately to avoid defeat in the dying minutes they hardly made an impression. The clash between the two top clubs in Sussex got off to a punch-up start. Twice in the first 15 minutes players had to be pulled apart and then it settled down to Lewes trying to find their form and Brighton keeping the Lewes three-quarters in check. Ever since they beat Brighton in the Cup six weeks back Lewes have been excelling and there is no doubt they can win, but this time Brighton had the fire and enthusiasm. They hustled Lewes with a pack well experienced from their recent battles from their strong fixture list which prevented Lewes finding their rhythm. They had a magnificent defence, inevitably with a double line of defenders. It was soon quite obvious that unless Lewes could click into their usual form they were in line for their second defeat of the season.

The first punch up came after seven minutes was between Brighton prop Graham Nicholas and Lewes lock Andy Herman. Then Brighton went ahead after 15 minutes with possession from a line-out, punted cross-field by veteran fly-half John Woodley on the left, Hopkins dived over next to the right corner flag. Lewes left-wing Ron Bennison tackled him as he went over and again another punch-up started, even after Hopkins shirt had been pulled over his head his arms his arms were still flailing.

Lewes had lucky let offs, especially when Harbidge missed a penalty. He succeeded with a kick after 36 minutes. Right on half-time Lewes full back Bob Mainstone put over a penalty from an angle inside the 25. It should have been an ideal platform to a second half fight back, but then there was hardly any urgency until time had almost run out.

Evening Argus Jan 1974

BRIGHTON'S 24-6 victory at WORTHING's Castle Road ground was as easy as the scores suggests. Brighton efficiency and inventive flair reaped its reward in the form of one goal, three tries and two penalty goals, while the home team could muster only two penalty goals in reply. Although Worthing opened the scoring with a penalty goal from Mike Bamsey after a scrum infringement.

Brighton pulled back with a try from right-wing Kevin Hopkins,. his speed took him clear after following up a kick by Brighton's star man Jamie Mitchell, at outside-half. Mitchell's finely angled kicks were a feature of the game, and as well as providing a flow of passes for his team-mates he was rewarded with a try himself when he kicked ahead, gathered in style and went over in the corner.

Mitchell's try came after Peter Harbidge had kicked a penalty goal to give Brighton a 7-4 lead interval lead. Chris Kerin scored a try equally as good as Mitchell's effort, and Harbidge converted to widen the points gap after the interval. Cudmore kicked a penalty goal for Worthing after a line-out incident, but John Jennings, Brighton's scrum half, completed the scoring when he went over in the corner.

Evening Argus, Dec, 1976

BRIGHTON, who last week beat Streatham-Croydon continue on their successful road to moulding a side which can play open rugby.

They are certainly scoring tries, just as their 30-21 defeat of East Grinstead proved. They scored six tries and Ian Robinson converted three of them. Grinstead managed only one try by Les Ward, and the rest of the points came from Chris Lewis's boot with five penalties and a conversion.

Brighton's tries came from Chris Kerin who is back on the wing in place of the injured Nick Tetlow, Malcolm McNeil, skipper Geoff Hindle, Kevin Hopkins, Ian Griffiths and Mike Brownhill. Brighton will have to stamp out a tendency to give away penalties, if they are to have a successful run in the cup, however, they gave away three penalties in five minutes to transform a commanding lead into a meagre 20-15 margin at one stage.

Over the years I have begged, borrowed and swapped cards to enhance my collection..
I need, 1901-02, 1921-22, 1924-25, 1996-97, 2000-01and 2001-02..!!

Brighton Football Club (R.F.U.) 1st XV 1974-75
S.O'Sullivan, K.Hopkins , D.Tatum, I.Robinson, M.McNeil
D.Malby M.Pocock, S.Fry, G.Hindle
G. Nicholas, B.Holt, (President) M.Brownhill (Captain) P.Harbidge
C. Kerin, B.Lowe, N. Tetlow

Brighton's third team are in danger of eclipsing even the first teams achievements the way they are running up the points, with former Sussex fullback Mike Jackson leading the way with 108 points, and they have tallied 398 for, to 28 against in just nine games. Jackson's ton-up has stung a few pockets as well. He was challenged to reach 100 points by Christmas.. It seems only fair that it should be double or quits on him reaching 200 by the New Year.

Brighton Gazette Feb 1976

BRIGHTON REACH FOR KO CUP GLORY

BRIGHTON must overcome a hoodoo if theu are to beat Crowborough and win the Sussex Knockout Cup on Sunday. For the ground chosen for the final seems to hold a jinx.

The match is at Lewes---full of unpleasent memories for Brighton. They won the first Knockout there in 1971---but since then they have come away from there with nothing to show but exasperation. "there must be something about this place that we don't like" said Club Captain Graham Nicholas, "We always seem to lose there, but this time we'll just have to make sure that doesn't happen" Nicholas believes his side will start slight favourites, "It's obviously going to be an evenly contested game, but we've run into form at the right time, and are quite confident. A point in our favour is that we have a tougher fixture list than Crowborough, and that should stand us in good stead. We're constantly geared for big matches"

In beating Gravesend 17-3 on Saturday, Brighton produced some of their best rugby of the Winter, and Nicholas is hoping that they will hold on to their form long enough to carry them through to the weekend.

"We're going to have a busy time . Apart from the cup final, we will be playing Warlingham tomorrow, as arranged, he said.

There are those who thought the Warlingham game should have been cancelled, leaving the weekend clear for the final. But Nicholas felt it was unfair to cancel the fixture at the last minute. "We've a good relasionship with Warlingham. We've played them over many years, and it would be wrong to let them down. The only risk we run is losing players through injury, but a player can be injured in a training session just as easily". The same fifteen have been picked for both Saturday and Sunday games Crowborough also have a game on Saturday against Chichester.

Nicholas is looking to wingers Frank Samsom and Kevin Hopkins and back-row forwards Stu Fry, John Pope, and Malcom McNeil to provide the spark. "These might be key players, but we're an experienced alround side, and each individual has the ability to win the game". Brighton Team; I. Robinson, F. Sansom, J. Mitchell, M. Brownhill, K. Hopkins, I. Griffiths, R. Lowrie, G. Nicholas, G. Beard, S. Weatherhead, M. Pocock, M. Meik, M. McNeill, S. Fry, J. Pope. Reserves ; C. Kevin and P. Harbidge

Roger Lowrie, (scrum-half) in his coiled-spring position, ready to unleash his *flying* spin pass that would cut you in half if you were not concentrating.

Evening Argus Feb 28th 1978

Carved Up

While Lewes were dealing with Crawley, BRIGHTON were being carved up by London Irish Wild Geese. With every Irish player having appeared for the first team this season, they swept through 33-0.

One former Crawley player is revelling in his third team status at Brighton, though Max Pocock, a former County lock, has scored his fourth hat-trick of tries this season and in five games scored 14 tries.

I do remember these games as I was playing full back and Max who was a regular first team player somehow found his way into the "A" team. Why is speculation but he insisted on playing on the wing.

It was highly amusing watching the face of his opposite number as he walked on the pitch with a number 11 on his back (Max is in the 1st team photograph 1974-75).

I cannot leave the 70's without mentioning the "William Webb Ellis" Morris men. (Made up of players from Brighton and Lewes) It was great fun watching these guys on a Sunday lunchtime, somewhere outside a Pub in deepest darkest Sussex, with bells on their legs and hankies flapping in the wind, and the crack of stick against prick!

Participants included ; Alex Pincus, Max Pocock, Graham Howe, Keith Dixon, and Paul White... And of course, our present President Mr Steve Russell.

I hope this is deemed sufficient enough to embarrass 'El Presidente

Chapter XIII

The 'Brighton Boot' 1979-89

It was September 1979, that the first Brighton Boot, "newsletter" was issued. Personally, I found them hilarious and if it was possible I would reproduce them all.

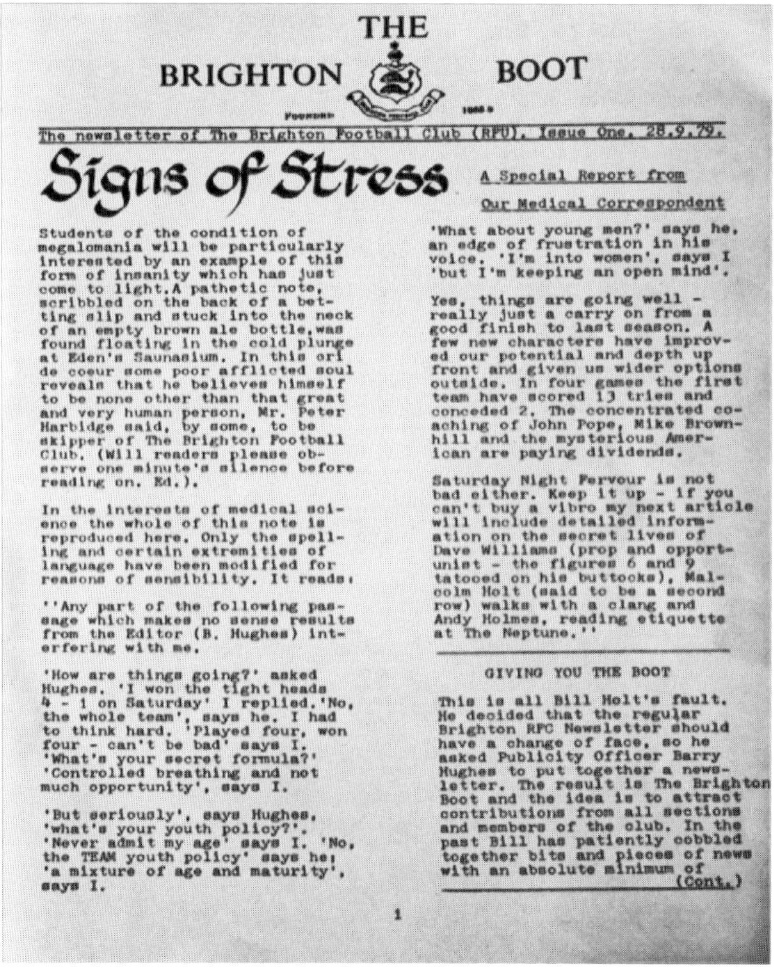

THE BRIGHTON BOOT

The newsletter of The Brighton Football Club (RFU). Issue One. 28.9.79.

Signs of Stress

A Special Report from Our Medical Correspondent

Students of the condition of megalomania will be particularly interested by an example of this form of insanity which has just come to light. A pathetic note, scribbled on the back of a betting slip and stuck into the neck of an empty brown ale bottle, was found floating in the cold plunge at Eden's Saunasium. In this cri de coeur some poor afflicted soul reveals that he believes himself to be none other than that great and very human person, Mr. Peter Harbidge said, by some, to be skipper of The Brighton Football Club. (Will readers please observe one minute's silence before reading on. Ed.).

In the interests of medical science the whole of this note is reproduced here. Only the spelling and certain extremities of language have been modified for reasons of sensibility. It reads:

''Any part of the following passage which makes no sense results from the Editor (B. Hughes) interfering with me.

'How are things going?' asked Hughes. 'I won the tight heads 4 - 1 on Saturday' I replied. 'No, the whole team', says he. I had to think hard. 'Played four, won four - can't be bad' says I. 'What's your secret formula?' 'Controlled breathing and not much opportunity', says I.

'But seriously', says Hughes, 'what's your youth policy?'. 'Never admit my age' says I. 'No, the TEAM youth policy' says he; 'a mixture of age and maturity', says I.

'What about young men?' says he, an edge of frustration in his voice. 'I'm into women', says I 'but I'm keeping an open mind'.

Yes, things are going well - really just a carry on from a good finish to last season. A few new characters have improved our potential and depth up front and given us wider options outside. In four games the first team have scored 13 tries and conceded 2. The concentrated coaching of John Pope, Mike Brownhill and the mysterious American are paying dividends.

Saturday Night Fervour is not bad either. Keep it up - if you can't buy a vibro my next article will include detailed information on the secret lives of Dave Williams (prop and opportunist - the figures 6 and 9 tatooed on his buttocks), Malcolm Holt (said to be a second row) walks with a clang and Andy Holmes, reading etiquette at The Neptune.''

GIVING YOU THE BOOT

This is all Bill Holt's fault. He decided that the regular Brighton RFC Newsletter should have a change of face, so he asked Publicity Officer Barry Hughes to put together a newsletter. The result is The Brighton Boot and the idea is to attract contributions from all sections and members of the club. In the past Bill has patiently cobbled together bits and pieces of news with an absolute minimum of (Cont.)

1

The first of Barry Hughes's "Boot"

Evening Argus 1980

BRIGHTON ARE BOGGED DOWN

by Mike Buckingham

Brighton 3 Worthing 0

PLAYING under terrible conditions---a quagmire underfoot and a near gale blowing.

Brighton found it hard to play their fluent, running style of rugby against Worthing.

The young Brighton side---three colts are now playing in the senior team---kept up relentless pressure. Worthing defended stoically, doing well to contain the home side.

Although the conditions called for the ball to be taken forward at the feet, Brighton persisted in trying to distribute the ball to their flyers, Dave Williams and Ian Barratt, on the wings. It was not until the second half , when Robinson's territory gaining kicks kept the Worthing pack turning back on their heels, that Brighton looked like breaking the stalemate. In the event Brighton had to be content with a Norman Allen penalty five minutes from the final whistle.

Brighton Extra 1st, 13, Worthing 2's 0

Skipper, Tony Mushens, watching from the touchline for the fourth week, was very impressed with his side's performance against as strong Worthing XV. Ray Mullen kicked two penalties, Danny Craze scored a well taken try and Ian Humphries dropped a goal.

Brighton "A" 22, Worthing 0

Brighton had the maturity in their 22-0 win over Worthing to play exactly the kind of rugby required by the conditions. Wise hands like Don Rees constantly denied Worthing given the Brighton backs a field day. Tries came from Jones, Lowrie, Davis, Hales and Shipman, while Wristy Knowles added a conversion.

The Brighton whitewash of Worthing was completed with a 24-4 win for the Extra "A", Scorers were Gareth King (1 try) Mike Jackson (two penalties, one dropped goal and one conversion) and Ian Chapman, (two tries)

***Brighton Colts** thrashed **Bognor Colts** by a massive 47-0 at Waterhall*

A "Cheeky" photo from the 1981 Brighton v Lewes game

Jane Warner (Sun page 3) just popping into the 1st XV changing room. We must thank Sally Ann Voak, wife of Pat Ward-Lee for enticing the Sun page 3 Girls down for the odd match and Social event.

On the 24th January 1981, while putting out the flags at Waterhall, unfortunately, our President Bill Holt passed away. Below is an poignant extract from the memorial floodlights programme.

BILL "MUSH" HOLT

An Appreciation by Peter Harbidge

William Robert Beric Holt, known as Bill or "Mush", arrived 02/12/30 left 24/01/81. He went to Brighton College and starting working at 16 on the land, and never really left it. In between he married Ann, with her they raised umpteen children, the odd business or two, ran several farms, was a local Justice of the Peace, regular Churchman and President of Brighton Football Club (RFU).

Those are just some of the facts, but Bill was many other things to lots of people and I can only give you my version of this larger than life man. Perhaps my first contact with Bill says a lot about his approach to life. I joined Brighton in season number 98 (seventeen years ago). I was a new centre who kicked a bit. Bill was hooker in my first home game at the superb Withdean Stadium. I had a good game, scored a try and converted a couple of penalties. I was pompously enjoying the bar afterwards courted by admiring players as new kickers often are. Bill wandered over, said "Hello, and well played, here have a pint" I accepted graciously as new kickers do, only to find he had given me two pints, one in the hand and the other in my pocket.

It could have been worse. He once offered manure to a friend who readily accepted. Asked how much he wanted, he replied "as much as you can spare Bill". Bill delivered a tip-up lorry full.

Sadly many of our newcomers will not know Bill. Well, he was something special. Not a great dresser--usually in Wellington boots, mud covered trousers, shirt tail dangling, one sleeve up, one down, An impromptu crusher of full cigarettes packets and crisps. For years Ann stoically dressed Bill, but he could crumple the uncrumpable, stick mud on the unstickable. His tailors never grasped that Bill's arms, legs and waist changed size according to his mood.

Just once I saw him immaculate in a Dinner Jacket and Crimson Cummerbund. Shortly before people left to go to the annual Ball, the

Clubhouse drains were blocked. When Bill and his Dynarod were dragged back up from his beloved drains he once again looked his comfortable self.

Not a Gourmet, or perhaps his passion for eating Tulip, Daffodils, cigarettes and toxic paint put him ahead of his time. There is a Frenchman in Northern France who still tells the story of the mad Englishman who when offered a Gauloise took the "bleu packette" and ate the lot---sacre bleu.

Not a gentleman on the field. Bill was a regular choice hooker for Brighton 1st XV at 16. He learned to look after himself young. He used his full self defence system. Knees to introduce himself, boot to reach the second row and teeth for nearby ears. It took the combined resources of several refereeing associations and a mix of captains to persuade him to at least confine his footwork to the man lying on the ball. He approached a ruck like a combine harvester---if it moved bag it.

Bill was generous, both flamboyant and discreet. Many a fiver was loaned without a murmur, but when he chose to push the boat out the river banks ran awash---so did we. An incredibly hard worker---when he decided to do something, he did it. If the committee wanted a float for the Carnival, he and his Dad-in-law built a castle on wheels.

Or a Mississippi Paddle Steamer with moving paddles, or a Galleon---with Canon (we didn't win the year of the Galleon---Bill

over did it. As the Mayor and entourage arrived to judge, the canons fired. The Drive, Hove was completely smogged out for an hour)

He put the fires out more than once. When an ex-Mayor set fire to a local photographer's hat Bill used the photographer's pint to put the fire out before his hair got out of control.

This may have led Bill to acquire his own fire engine, he perhaps felt he would continue to need one.

Lille was his favourite away fixture. His various speeches are the main cause of our EEC budget problems now. He did and said outrageous things and the French loved him for it. He revelled in doing the unexpected. When Lille and Brighton drew in "Le Grand Match" Bill furtively hacksawed the silver down the middle. At the presentation the cup stood whole and bedecked with ribbons. As the two captains took a handle each at the climax of the ceremony to acknowledge to the acclaim of the multitudes, the cup and their aplomb disintegrated.

At Committee when discussing the latest atrocity of a Club Member, Bill would insist "the Club is bigger than the man" it was his way of saying, none of us are indispensable. Well, of course, he was right---but some are less dispensable than others.

Bill's sad and early death left a big black hole in many lives. He will long be remembered and missed for so many things, so perhaps the floodlights have more than a touch of symbolism about them.

When they blow the whistle tonight and switch on the splendid memorial floodlights give a moment's thought to Bill Holt---he would have liked that---they were his idea

Sunday 22nd April 1984, was the official "turning on" of the Bill Holt Memorial Floodlights. A game was played at Horsdean, where Brighton Football Club (RFU) played Oxford RFU. The story of the lights is as follows ;

On Sunday 26th September 1982 Charlie Day, Jamie Mitchell, Roger Lowrie, Dave Taylor and Andy Holmes set off for Dover to begin dismantling the floodlight towers, which Brighton Football Club had bought from Dover Harbour Board.

At 6:30 that evening most of the dismantling had been done and the following weekend the same crew plus John Wallace stacked the towers onto a low loader and headed for home. The lorry got stuck on the ramp into the ground and had to be unloaded in a downpour, but this minor unpleasantness was a small price to pay for an incredible bargain.

We had originally been quoted between £15,000 and £18,000 for the installation of a less comprehensive system that we eventually got. Between them, Dennis Nolan, Jamie Mitchell and Pat Ward-Lee got wind of the Dover sale and eventually won the tender at a very competitive price.

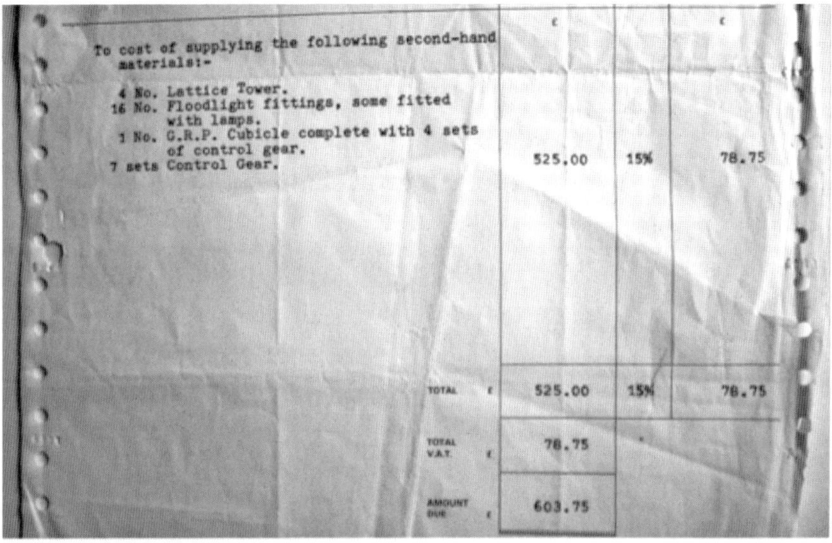

	£		£
To cost of supplying the following second-hand materials:- 4 No. Lattice Tower. 16 No. Floodlight fittings, some fitted with lamps. 1 No. G.R.P. Cubicle complete with 4 sets of control gear. 7 sets Control Gear.	525.00	15%	78.75
TOTAL £	525.00	15%	78.75
TOTAL V.A.T. £	78.75		
AMOUNT DUE £	603.75		

In order to erect the lights the base had to be set in 3 metre concrete blocks and for this Dominic Filmer-Sankey and Bob Chessel, with a JCB and Dumper, were called in. Concrete mixers fed by Chessell, Kevin Hopkins, Danny Craze and Duncan Sinclair supplied the mix for a varied crew including Ray Stenning, Ken Vogwill, Pete Rowlandson and Jim Poor who wheeled it into the holes. A couple of the aforementioned managed to get a barrow, gumboots and self in as well. This extremely arduous task took several hours and all the crew must be congratulated on sticking at it. In the afternoon Dennis Nolan with a jack-hammer made a cable duct through the changing room floor. The following weekend Frank Howard organised a crane and yet another working party headed by Jamie Mitchell lifted the towers into position. Paul Day showing his ancestry swarmed up the towers and unhooked them.

Pat Ward-Lee headed the wiring-up party, in some terrible weather found and joined up the underground cables and completed the circuit.

With Jamie's finishing touches at the top of the towers the lights were ready for action barely a month after our first trip to Dover. The whole operation was arranged and completed by members of the club. By no means all who helped are mentioned and we want to pay tribute to everyone who assisted in any way.

We were still paying off the loans arranged to cover the installation, but with a bit more enterprise, the whole lot should be paid for by the end of the 1984-85 season.

The Club is justifiably proud of its achievement and the team work involved has given our playing record a lift up as well. When Linda Lusardi kicks off at 7:30 pm on Sunday 22nd April 1984, the floodlit match will provide satisfaction to the large number of people whose physical efforts have made it possible. Thank you very much.

Linda Lusardi

The 1980's was my decade playing for the 1st XV. The captains I played under deserve and warrant more than I am able to give them in this book, Geoff Hindle (his dummy was well known South of the Thames, but still he sold it!), Neil Thomas ("Pound for Pound", very competent and his record as Captain proves it), Bob Avery (The Welsh Wizard, pure class), Mick Avery ("The Jean-Pierre Rive of the Valleys") and Charlie Day ("Just make sure you get that Ball in front of me Honeysett!")

Below is a 1st XV playing report written by Charlie Day and published in the "The Brighton Boot" Issue 14, Feb 1983, includes so many names that have "Disappeared" "Sailed Away" or "Unfortunately left us way before their time". They need to be remembered and maybe some light can be thrown on their whereabouts. In my humble opinion they were, and some still are, a fantastic bunch of guys that only the camaraderie of Rugby is able to achieve.

1st's FIGHT BACK

A good win at Worthing in the merit table just before Christmas and a reasonably stable side since, has seen us win or draw all but two of our last ten games. Some good wins against Sussex sides including both Lewes and Worthing have enabled us to clear any relegation danger zone at the bottom of the merit table, but we must beat Hastings & Bexhill to make absolutely sure of staying up. One of the games we lost was against Old Reigations and was played on New Year's Day..!, needless to say many of the players were feeling a little worse for wear, the second was against London Irish, at Sunbury, we had to remove the gates from their hinges to get into the ground before we could begin to play, only to find we had to play short halves to enable us to watch the International!

The game against Beckenham saw probably one of the oldest sides put out for Brighton 1st's for a couple of years, with only six players being anywhere near their early twenties (I was 28) It would be unfair to mention certain names as these veterans beat Beckenham, who had been beaten only twice this season. John Pope has done a good job in getting a mainly unchanged pack to work as a unit. The pack being Charlie Day, Andy Smith, Dominic Filmer-

Sankey, Andy Holmes and Malcom Holt and the back row, Dave Brown, Mike Dooling and Des O'Hara with John Pope, Sean Maquire and Peter Rowlandson standing in for a couple of games. The fruits of their efforts were shown with tries being scored by the pack in the last four games, Mike Dooling and Des O'Hara scoring two each and Sean Maquire scoring another.

Geoff Hindle had gone to work on the backs and has got some slick moves going (without giving details for obvious reasons) the wingers Kevin Hopkins (4 tries) and Bill McMenamin and John Honeysett two apiece, making good use of them. Frank Samson and Mark Appleton were unlucky not to score tries after making some great breaks through the centre. Adrian Knight got a good try against the Wild Geese and Geoff Hindle got his name on the score sheet against Lewes with a very timely drop goal. John Honeysett and Frank Brown have been our main scorers with the Boot. With Graham Twyneham back playing and some injured players coming back soon, we should look forward to some good results for the rest of the season.

A secondary article by Malcolm Holt is worth a mention, as he indicates more than a few of our colts departing to London Clubs

Looking at the games played in 1983, the second half of 1982 - 83 season and the first half of 1983 - 84 season. We played 39 games, Won 29, Draw 3 and Lost 7.

1983-84 season (02.09.83. - 31.12.83)

Lost Home Game - Sussex
Drawn Home Games - Hove, Guildford,
Lost Away Games - Reigatians, Wild Geese (London Irish 2nd's), Surbitonians, Walcountians, Horsham and Crawley.
Drawn Away Games, - Blackheathens (Blackheath 2nd's)

Having started the New Year with a good result over Old Reigatians, it is interesting to look back on 1983. As can be seen above, it has been a particularly successful year despite a terrible start with a very hungover 28 - 0 defeat on 1st January last year by

a seemingly teetotal Reigatians side when all players who were sober enough to stagger onto the field covered themselves in dishonour.

Fortunately the first half of the season which started so badly picked itself up. This was attributable to the availability of several key players who had earlier not been available due to injury or other commitments, and undoubtedly the work put in by John Pope with the forwards both on and off the field, was a major contributing factor, with the current season half way through and the current playing record being what it is, the future is very bright.

The only blemishes on the season was losing to Horsham in the merit table and Crawley in the Cup. both these losses can be put down to bad preparation, both physically and mentally. And probably against Horsham the wrong sort of tactics.

It is essential that now we have the best training facilities in the South East these are used by more players and that attendance at training play a more significant role in selection.

Another feature of the current season is that the loss of a lot of our good young players will only be short term and we can look forward to their return to the Club having gained valuable experience at top level rugby. These include Mark Appleton and Adrian Knight at Harlequins, Mark Jenkins and Rob Thompson to London Welsh, Richard James at Blackheath and Andy Holmes to Angouleme. We wish these players and all the ex Brighton players success in their present Clubs.

The second half of the season offers the chance of winning the merit table, more attractive floodlight fixtures, and the prospect of organising the fixture list so that in 1984 - 85 we join the Southern Merit table. The future looks good and there is a very discernible mood of optimism throughout the Club. Not the least of the reasons is floodlighting which has given us a real advantage over our rivals. Good facilities, good leadership, good results . All hallmarks of a successful Club.

Malcom Holt

Merit Table (at Feb 20th)

Club	Played	%
Crawley	4	100
Horsham	5	80
Bognor	6	67
Lewes	8	63
Worthing	6	50
Brighton	9	50
Hove	9	50
Eastbourne	7	43
Sussex Police	5	40
East Grinstead	5	40
Hastings &Bexhill	3	0
Seaford	4	0

Certain gentlemen command an audience and personally I believe Peter Rumney was one of these. Peter was "Old Brightonians R.F.C." and I came across an article that I believe was published in 1988.

THE OLD BOYS' NETWORK

If you drink at Brighton Rugby Club (and the best people do!), you'll mingle with a large cross-section of rugby players and enthusiasts. None is more knowledgeable about the game than Peter Rumney, a charismatic character who works hard in his role as Secretary of the Old Brightonians R.F.C.

The "OB's" as they are affectionately named, share our ground, providing an additional choice of quality rugby (along with the Sussex Police) for or Saturday afternoon visitors.

In the past, the Old Brightonian headquarters have included a Beach Yacht Club, a Seaside Hotel and an Angling Club, with all the accompanying problems of location and parking - so they are extremely happy with the excellent facilities we enjoy at Brighton.

We asked Peter Rumney to give us some background details about Old Brightonians;

Peter writes ;

"The OB's were founded in 1926 and flourished in the pre-war years. But. Brighton College remained in Brighton during the war years, which resulted in falling numbers - so efforts to restart the Club in 1946-47 failed, and the Clubhouse and ground at Chessington were eventually sold.

The College has always had close links with Brighton Football Club (R.F.U.). This included a regular 1st XV fixture, until the RFU restricted the age for schoolboy opponents to 21. So, when they resumed after the war, many OBs started playing for Brighton, forming a large percentage of the Sussex senior team captained by Dick Braybon, who is now a Brighton Trustee. Players included such personalities as Eric Wormesley and David Benjamin.

In 1958, a group of OB's in the Brighton Club decided to reform the OBRFC as a Sussex Club, hearing this Lewes RFC arranged a pre-season fixture which the OB's won by one try to nil - scored by the College master in charge of Rugby Jim Wainwright, a Cambridge Blue and Esher player, and father of the present Scottish captain.

Several Brighton players, including the late Bill Holt, Eric Wormesley and others had the odd game with the OB's to assist with numbers. As rejoining secretary, I gained valuable administration experience on the Brighton Committee which has served me well in my role as a Sussex RFU official - from 1961 up to the present day.

Naturally, the OB's link with the College itself is very strong. The master in charge of Rugby at the Brighton College is Mr John Pope, of Rosslyn Park and Brighton, who is a former Sussex Captain.

Mrs Ann Holt, JP, widow of Bill Holt, well-known for her hard work as Brighton Treasurer, is on the Association of Old Brightonians Committee and the Secretary, Tim Lordsman, is currently playing for the OB's.

Finally, something for the record books ; our Club Jerseys have been laundered brilliantly, for the past 25 years by a parent, the former Mayor of Hove, Cl Mrs Margret Adams, and her husband Bill. Hopefully, this is a sign of the continuity of our Club.. and the clean game we aspire too!

Peter Rumney

(Peter passed away November 2007)

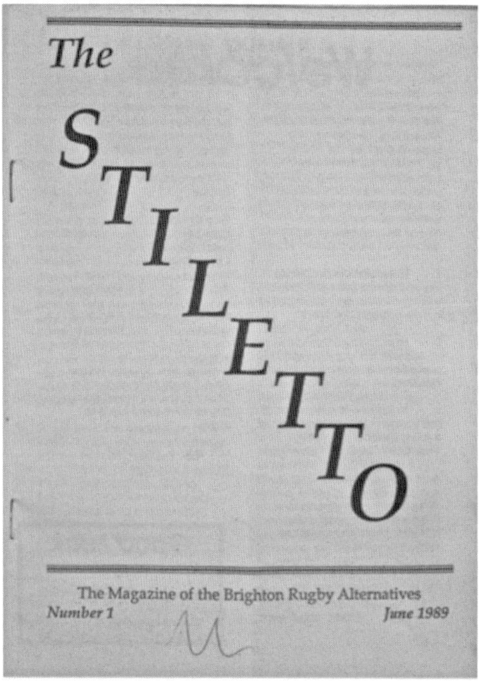

The STILETTO

The Magazine of the Brighton Rugby Alternatives
Number 1 June 1989

The Fist edition of the "Stiletto" June 1989

The "Stiletto" was the girls answer to the "The Boot" a Bi-monthly magazine produced by the BRA's (Brighton Rugby Alternatives), and I quote from this edition.

WHAT IS A BRA?

Not necessarily a female or feminine but tending to be so. A BRA is the non-playing counterpart of our heroes on the pitch, which usually means we're the Mrs/Miss/Ms section and they are the Mr's as long as rugby traditional reigns strong, and we hope it does. Some of our recent innovations have caused this thin dividing line to tremble and shake, usually with raucous laughter. Note such irreverent forays as 'The Men Wearing Female Lingerie versus The not so lady like Ladies All Conquering team" and then the Mr & Mrs Competition, that infamous debacle, where prominent waring couples stood side by side, to jointly reveal all to the gathered crowd. Only one couple were married, one couple had separate rooms, and one couple obviously got together on a very dark night indeed.!

Such human and vulnerable moments ironically often lead to greater group unity or that all consuming feeling that we are all lumped together in this embarrassing mess and there's no way out.

Allegiance to one particular player is not a prerequisite (sighs of relief). But, loyalty and devotion to Brighton Rugby Football Club is a necessary quality to have, or to cultivate. So, whether single or married, unattached or axed, hopeful or not quite sure, all are welcome to our merry band, if you enjoy Rugby and it's unique social mix, or you think you might, and by virtue of your gender you feel a bit left out, on the sidelines, get in touch and join the BRA's.

The above photograph is not the game mentioned in 'The Stiletto' but gives an indication of the fun times we had at Horsdean

Going Down Under

In 1988 Danny Craze and myself found our way down under to play a season with Brighton Rugby Club, Adelaide, South Australia. This tour was an excuse to liaise with our Australian counterparts on their forthcoming tour to Brighton England. I may add that Brighton Football Club, England, travelled to Brighton Rugby Club in 1986, for the 'First International Brighton Rugby Club Festival'. South Australia.

'SECOND INTERNATIONAL BRIGHTON RUGBY CLUB FESTIVAL'

Emissaries from Adelaide have informed us that they expect a contingent of at least 50 people here in September 1989 to contest the second Brighton games. Brighton Rugby Club, Melbourne have also indicated that they will have a good sized group here as well.

New Brighton are coming down to play and enquiries are being followed up with the Brighton Rugby Club of Soweto and in other Brighton Rugby Clubs around the World. We expect to find one in Uttar Pradesh. Obviously, we are going to need the odd billet or two, for all these people, and Barry Hughes, who did so well from such a bad start when he fell of the bus at the feet of his hostess on arriving in Adelaide for reasons it's hardly necessary to explain to you, dear reader will be the accommodations officer. Peter Thompson would just try to put them all up at his own place, so he'll be in charge of entertainments. Peter Noble whose reputation in Adelaide has not diminished with time, can be in charge of special affairs. I'll be trying to raise a few bob with which to entertain them in the manner in which they looked after us.

We would be delighted to hear from anyone who will help in any way. The outline plan is to have a series of inter Club games during the second week of Sept, with lots of other entertainments in between. It is all intended to be light hearted.

This Club has already benefitted this year from contacts we made and the potential for other Brighton players in Australia is enormous.

You are welcome to play and work there at their invitation.

I am pleased to say that many friendships and cultural exchanges have materialized following those early days in the 1980's and Dennis Holyoak 'President' will visit and help us celebrate our 150th and in November and visit Twickenham to watch England beat Australia.

ChapterXIV

HORSDEAN - THE END OF AN ERA

Since the formation of Brighton F.C. (RFU) in 1868 we have used approximately 20 different locations in Brighton and Hove for playing facilities. Post-match watering holes are even more numerous. Eventually in 1970 the foundation stone was laid at our Clubhouse at Horsdean after 102 years of waiting. However, our honeymoon was short lived for within two years of laying roots it became clear that our new ground and Clubhouse was within the path of the New Folkestone to Honiton A27, the Brighton By-Pass.

Plans for the newly proposed A27 then spent numerous years going backwards and forwards to the drawing board and being financial discussed by every accountant South of the Watford Gap Then of course the lovers of "Trees" and "Great Crested Newts" also had their say. as you can imagine not much was discussed at the Club, "What will be will be".

Years passed, before the powers that be, had agreed to start the legal proceedings with the infrastructure of the proposed road.

Suddenly it was happening. The Club had decided to create a "By-Pass Committee" which would answer to the General Club Committee. I would like to take this opportunity to say a personal thank you these Ladies and Gentleman who worked so tirelessly, ensuring we would benefit from the best Clubhouse and facilities in Sussex and beyond.

In 1984 The Brighton Borough Council agreed to the compulsory purchase of the land (including Horsdean) which was the first stage of land purchase prior to actual Motorway Construction.

The Department of Transport has agreed compensation for replacement of the original clubhouse on a like for like basis. It was at this juncture that the "Dunkirk Spirit" came into action.

The A27 taking shape on the South Downs

The demolition of our Clubhouse at Horsdean

Extract from the "Brighton Boot" Sept 1984

WORKING PARTY from 9 to 12am in which we aim to complete the painting of the clubhouse. We will need 50 people to work shifts to get the job done before we are valued for By-Pass Destruction Day (D-Day) .

Charlie Day will lead the assault. On the same day we will be hosting the Rugby section of the Inter Town Festival in which several junior teams from the local area will be taking part. We have decided then to hold the first "Wine and Cheese" morning, both to restart the season and provide the parents of the boys and girls taking part with a pleasant welcome to the Club. We've positively committed to attracting new members and this is a good opportunity to do so. The lure of a drink for the workers might attract a few more painters as well.

In 1988 a public enquiry into the new road gave the go-ahead for the road to proceed and from that point in time the Club has been negotiating with Brighton Borough Council for possible new sites.

I remember, one day going with Adrian Biggs, a "By-Pass Committee" member and working colleague, over to Waterhall. We parked up and walked to the end of the valley. It was a tip, literally, a refuse tip but looking down the valley the vista was sublime. I was surprised, but quite elated that this could be the future of Brighton Football Club (RFU). In a recent conversation with John Wallace he told me it was down to Adrian that we are where we are now. His proposal was submitted to Brighton Borough Council and after due diligence it was agreed.

The site at Waterhall Valley was agreed by the Brighton Council in December 1989 and the Club started to negotiate a suitable lease and license for pitches since that date.

Building work started in August 5th and the current timetable should have them finished by the end of February 1992.

The A27 taking shape, parallel to "Mill Road" and in the far distance of Waterhall valley, the top pitches on the newly formed plateau.

A Brighton XV v St Francis at Horsdean 1990, this photograph graced the pages of the Evening Argus, even though the conditions were somewhat "dirty" I can still pick out ; Dick Thoms, Chris Cleary, Alan Beck, Nick Coral, Nick Henry, Danny Craze, and Dannie Venter.

During the late 1980's the 1st XV captain's role was split, and a Club Captain was elected to help with administration duties. Peter "Colin Cowdrey" Thompson, "Tommo", was elected to this position and felt it was his duty to accompany the Brighton Football Club (RFU) on their tour to Wales and report his findings back to the Committee.

What did we do on our Holidays!

It was hard work organising a tour, but it is most gratifying to see the lengths some men will go to get on tour. Take Brian Spring for example. cast naked onto the streets of Brighton with less than an hour to make the coach he did no more than dash around the town and spend £140 on clothes in order to attend our missionary journey to the Land of Someone's Fathers.

You may be surprised to know that it began to rain as we cleared customs at checkpoint Severn Bridge, by which time we had taught Mark Wallace the rudiments of three-card brag. His contribution to the Thompson touring fund was most welcome.

It continued to rain when the good citizens of Caerleon were awakened by the sound of 22 rugby players sprinting to make last orders at the local hostelry. All that training paying off at last. Tour officials were duly appointed, most notably that of Major as team Beaver, whose first duty was to Beaver us some food. It was at this time the tendencies of John Easden and Jerry Smith became apparent. Martin Watts, at this time looked awful.

On Saturday morning it was, of course, raining and Martin Watts looked worse. A stewards enquiry was held during breakfast as to which effing clown had arranged a ten o'clock kick off against Cross Keys United.

Paddy Park proved to be everything one imagines a Welsh valley rugby club to be. A picturesque little ground on the only piece of flat land for miles around surrounded by dark and brooding hills shrouded in cloud and rain. Behind the main stand the river was in spate and the bleating of sheep, obviously pining for Mick and Bob Avery, echoed around the redundant spoil tips. This Wagnerian scene slowly became inhabited by strange shapes, bearing a passing resemblance to Human Beings, which turned out to be our opposition.

By now you will have heard many vastly exaggerated accounts of this encounter, so, I shall confine my comments to the modest. We were brilliant, World Class, Outstanding etc etc, and had it not been for the atrocious conditions would have been in a position to declare before lunch! As it was, we had to settle for Mick's penalty and a try from a person who resembled an enraged Rhino, handing off their entire defence. Respecting his extreme modesty, this person will remain anonymous.

A pleasant afternoon was spent at the Snelling Seven's sampling the local bitter and absorbing the Welsh passion for their national game. It was nice John Dawes recognised another national hero the moment Griff arrived! Talking of national heroes, the present incumbent of the Welsh number ten jersey, described by Mick and Bob's Father as an insipid little money-grabbing hunchback who should piss off up North with the other softies scored a succession of brilliant tries and smashed the tournament points record previously held by Phil Bennett. I think it's called national spirit.

I am sure that I would have enjoyed my Curry, but I blinked at the wrong moment and opened my eyes to find that it had been devoured by "Dustbin" Hoad. From this point events became a little confused ; but I specifically remember that a) it was raining ; b) Bronwen the Barmaid had huge tits ; c) Martin Watts looked awful ; d) Jeremy Smith looked distinctly sheepish at the end of the evening. (Note to Boy-This is a double entendre. See any front row for explanation.

It is said that necessity makes for strange bedfellows, and they don't come any stranger than Mick Avery and Chris Cleary!

On Sunday morning it rained. Some of the more Corinthian chaps decided to visit the local golf course. The front row Union, playing off scratch as they neglected to wash added a new dimension to the game by blasting salvoes of drives at the groundsman on his tractor! Excellent sport.

And so to take on the vaulted might of Newport Saracens. As a contrast to the previous day, their pitch lay on the expanses of the River Usk floodplain, with mementoes of the Welsh industrial heritage that has contributed so much to their national tradition standing starkly against the lowering skyline. Remarkable, then, that in such a landscape a man from the idyllic sun-drenched, palm-fringed shores of the Pacific Islands should so outstandingly well, In a side that reminded me of a combination of the 1973 Barbarians and the current All-Blacks, Joe Barro was brilliant. The senior tourists immediately decided to teach him Hi-Ho, spoof and impecuniosities so that he may be fairly compared to other great Brighton Wingers like Kevin Hopkins.

For the record, we won 22-18 after being 12-4 down at the half. Much of the credit must go down to the Skipper's tactical acumen in taking off this writer at half time. It was a superb all round performance and one of their players was heard grudgingly admit "for a bunch of English Poofs we were OK". Praise indeed from the Welsh and guess who were singing in the bar afterwards.

Once again things became rather blurred, but I seem to recall that ; a) Mick has 65 good looking sisters in Caerleon ; b) Martin

Watts looked awful ; c) John Easden was heard to be intimately discussing his new friends GCSE results and d) I do not recommend viewing Boy naked as a method of pre-coital stimulation (for either partner). It also seemed to rain heavily in my room. We crossed the Severn Bridge into glorious sunshine on Monday morning with Mark Wallace determinedly donating the rest of his tour funds to Dave Slocombe in order that he could buy the statutory Cat for Caroline so that he can go next time. A quiet lunchtime drink in Maidenhead saw Mark Slade forced to drink his own weight in Vodka for attempting to buy a coke and Pat Kilby downed a Richard Lee cocktail, known as a Burst Boil.

Thanks to everyone who came and contributed to one of the most successful Brighton tours I have taken part in and to those not mentioned in the above account, thanks for the beer. Your secrets are safe with me for the time being.

Tommo

THE BRIGHTON BOOT'

September 1989

Start of the season message from our Captain.

It is with anticipation that we look forward to our last season at Horsdean before moving to Waterhall, which should be our final resting place. There would be no better way to arrive there than as a league winning side.

As Captain I have no miracle solution to get the results necessary to win the league. I have not "signed" anybody in the close season and we do not seem to have attracted many new faces for our coming campaign. This does not worry me as I feel with honest endeavour and positive commitment the 1st XV can do well this season. At times last season we looked as though winning the league was a formality; destroying the likes of Chichester and Burgess Hill and also beating Horsham and other London 3 teams. It is as a result of the groundwork that I feel we have the potential to do well again.

I have always advocated "no train-no play" for the 1st XV as I honestly feel that team play benefits from the co-operation of all

1st XV 1988

Back Row ; Pete Relton John Blackburn Simon Backhouse Brian Spring Peter Noble Alan Crowhurst Pat Walker
Front Row ; Mick Avery Nick Henry Justin Burt Neil Thomas (C) Chris Cleary Steve Dunnhill Keith Basnett Dave Trower

players. I am realistic enough to understand that this policy has to be flexible as other commitments i.e. work and family are important, and as long as players keep in touch if they have problems then this is perfectly acceptable. With regard to training I am proposing that the 1st XV train as a squad on Thursday during the season. The situation of having 6 players on a Tuesday and 8 on Thursday is farcical and almost makes training irrelevant . A well supported and organised 1st XV session on Thursday, perhaps from 5:15 to 9:00pm, seems a better proposition. I want all 1st team players to commit themselves to this one night of training! I would like to thank Jeremy Smith for taking on the Vice Captaincy and I feel with Charlie Day and Kevin Hopkins taking over coaching duties, that their experience will be invaluable and their support absolutely essential.

It is only with 100% effort, commitment and loyalty that Brighton F.C. (RFU) can do well this year.

All the best Bob Avery

Chapter XV

Waterhall

NEW, LUXURY HEADQUARTERS FOR BRIGHTON FOOTBALL CLUB (RFU)

The Town's most exciting sporting venue will be open in 1990

The 1990s are all set to be a fantastic decade for sport. With more leisure, better facilities, and more time to enjoy them.

Right in the forefront of this exciting period of sporting development is Brighton's most forward looking sports club---Brighton Football Club (R.F.U.)

The Club has suffered EIGHT YEARS of uncertainty generated by the new Folkestone to Honiton Trunk Road, part of which (the A27 Brighton By-Pass) is scheduled to go straight through the Club's present Clubhouse and main pitch when work starts next year.

But, thanks to the efforts of Brighton Corporation and our local MPs, Julian Amery and Andrew Bowden, MBE, the club has now secured a fabulous new site at Waterhall.

The site, at the top end of the beautiful Waterhall Valley, Mill Lane, Brighton, is nothing short of sensational. It comprises space for four pitches and a two storey Clubhouse, with easy access and ample space for parking. It is backed by the rolling acres of the South Downs and attractive "Greens" of Waterhall Golf Club. The clubhouse will have commanding views along the valley---with an imposing vista of one of Brighton's best loved landmarks, the Old Mill.

Brighton is already the top venue for Sussex rugby --- with major County Matches played under floodlights on our main pitch every season, and many more other top games on our ground. The new facilities promise to attract many more important fixtures---now that the Courage League is now established. There is also plenty of scope for other sports---and the club will be setting up its own Cricket section next Summer.

Because of the incredible potential of the new site and Clubhouse, Brighton's Committee has engaged a top architect to design the Clubhouse---James T. Laidlaw, B.Arch (Hons), RIBA. With important input from experienced players and experts from the Club itself. Mr Laidlaw has produced a fantastic design. Plans are currently before Brighton Council Parks and Recreation Committee---and, following their approval, these will be submitted to the Planning Department.

Although the Club will be receiving compensation for the loss of the existing Clubhouse, the fact remains that we now URGENTLY need to raise £150,000 to cover the additional expenses of our new luxury and the move itself.

1st XV 1988-89

Dick Thoms (Asst C), Brian Spring, Alan Coe, Martin Watts Peter Small (Coach) Chris Cleary, Simon Dean, Paul Harrison, Chris Watts, Richard Lovegrove, Kevin Hoad, Nick Henry, Peter Noble, Michael Brett, A.N. Other, Mick Avery (Capt), Justin Burt.

EVENING ARGUS, Friday, December 14, 1990

RUGBY VERSUS SOCCER IN A PITCH BATTLE

A squabble has broken out over Brighton and Hove Albion's possible move to Waterhall.

Brighton Rugby Club have told the Albion to keep their hands off the Waterhall land, mentioned as a suitable site for an £18 million, 25,000 capacity, all-seated stadium for the Seagulls.

The rugby club say they have been promised the Brighton Council-owned land.

Rugby club president Pat Ward-Lee said "The Albion have absolutely no claim on this land".

"It has been promised to us through the goodwill of Brighton Council following the loss of our existing grounds under the Department of Transport A27 bypass scheme".

"I was totally surprised when the Albion said Waterhall was one of the sites they were looking at. Our pitches have already been levelled and the grass has been sown. The club house is going to be built after Christmas. To even think of another move could lead to the demise of the club".

But John Farmer, chairman of the stadium developers Wyncote, says there is room for both clubs. "We wish to see the rugby club as part of the overall scheme. They have nothing to fear from us. I do not see that we are in competition with the rugby club. If the stadium ends up at Waterhall there is ample scope for the rugby club as well as the football stadium. Far from trampling on the toes of the rugby club this could be a way of enhancing facilities there"

4 October 1991

A message from the Chairman

NEWSLETTER TO ALL NON-PLAYING MEMBERS PAST AND PRESENT

Another season is now well underway, and without doubt it is one of the most important in the long history of the club.

I am writing to you at length to tell you how things stand with the Club as of now, to raise the old chestnut of non-playing subscriptions, to make a few promises and finally to beg such donations as you may be prepared to make.

The Club

When we were moved from Horsdean early in April we had no terms of our new lease at Waterhall agreed with Brighton Council, nor did we have a firm idea of the compensation we would receive. We had no home either. What we did have was planning consent for the Clubhouse, terms for a lease (and licence for the pitches) that were not acceptable to us, and a potential shortfall in funds to build the Clubhouse of an amount we could not hope to make up.

Since then I am pleased to be able to report considerable progress. The terms for the lease and the licence have now been agreed by all parties, and the documents have been signed although for reasons I will explain later, they have not been returned yet to the Club. The terms that the Club agreed to are not ideal for us but the best that we thought achievable. We have a 45 year lease on an index linked ground rent of £250 per annum. At the end of the lease, as would have been the situation at Horsdean over a similar period, we will have to negotiate new terms that reflect the value of the Clubhouse then. The licence is for the same period at a cost yet to be determined and includes 3 out of the 4 Rugby pitches and the Cricket square on the new plateau adjacent to the Clubhouse. Brighton Corporation have given us assurances that we will be allowed use of the 4th pitch when we can show our regular need for it, and from our point of view when we can afford it. In the meantime it seems likely that the Sussex Police RFU will get the 4th pitch, and continue to use our Clubhouse facilities as they have for the past few years.

The pitches were laid and seeded in October last year. After a poor start much further work as been done on them this summer and they are all in magnificent condition. At the earliest we might be able to play a few games on them towards the end of this season, but this time next year they should be in full use.

Compensation for the buildings at Horsdean has been agreed subject to adjustment due to indexation which could work against us, but we are still negotiating the remainder of our compensation claim for items broadly termed "disturbance".

Although the terms of the lease and licence for Waterhall were agreed in August, we have not had them back from Brighton Council because of a dispute by us as to who should bear the costs of preparing the documents, a sum in excess of £7500. Despite the holdup (take this word whichever way you like), it was decided that work on the new Clubhouse had to go ahead if the building was to be completed in time for us to start using it well before the end of the season. After seeking revised prices, the contract was awarded to J.R. Tasker & Co., and work began in August. At the time of writing the site has been cleared, foundations and services are in, brickwork is above ground level and Taskers are on schedule for completion towards the end of February.

The cost involved is higher than anticipated, and to get down to a budget that is believed to be within our reasonable means, some of the external works, and the more luxurious internal finishing's have had to be trimmed. What we should end up with when we move in will still be the finest facilities for Rugby in Sussex.

On present costings we anticipate that we will have a shortfall of around £50,000 on the building contract costs less our compensation and money already raised. Because the lease is still not in our possession, we have been unable to apply formally for a number of grants and zero interest loans nor can we be clear exactly how much we may ultimately raise in this way. We are hoping this will cover at least 50% of the initial shortfall.

We are planning and have in progress various fundraising activities and hope that these together with donations may make good the difference. If we fail to raise enough then inevitably it will be necessary to trim further our spending, as the Club is not in a position to borrow any substantial amount on commercial terms.

The playing side of things has, under the circumstances, started promisingly. Although we have no great expectations of gaining promotion from Sussex Division 1 this season, we have a number of very useful new players, and in Peter Small and Bob Avery and excellent Coach and Assistant Coach. We do not reckon to be troubled with relegation fears and could do unexpectedly well if everything comes together at the right time. This season, with no real home, must be viewed as a transitional period in which we must maintain what we have whilst building for the future.

Until the new clubhouse is ready for use, we are camping out at Waterhall for the home games in a Portacabin using whenever possible the existing Corporation changing facilities there as well. We have the 2 existing pitches nearby and the north pitch at Horsdean (which was not touched by the Bypass, but which needs a map to find), and will have them until our new plateau is handed over to us for regular play. After matches teams go to The Sportsman at Withdean for tea and Bar facilities. From early October we will also be using Withdean for training.

The last few seasons have been extremely difficult due to the threat of the Bypass and the air of uncertainty prevailing as a result. However, the spirit in the Club is truly excellent, and a real effort is being made this year to right a few past wrongs, with the target of our Clubhouse and a new era in sight.

David Malby

BRIGHTON FOOTBALL CLUB'S ARCHITECT

The Club Committee after due consideration have appointed a top London Architect---James T. Laidlaw, B. Arch (Hons), RIBA--- to design the new Clubhouse. Mr Laidlaw, who has a thriving business in London's Mayfair, specialises in new building and refurbishments. He has a considerable experience in designing sports pavilions and clubhouses----among his commissions are the impressive Rugby Pavilions at Haddington Rugby Club, the clubhouse at the Eastleigh Unity Club in Hampshire. He says ; "It is no longer enough for a Rugby Club to be a functional building with a good Bar and adequate changing rooms. These days, a sports clubhouse must be luxurious enough for social events and business functions---sometimes on a very large scale indeed. It must also have facilities for the disabled, indoor and outdoor viewing areas, smaller intimate areas for meetings---and attractive powder rooms" His latest projects have included a new Penthouse flat in Holland Park, five luxury flats central London, and a house in Hampstead. So, Brighton Rugby Club is confident that he can bring a feeling of luxury and excitement to our new building.

Mr Laidlaw feels strongly that the historical side of the Club should be reflected in the building itself---together with new artefacts such as wall hangings, carvings and sculpture. The Club will be enlisting the help of Colleges and Schools in Brighton to provide us with even more treasures for the future. He says ;

"Brighton now have the opportunity to establish a Clubhouse to be proud of---and I intend to provide a building which will fulfil this opportunity. I am delighted that they have selected me for this job"

Personally, I'm somewhat confused with his penultimate paragraph, "The historical side of the Club should be reflected in the building itself"? Although I think the design is marvellous, it is not fantastic. There is no wall space for the numerous "artefacts" and a large room for functions is needed. The structural design of the two columns to support the roof is brilliant. Shame it obstructs the doorway and natural footfall to the bar. There is another way of observing J.T.L's handy work. Stand on the apex of the balcony, face the bar and look down at the tiles, can you see his initials? also within the tiles in the Clubhouse entrance, BFC RFU? And I can dispel the rumour it was built to look like a ship?

The pitches have been seeded and the 'Clubhouse' has started to rise

The roof trusses are up, and shows the structural integrity of the columns

The Interior taking shape showing it's capacious design.

The exterior showing near completion, only the roof to be fitted

1st XV 1992-93

BR; Paul Halsey (Coach), Jason Rasih, Nick Hart (Physio), Kieran Constadine, Nick Koral, John Blackburn, Chris Bourne, Jury Button, Garry Miles.
FR; Steve Morris, Tim Packham, Greg Doughty, Brian Spring, Paul Morley, (Capt), Tim Parkman, Greg Heath, Martin Watts,

LONDON DIVISION SOUTH EAST 3
Matches played to include Saturday 31.10.92.

	PLD	WON	DRN	LST	FOR	AGN	DIF	PNTS
BRIGHTON	5	5	0	0	88	46	+42	10
HORSHAM	5	4	0	1	138	35	+103	8
BECKENHAM	5	4	0	1	70	36	+34	8
O.BECCEHAMIAN	5	3	1	1	69	52	+17	7
EAST GRINSTEAD	5	3	0	2	45	51	-6	6
CHICHESTER	4	2	1	1	47	62	-15	5
HOVE	5	2	0	3	91	72	+19	4
TUNBRIDGE WELLS	4	2	0	2	45	68	-23	4
GILLINGHAM ANCH.	4	1	0	3	29	38	-9	2
DARTFORDIANS	4	1	0	3	54	89	-35	2
ERITH	5	1	0	4	34	82	-48	2
O.BROCLEANS	3	0	0	3	35	42	-7	0
CRAWLEY	4	0	0	4	34	106	-72	0

THE OFFICIAL CLUBHOUSE OPENING

Pat Ward-Lee, Frank Howard, Danie Serfontein

Evening Argus, Tuesday, September 22nd 1992

On Sunday 20th September 1992, new clubhouse at Waterhall has been officially opened by the Rugby Football Union president Danie Serfontein.

The ceremony was the final chapter in the long saga of Brighton's move after their former base at Horsdean was swallowed up by the Brighton by-pass.

Mr Serfontein said "It's obvious that Brighton is a vibrant club which is going somewhere. The club is very precious to the RFU as it believes in progress".

The ceremony was attended by representives from other Sussex Clubs as well as former Brighton players. The oldest was 91 year old Edgar Hunter who was Brighton's first choice Hooker between 1927-1932.

I have been surprised by the lack of photographs covering this event, hence the previous photograph is a copy of the one printed in the Argus.

To commemorate the opening a Rugby match was played between Brighton and Sussex, with a 25 - 3 victory to Sussex.

A Grand time at the Gala Opening
Mike Buckingham, Paul Morley, Nick Henry, Steve Morris, Mike Sutton

Evening Argus, Tuesday, March 30th 1993

BRIGHTON RUMBLE ON TOWARDS TITLE

Unbeaten Brighton have taken another step towards the South East title with a 25-9 win over Tunbridge Wells. Brighton's ninth win in ten starts keeps them two points ahead of second place Horsham and stretches their unbeaten run in London League Three to 22 matches.

Tunbridge Wells backs lacked penetration, gave Brighton some anxious moments as they started to run the ball, and landed to penalties before Brighton opened their tally.

At half-time Brighton had a slender 8-6 lead through Martin Watts try and a Greg Heath penalty. In the second half, Heath converted tries by Kieran Considine and Jury Buttton and added one penalty.

I cannot let the 1990's pass without mentioning Mark Appleton who unfortunately left us far too early. His inclusion in this publication will guarantee he will not be forgotten to future generations.

MARK APPLETON
(from the memorial Match programme)

On Sunday 5th September 1993 the first memorial match for Mark was played at Brighton F.C. (RFU). But who was he, other than my friend? Let give you an insight into the man from the memorial programme ;

"Where would one start to describe Mark Appleton and his achievements. It is probably best to say that by nature he was an outdoors man; never more happier than if he was stalking his prey through the woods on a quiet Summer's morning, or stalking his prey on the rugby field on a noisy Saturday afternoon. As a rugby player he shall be remembered for countless bone-crushing tackles on his opposite number. Mark began his rugby playing days at St Christopher's and Mowden preparatory schools in Hove.

At Mowden he was already showing his destroying capabilities by being selected for the 1st XV when most of his team mates were 4/5 years older. Mark continued his rugby career at Brighton College despite a bone marrow disorder in his leg that hospitalised him for several months. Under the watchful eyes of John Pope, the rugby coach at Brighton College, he played fly-half in the unbeaten XV of the early 80's. Marks connection with Harlequins allowed him to play a season with North Shore in Auckland, New Zealand, a season with Aspen, Colorado, USA, and tours in Spain, Italy, Holland and Ireland. Playing at Harlequins made Mark a more complete player. There he forged many strong and loyal friendships with other players such as Tim Bell, Peter Clovey and Jimmy McCall. It was with these guys that playing, training and winning became a commitment week in week out.

Mark also acquired the nickname of "Abbo" because of his rather large leg muscles! Aided by his studies at Plumpton Agricultural College he managed the family farm gradually stamping his mark on this business, determined to experiment and return the land to more vegetable production and greater profit. Hunting and Fishing was Mark's relaxation and moreover his passion. His home was the woods and the fields and he always spoke of his love for the wilds and it represented a large part of his life. He hunted with his

Mark on the Farm

father Graham in Scotland, Austria, Germany and Mongolia. Many a patient hour they spent together watching, walking, spying and stalking. Mark was a determined person who made an impression on every individual he met. Such a person you only meet once in a lifetime. We love and miss you Mark but time will not dull our memories of you. Personally I have many fond memories of Mark, I do remember being at a party, when a "Banshee" came running in dressed all in black complete with Ski face mask, brandishing a "Chain Saw" running at full power...!!! Yes, it was Mark and the Chain was off.. But bloody hell...!

The Mark Appleton Memorial Medal

I have no idea the result of the game, but let me give you partial list of the participants ; Audley Lumsden, Steve Moriarty, David Cooke, Micky Skinner, Bill Cuthbertson Tim Bell, Jason Burrows, and for Brighton F.C. ; Mark Jenkins, Nick Killick, Bob Jackson, Jeremy Smith, Marc O'Connor, Peter Noble, Rob Thompson, Richard Thoms, Dave Harris, David Lowrie, Graham Stone.

Laz Mahoney, Pat Kilby, Colin Salter, Ed D'arcy, Alan Beck, Jon Prytheric, Stefan Radiojic, Andy Chapman, Jim Ward, Pat Walker, John Honeysett, (Capt) Pete Cimiwic Dave Lowrie, Jim Farr Ray Greenwood Dave Trower

In the early 1990's it was quite standard for us "older members of the Club", on a Saturday to leave the Clubhouse mid-evening and head off, usually to the "Bugle", a popular watering hole for the players and fine establishment at the time, Thank you Ian & Eileen. Then a motley crew would go to "The Junction" a interesting little nightclub in Pool Valley. I decided, one evening to approach the owners to discuss the possibility of sponsorship, and I may add they also owned the bar above "Charlie's" and the Hotel above that. During our conversation "Dougie", one of the owners mentioned that "since the Rugby Club had used the night club the level of trouble has decreased by 85%". Consequently the above photograph shows Veterans showing off their new playing strip! As well as playing a few local fixtures, the highlight of the year was participation in the "Dieppe Veterans Tournament". I played in their first Tournament which we won 26 years ago, even if there were only three teams...!

The Dieppe Veteran tournament is now in its 26th year and for the first 25 years was ably run by Fred Eloy, now the Mayor of

Dieppe. As I have mentioned we won in the first year and again in its twentieth year. We have reached the final on five occasions and soundly beaten by our nemesis, CSM Bucharest, on the three of the finals we have played them. The Bucharest team comprised mainly of policemen and a few of the 'Old regimes' henchmen, there lies another story.

Fred Eloy (Mr Dieppe)

The last time I played in Dieppe, and during my whole career, this front row was probably the best I've ever played with, Ed Wilcox, Mark Jenkins and Dave Harris.

MR PAT WARD-LEE

I mentioned to Pat, a long standing past president, and stalwart of the Club, if he would put together a short "Memoir" of his time at Brighton Rugby Club.

PAT'S RUGBY MEMORIES

"I was a keen player at school in the Midlands, starting at the age of 11. A few years later, at County level, I even played at Twickenham. However, my parents decided to move to Brighton and, at 16, I found myself at Varndean Grammar School. Pupils did not play rugby then, just cricket, athletics and soccer. It was not a good situation for a keen young player, but I was introduced to Brighton Football Club (RFU) by a school friend, Colin "Olly" Biggs. I went down, liked the setup and started in the B XV. Brian Poupard (famous for his photography on Brighton seafront, complete with a parrot on his shoulder!)and Jerry Carr ran the B XV in those days. I soon progressed up to the Extra A, then the A XV and then, what was called in those days, the Extra 1st XV. I was promoted quite rapidly to the 1st XV and was playing for them at the age of 18, one of the youngest members of the team. I started in the Club playing Hooker or Front Row, Tight or Loose Head Prop. As I continued to play, and grow, I became too big for Hooker, and was put in the Second Row and, throughout my career with the Club, I played there or occasionally in the Back Row at No 8.

Back in 1954, when I joined the Club, the lower sides used a field in Falmer, courtesy of a local farmer, arranged by Bill Holt, as well as Stanmer Park, where we used to shunt the cows off before we could play. We also used Preston Park for more important matches.

The standard of the First XV in those days was very, very high. We played against sides like Blackheathens, which was the Blackheath Second Side, and Rosslyn Park Stags, which was their second side and we also played 'Quins' second side and other top Club senior sides.

When we graduated to playing at Withdean Stadium, the junior teams used the second team pitch, and the first XV played all their major fixtures on the main pitch. We did very well in those days. My close friend Ian Heath was in the team, a Sussex star. I played in a game against an American naval touring side which had arrived at Portsmouth on an aircraft carrier. Unknown to me, one of the organisers of the match was Sally, my future wife, who was working for Brighton Publicity Department during her school holidays! She had been to various meetings about the game with legendary Brighton players like John Hale, George Ashby and the then President Ronnie Malby and knew one or two of the members .We didn't meet officially until she went to Brighton Tech' (now Brighton University) to do a rapid commercial course before going over to study in France. I was introduced to her in the canteen by Tony Randall, also a Brighton player studying electrical engineering, as I was, at the College. When Sally came back from France we met up again, she landed her first job in journalism in London, and the rest is history!!

In those days, there was no league structure so there was an amateur atmosphere. Lots of singing, drinking etc.! For instance, if we played Hove, we played one, two, three, four, five teams across the Club. This also happened with Lewes, Worthing and other local clubs.

Our main clubhouse for quite a while was the little bar at Withdean stadium. using the pub next door for some of our bigger events such as a reception for the American Naval Team (who lost the match by the way!) Not glamorous, but a great atmosphere. We also hosted a game for the London Ravens, an American football team based in London. They lost as well even though they were clad in various layers of padding!

The big change socially came when we established the Club in two arches under the Brighton Promenade. We painted them black, set up the bar all under the guidance of our President, Bill Holt. It was an instant hit with visiting sides despite the parking problems. We had some of the most memorable after-match parties there, still talked about today!

The next move was to establish a new Clubhouse and ground in Patcham, at Horsdean, with architect and player Derek Pickering in charge. The annoying thing was that we had to take down two of the floodlights at the end of our season each year to allow the Cricket Club to play. That was one of my jobs. We had a lot of fun there: Sally and I were joint Social Secretaries and I ran the bar. For one of our many brilliant events, we organised a large barbecue and cooked 300 pieces of chicken in our oven at home, and took them down to the Club. It pissed down with rain all day but the party was hugely successful because everyone sheltered inside the clubhouse and we drank the bar dry. The Chicken was great, crisped to perfection under a canopy by ourselves and Don Rees. Other memorable events were a ladies v men game, various games against local nurses, and some cabaret nights. We brought down Julian Clary who we had seen performing in a club in London but in those days his camp style of humour went down like a lead balloon. Soon after our move to Waterhall, we were much more successful with a male stripper morning with six professional strippers, hired by Sally, dressed as James Bond (to start with, anyway), smoked salmon and champagne and a large, women only, audience. I was the barman, staying fully-clothed throughout the evening.

The players' dinners and Annual Ball have always been a time for us to let our hair down. Certain people swung on chandeliers at the Grand Hotel, others raced down the main stairs on tin trays. My

biggest mistake was to organise one particular Players' Dinner. The dessert was very tasty chocolate profiteroles, delicious but also excellent missiles for a few people. Everything was eventually sorted out amicably with the hotel. I've dined in most of the big hotels in Brighton and I never been thrown out yet!

During my playing years, I have played under some great captains: Scottish International Charlie McDonald, George Ashby, Peter Harbidge, Derek Pickering, Geoff Hindle, Rod Hewson, Bob Bashford and other legendary Brighton players.

Matches against Lille and Dieppe turned out to be highlights of my career, on and off the field, for more than fifty years!

I hung up my boots at the age of 54 after a 1st XV match against Worthing when I was brought on as a sub (we were desperate!) I had no kit, and had to rummage for it from the "left" gear at Worthing Clubhouse. The boots were too small but I managed and we did win the game. I thought this was a good moment to announce my retirement.

During the latter days of my playing career, Bill Holt was our famous, and dearly loved President, combining the job with running his business and his duties as a local JP. He was responsible for the brilliant Brighton Rugby Club floats at the annual town carnival which won many prizes. We became firm friends. Our two families have remained very close ever since. That is the power of rugby. Sadly, Bill died in 1981. We will always miss him.

I was privileged to follow Bill, and another good pal, Denis Nolan, as President, remaining in the job for 13 years.

When the Horsdean Club was threatened by the Transport Dept. who were planning a new road we set up a very strong committee, The Bypass Committee. This was to ensure that our needs were met in the event of the ground and clubhouse being wiped off the earth and to protect the Club from any moves to force us to join up with other local rugby sides. Members and friends were a group of professionals with legal, PR, architectural, and engineering skills including David Malby, Ann Holt, John Wallace, John Woodley, Graham Nicholas, Sally and myself. The committee was in session for 10 years. After the initial, prolonged negotiations and, exactly 10 years after our Committee was first set up, we finally achieved our goal of moving to our current ground at Waterhall. Although it had been a Council tip and much flint picking was required to make it a safe, playable pitch, the position and elevation were superb. After due consideration, and to the surprise of the Council, we went for it! The floodlights originally at Horsdean were too good to lose, and were stored by John Honeysett on a reservoir in Dyke Road, we moved them to Waterhall, with much help. John Orrell was involved as was Roger Lowrie and myself to oversee the new cable laying, jointing and erection, and commissioning for the first game under lights.

The journey to that point was very, very hard work, with long meetings in various pubs and clubs, and much slogging away, trying to convince Brighton Council that our Club had to be moved to a prestigious venue. We won – and spent many hours digging out bagfuls of sharp stones and rubble! We hired a top London architect, Jim Laidlaw, a friend of John Wallace, to design the Clubhouse which is still one of the best in Southern England. The opening ceremony took place on Saturday 20th September 1992, performed by the then-President of the RFU, Danie Serfontain.

Punchy, effective publicity was required to kick things off, and many Page Three girls helped us with press coverage, stunts and events under the guidance of Sally, Frank Howard and Adrian Biggs. It worked!

We have always been a great social club, stuck to our guns and taken pride in our players, sometimes under very difficult circumstances. Each time we moved, there were problems. However, the indomitable spirit of Brighton Football Club, is what we are all about.

Pat and Sally Ward-Lee at the 2018 Annual Ball. (Photo Dave Beech)

RONNIE MALBY

1920 - 1993

Honours Cap	**1946-47**
Club Captain	**1950 - 52**
Vice President	**1954**
President	**1957 - 61**
Club Trustee	**1970 - 85**

Although born in London, Ronnie grew up and lived the rest of his life in Sussex. After leaving Brighton College at 16 he played his early club rugby for Blackheath and Old Brightonians. Ronnie joined Brighton FC in 1946 when the Club started again after the War. Through his skill on the field and his administrative expertise he contributed greatly to Club's sound recovery in the post war years.

In 1948 he took the post of Team Secretary, an onerous position with accompanying difficulties that only those who have held it will appreciate. With the help of Gerry Carr and Bob Skeet's daughter, universally known as 'Skeeter', Ronnie introduced a highly efficient carding system. He and Skeeter looked after the 1st and Extra 1st XV's and Gerry took care of the Club's other sides. Ronnie played regularly for the 1st XV and Sussex at Wing Forward, and captained the Club between 1950 and 1952.

Ronnie was a man of many talents, and as, for years, the Club was his greatest interest, in retrospect perhaps it is appropriate to recall what he regarded as his greatest achievement for the Club.

During Brighton's Smallpox epidemic in 1953, when vaccination fever was hitting the playing membership hard, he raised an unbeaten 1st XV that season.

Ronnie was also a generous man. He ran his own business and quite a number of older Club members will remember him for the jobs he provided in the post War years. Although perhaps not able to field a full 15, at one time LNP could have put out a very reasonable 7's team.

Over many years he devoted an enormous amount of his own and his staff's time to the Club affairs. After serving as President, when the Club had the opportunity of securing its new ground at Horsdean he became a Club Trustee, chaired the Clubhouse Committee and contributed financially to the building of the Clubhouse. More recently he donated £5,000 towards the cost of erecting the floodlights at Waterhall which we are officially opening tonight. This act of generosity was typical of the man.

There was a lighter side to his character and Ronnie enjoyed his Saturdays during the season to the full. To many who remember the 50s it as a golden era of Club Rugby which we are unlikely to see again. Today, the relatively harmless acts of high spirits enjoyed by Ronnie and others then are taboo. Antics like trailing fireworks under following cars on Reigate Hill, causing mayhem on the Big Wheel at Battersea and privatising countless road signs are now considered acts of vandalism, often involving the long arm of the law and serious penalties. Of course there was no breathalyser then and a good deal fewer cars on the road.

On one occasion Ronnie narrowly escaped injury on at least two counts. He was returning from a game at Reigate in his new Riley when a corner taken too fast resulted in a pranged wing and a broken farm gate. Later that evening he and his wife Una were going to a Club Dance at Withdean and , so that she didn't see the damage, he asked her to drive. The road was narrow and when an oncoming car dazzled her there was a slight brush with the edge of the road. Ronnie got out and surveying the damage that had been caused earlier remarked casually "A bit of a mess I'm afraid, but don't worry I'll get it repaired in the morning". The real culprit's identity was never revealed until now!

Adrian Biggs, a Vice President and former player, remembers Ronnie well for his find attention to detail and his knowledge of the Club's rules which remain a mystery to most of us today.

One of Ronnie's contemporaries, Dick Braybon, Also a former Captain, President and another Club Trustee, recalls a few items from Ronnie's time that are very different today.

When Ronnie was captain, the Brighton 1st XV played home matches between October and February on the outfield of the Sussex Cricket ground, on the south side in front of ' the Cowshed'.

In 1953, the first match of the All Blacks tour was played against Southern Counties at the Hove Greyhound Stadium.

Things were a lot cheaper then too. The Club's Annual Ball at The Grand cost 15/- per person, including the meal and a Cabaret (that's 75p today for those too young to remember shillings and old pence). If you couldn't afford the meal, you could go for the dance only at 5/- (just 25p!).

The Malby connection with the Club has been continued through Ronnie's sons David and Donald. Donald played for a few years in most XV's including the 1st's but is best remembered for his years of hard work running the Bar at the Arches and Horsdean, recognised by rare distinction of Honorary Life Membership. David, a regular 1st XV player who represented Sussex and the Sussex Martlets, is presently Club Chairman.

The Club will not forget Ronnie. His contribution was immense and undoubtedly helped to build the Club we have today. Thanks to stars like him, the present generation of Brighton players and supporters is continuing a tradition of great rugby, family involvement and friendship that simply has no comparison, anywhere.

1996-97 Handbook, and that doesn't look like Mel Heath?

MIKE BROWNHILL

Obituary taken from the programme Saturday 13th September 1997.

Members will be very shocked to hear of Mike's sudden death on Wednesday night. He was 61.

An immensely talented wing, he played for Leicester, captained Cardiff and was an England trialist before joining the Club. He captained the 1st XV from 1970 -1975 and frequently played for Sussex before hanging up his boots.

He maintained an active role in rugby, for the past several years as Sussex Team Manager.

A Prominent JP he was well know throughout the town and will be sadly missed by us and his many friends.

ALAN McCARTHY
President 1995-1997

Since John asked me to write a piece on my tenure as President I have been desperately trying to remember what happened during my two seasons, to the point where I even needed John to confirm which years they were.

As I recall they were two relatively successfully seasons narrowly missing promotion in 1995; more about this later.

I guess the three most prominent memories relate to: the front row, the coach, Neil Thomas, and Chairman, Alex Pincus (for all or part of the time), and the role of being President over twenty years ago.

For fear of retribution, I shall not mention the names of the front row! Suffice to say, they were one of the most physically aggressive and talented group that I had ever been associated with. One in particular, struggled to control his aggression, consequently being sent off several times during 1995. Similar characters play rugby at all levels and the key to their success is channeling this aggression. No doubt the coach has a key role to play in this.

This brings me to Neil Thomas. There is no doubt that Neil developed a formidable team that almost won promotion in a tough league. A major part of his success at coaching came from his motivation of the team. I am sure Neil will not mind me saying that much of that came from the emotional aggression that he brought to the role and not doubt translated to the team. Some, eg aforementioned front row, clearly struggled to channel that aggression! The emotional commitment also occasionally spilled over into some carefully chosen words of advice to the referee that were not always well received.

It is clearly important in an emotionally charged environment to have a calming influence within the club and the Chairman is often looked to for that role. For the most part I was very fortunate to have Alex Pincus in this role. But those of you that know Alex, will recognise that he does have occasional lapses of control himself; Peter Harbidge has a marvelous story of Alex attacking someone during the opera which I am sure he would be happy to share. So picture the scene at Heathfield in a tight game against one of the strongest sides in Sussex at the time. It was not the prettiest of games and our players, particularly again the front row, had clearly been "motivated" for the game. The referee had, in the eyes of Neil Thomas, made one or two errors, and was consequently getting the fully volley of abuse (unquestionably deserved!) and was getting extremely agitated. Whilst trying to calm matters I became aware of a scuffle on the touchline only to discover Alex in a fight with the Heathfield Chairman. Fortunately not many if any of the wild haymakers made contact.

We were not the most popular team amongst referees at this time. However I am not sure it justified the five (I think) sending offs from our front row during the season. The last one of which was in a game that determined whether or not we would gain promotion and which we consequently lost to miss out on points difference; it was the only game I missed that year through holiday and I remember the huge disappointment to this day. The sending offs did not enhance our reputation and resulted in us being summoned to the RFU in London. You can imagine the slight apprehension I felt when Alex and I entered the room to meet the alacado's at the RFU; how would we explain a punch up at the home of rugby? As it was, Alex was exemplary, all was well and no punches were thrown.

So this brings me to the role of President twenty years ago; I think a picture is emerging. Being asked to be President after having played for the club for over twenty years was a huge privilege for me but I think I should have taken more advice from Pat Ward-Lee, who had been President for the previous 12 years. I am not sure what I expected, but I guess it was more of an ambassadorial role, swanning around making the odd speech and buying a jug for the players (much as Steve does now!).

But no, it felt more like rugby's equivalent of Kofi Annan (RIP). Added to which, often on a Friday night I found myself ringing players (you guessed it, invariably front row) who for one reason or another were not certain of playing the next day. Also, I was still attempting to play veteran rugby at the time and was ably, and persistently, assisted by the late great club stalwart, Frank Howard (he of the blood soaked sponge at time of injury). So, the rest of my Friday night and many other evenings were spent talking with Frank about veteran rugby.

Suffice to say, the President did not have the same infrastructure, particularly around the playing, that is enjoyed today. It seemed all consuming, occasionally frustrating and agonizingly close to very fulfilling. Nevertheless, as I have said, it was a privilege to be President, but I am grateful for my sanity that it was only for two years before I was appointed to a new job that prevented me from carrying on.

Alan McCarthy, Neil Thomas and Martin Johnson

ARGUS, Tuesday, November 11, 1997

PETERS FIRES UP SURGE FOR THE TOP

Brighton are back in the promotion picture in London Three South East after producing their best rugby of the season against Tunbridge Wells.

They ran in three tries in a 22-16 home victory and only excellent Wells defending, particularly in the second half, prevented them winning more convincingly.

Centres Alex Balls and Chris Jones and winger Joe Brooking got first-half tries with fly half Tony Flowers, back after a year with Havant, celebrating his return with tow conversions and a penalty.

Man of the match was second row Simon Peters but scrum half Paul Hancock ran him close.

Katie Price, Matt Sellens John Honeysett, Mark Gibb and 'Spanners'

Mr Andrew Goodhall of Brunswick Development, became our main sponsor and a number of Brighton Football Club members were grateful to Andrew for organising a table at 'Donatellos' in aid of the 'Evening 'Argus Christmas Appeal'.

During the course of the evening, we were joined at our table by June Brown (Dot, from the TV programme Eastenders) the 'Can Can' Girls from the London Palladium. However, the highlight of a fantastic evening was when Katie Price (aka 'Jordan') joined us and graciously poised for a photograph..

Brunswick Developments came onboard as our main sponsors in 1998. The first £50,000 instalment of Goodhall's £200,000 was paid in the summer and some of the money was used to attract top players to the Club. This was obviously a shrewd move by Brunswick Developments as Brighton & Hove Albion had started to show interest in 'Waterhall' as a potential site for a new ground. Andrew was also determined to see Brighton, and Hove Rugby Clubs merge and had instigated meetings with each committee. Members from both clubs were never going to allow that to happen.

RECOLLECTIONS OF BRIGHTON FOOTBALL CLUB RFU

By Alex Pincus (President 1997-2000)

I first played for the Club in 1957 whilst whilst on Holiday from my schooI Epsom College. I was contacted by Peter Rumney who was captain of the 'A' XV and heard that I played rugby. I remember my first game which I think was in the 'A' away at Reigate. We travelled there by Coach and It was my introduction to alcohol.

However this was not my first contact with the Club. My father Joe was a Doctor who was born in South Africa. One of his friends was Maurice Rosen who was Secretary of the Club. The Rosens who were in the fur business lived in a house which overlooked the Hove County Cricket ground.I recall being there one day when Maurice's son Mike who was playing for Sussex vaulted their garden fence after a game. Mike subsequently changed his surname to Anthony and was a prominent member of the Club. At that time probably in the early 50's Brighton was probably the only Rugby Club in the world which boasted two members who were furriers. The other being David Benjamin.

In the late 50's many of the playing members of the Club were war veterans in particular the Hale brothers who were New Zealanders the elder brother John was particularly fearsome both on and off the field. Others were Dick Waite and Rod Hewson.

I managed to get a few games in the First 'XV' but wasn't really good enough so settled into the Ex 1st and 'A' XV. I introduced my friend Graham Nicholas to the Club and he went on to be a long serving Club Member and 1st team prop. I clearly recall one of my first encounters with Bill 'Mush' Holt and Ann who I think were not then married. Bill had a Morris pick-up truck always full of bags of building materials and implements. In one of my few games for the 1st Bill managed to get sent off for doing nasty things to his opposing hooker. I won't be more specific as today that offence would have elicited a very long ban.

Other memorable names were Derek Smith a patrician 2nd row and of course the evergreen Mike Buckingham. Also Derek Pickering an outstanding back who was my direct contemporary at Brighton College Junior School in the late 1940's. Another contemporary was David Laing.

We played at Withdean Stadium but prior to that the Club played in Preston Park and I think they turned down the chance to buy a house overlooking the park which could have been a Club house.

I had a spell away from the club as I joined my newly formed old school team Old Epsomians who played in Walton on Thames. After a couple of seasons I rejoined Brighton in the early 1970's and played mainly for the 'A' XV for many years. This was a golden time for the Club with the First XV winning the Sussex Cup.

Other memorable names from this period are Peter Harbidge who had joined from Old Anchorians. He had also played semi professional soccer for Gillingham. Geoff Hindle from Cheshire an outstanding fly half. John Jennings at scrum half as well as Ian Barnard ,Stuart Fry and Bob Bashford.

I enjoyed playing for the 'A' and we also had a good side with emerging players as well as former 1st and Ex 1st. We had three farmers playing for us in the A .John Baker, David Robinson and John Randle. The only problem was their non availability at lambing time ! I played in the second row with Ray Dunk and other team memebers Alan Wood ,Colin Salter, Don Rees, the Biggs Brothers and Adrian Shillaker .We also had Mike Jackson as a regular. A former 1st XV and ex Rugby League. He was a great asset to us on the pitch but dangerous off it. Especially after a few beers. A great character.

In the 80s the club regularly ran 5 senior teams as well as a very good under 18 Colts. I was fortunate to run the Colts for a couple of years and the then rules allowed one old fart to play. So I revelled in playing some of the best rugby of my life. We had a very good side with Steve Foxton, Adrian Knight, Robert Thompson and Peter Noble. All became regular 1st Team players.

The social side of the Club was excellent. There were regular dances at Withdean then at Horsdean when we moved there in the 70's.We also established a ClubHouse in the Arches between the Piers on the lower esplanade. The Arches were opened by the Mayor of Brighton Frank Masefield Baker.

He was very eccentric and during the proceedings he set fire to John Hindmarsh's hair which was heavily oiled. It went up in flames probably a couple of feet high. Fortunately no harm was done to kind of crazy behaviour associated then with Club rugby. There were many other memorable episodes ranging from chandelier swinging at the Grand Hotel to naked horse riding during a Lille visit. Many of them involved Mike Buckingham.

In 1977 as part of the Queen's Jubilee weekend 3 of us from Brighton, myself Max Pocock and Ian Griffiths joined with 3 Lewes players to form the William Webb Ellis Morris men. The idea was to raise money for charity. We had such a good time that this carried on for another 10 years. The idea of participating in a weekly event in the summer that included free beer attracted other Brighton players including Peter Harbidge, Keith Dixon, Gerry Wicks, Graham Howe, Paul White and our own President Steve Russell.

When I finished playing in the early 80s I became a strong supporter but it wasn't until 10 years after that I was persuaded by David Malby to get involved with the move to Waterhall.

There followed a further 15 years on various Committees including a couple as President.

Although much of it was enjoyable the pressures of trying to manage the change from amateur to the professional era were considerable. It was around this time that I became close friends with Malcolm Holt and after a challenging period I managed to persuade him to take over as President.

I think it's fair to say that he established the foundations for the success that the Club now enjoys.

It's been a roller coaster ride during the over 60 years that I have been involved with the Club. However I have made close friendships that have lasted to this day and I even manage occasionally to cycle with some of them along the seafront in Brighton and Hove. Nowadays I am a volunteer for the Wooden Spoon Rugby charity and am joined on the Committee by Ann Holt and Peter Harbidge

As the Club celebrates its 150th birthday I am very grateful for the call that Peter Rumney made to me in 1957.Its good to see the Club going from strength to strength and hopefully someone might read this on our 200th Anniversary in 2068.

MINI AND YOUTH

by Neil Thomas

In January 1999 Mark Whitlock and Neil Dermott decided to take the short journey east to Waterhall to set up a mini and youth section at Brighton.

They only had two players – their sons Kris and Scott - but through hard work and determination they managed to set in motion a new section with teams in several age groups.

Word soon spread and the club developed links with local schools. These links introduced young players who had never considered rugby previously. Soon the club was able to boast good numbers at all ages from 7 to 18.

Former first team stalwarts, including Paul Morley and Steve Morris, took up the coaching reins to develop the youngsters further.

Brighton sent teams to the annual East Sussex Festival and made their presence felt. Mark Whitlock's under 12's reached the final against a Horsham side, including Billy Twelvetrees, in April 2000.

As the teams became more competitive they went further afield with tours throughout England, Scotland, Wales and Ireland. Teams including Saracens, Rosslyn Park, Blackheath, London Scottish and

Richmond were regular visitors seeking competitive fixtures for their mini and youth outfits.

In 2003 Brighton's then under 11's took part in the Gulliver's Nationwide Tournament and reached the finals at Twickenham in May of that year. Other teams followed their lead achieving the runners up spot and overall winner at the home of English Rugby.

The section has continued to thrive and it is great to see Frank Taggart come back to Brighton as captain and forwards coach, having started his Rugby journey in the Mini and Youth ranks.

THE MILLENNIUM SEASON 1999-2000
*GIVE 'EM THE ******* TREATMENT*

by Ian Watkins - Director of Rugby.

It is now one year on from my first introduction to Brighton F.C. where I eagerly and enthusiastically prepared my first training session on the hallowed turf at Waterhall. As I stood waiting patiently amongst my cones, tackle bags and various articles of equipment including a bag of well used rugby balls, one by one my new set of players- all eleven of them - trooped gingerly across to the training field and promptly announced that three of them had never played before!

As Dick Toms, my trusty assistant and I made our way off the field after one and a half hours of coaching torment he assured me that things would improve (with tongue firmly in cheek) and so they did. The players started to trickle into the coaching sessions and it was quickly apparent to me that the fitness and standard of skills on display were very poor indeed. It was going to take a huge amount of work to introduce a style and pattern that we could develop in time for the fast approaching league campaign.

On a positive note I recruited Paul Britton (now affectionately known as 'MoG'- 'Man of Glass'), Jenks returned from G&G and it was decided to convert him from Prop to Hooker to which he responded with relish. We won't tell anyone about the night he lost several 'Heads' to the scrimmaging machine and after some, one on one coaching I was duly given the name 'Snakehips'.

Everything started to gain momentum until a bombshell was

dropped. I discovered that Bok and Danie decided to try their luck with the Saracens Development Squad and, to cap it all, on his first appearance at training, Shay Fitzpatrick concussed himself by running into a goal post! He missed our opening match, however from thereon we were able to develop a line-out called the 'Post' ball.

My squad was now looking paper-thin. A heavy defeat at the hands of Ruislip and unconvincing victory over Old Brightonians were followed by what I regard as a turning point, when we trashed London Division Two side, Old Juddians, 66-0. At last things were taking shape.

The weeks rolled into months and by Christmas we were second in the League and travelled to far flung places such as Folkestone where we took their two and a half year ground record, 14-13 the game was akin to 'Rorkes Drift.' The real highlight - apart from the victory - was the 'Caribbean Night' organised by Jenks and Mozza, when Major and I were plied with various cocktails expertly prepared by the duo on the coach, freshly cut pineapple, garnish and all. (I wish to make no reference to a female supporter being seen relieving herself in the bushes on the side of the M25).

There were highs and lows throughout the season including beating Cranbrook twice. Defeats by Heathfield and East Grinstead and the horrible Home Draw with Medway were offset by tremendous results over Sidcup, Chichester, Worthing and Eastbourne. Who can forget the titanic struggle with Lewes in the Sussex Cup where victory was snatched away by some dubious refereeing decisions at the line-out?

Since last season the club has flourished from that first sparse training session in July last year. There is a buzz and an expectation to succeed now. The fitness work that the players have endured throughout June have gone down well, together with the charity bike ride which helped them improve considerably.

*My thanks go to my two assistants Dick and Maj., and to my First and Second XV skippers Gibbo and Sean. Thank you all for your unstinting support, and, above all, the opportunity to put Brighton F.C back on the rugby map. In the meanwhile we'll continue to give 'em the ******* treatment.*

The Argus Tuesday January 18th 2000

BRIGHTON SLIP-UP GIVES WORTHING FRESH HOPE

Get set for a momentous title shoot out after Brighton lost their perfect record amid high drama at Waterhall.

Cranbrook outside half Dale Spencer stroked over a thirty yard penalty with the last kick of the game as Cranbrook grabbed a 22 - 22 draw from Saturday's thriller in London Three South East.

Now the battle for the top spot could hinge on events at Roundstone Lane a week on Saturday, when Ian Watkins' leaders visit old rivals Worthing.

Brighton should have won on Saturday after leading 12-0, 19-7, 11-14, but coach Ian Watkins said "A draw was a fair result".

He added "It was an excellent game. This league needs more matches like that. There was plenty of Blood and Thunder up front and some superb handling movements and support play.

The players were bitterly disappointed at the end but the result shows we can't rest on our laurels".

Well worked scores by Justin Burt and the influential Conrad Burke sent Brighton 12 points clear at the break, and it would have been game over but for a last ditch tackle by Donovan Smith on the flying Micky Poole right on half-time.

Cranbrook responded with a spell of pressure which saw them make room for Dave O'Brien to strike in the corner, but the hosts replied with a scintillating handling move for Poole to send Geraint Jones to the posts. Jones converted and Burke sent over a penalty, but tries from Paddy Donegan and Ben Tardiff kept the spirited Kent men in touch. The hosts played the more expansive rugby and were happy to move the ball wide from deep inside their own 22, even in those last nerve-jangling minutes.

But they missed three kickable penalties, while Spencer sent over two conversions from near the touchline for Cranbrook.

The Argus, Tuesday, February 29, 2000

BRIGHTON LOOKING TO CLINCH PROMOTION AT WATERHALL

Home is where the title is insists coach Watkins

Ian Watkins say his Brighton side edge closer to the title, then declared: "We can finish the job at home."

The unbeaten leaders need just one win from their two remaining games to clinch the Three South East Crown.

And Watkins wants his side to settle matters against Dartfordians at Waterhall a week on Saturday.

Watkins said: We've had a very hard run of games since Christmas and we've come through unscathed. We won't count our chickens, but we've got a great chance to lift the title on our own patch."

Heathfield had plenty of fire and physical presence up front but Brighton matched them in the pack and offered the greater flair behind the scrum during their 29-5 win.

They conjured tries for wingers Geraint Jones and Martin Watts inside 12 minutes.

Both followed passages of flowing back play, though Jones was fortunate to complete his run to the line after picking up a Micky Poole pass which went forward.

Jones added the goal points and also did the honours just before the break when a big lineout win by Danie Venter led to Julian Hutchens providing Gary Henderson with a scoring pass.

Conrad Burke made it 24-0 after the interval with a drop goal, prop Paul Watton rewarded Heath's best spell of the match with a try from a driving lineout but Brighton finished in style when Poole's break set up a Venter try.

The Argus, Tuesday, March 14, 2000

WATKINS : HARD WORK IS THE KEY TO OUR SUCCESS

Ian Watkins watched Brighton clinch their first title in 11 years, then revealed "It's all down to sheer hard work".

Brighton overcame a few big day nerves to score six tries and beat Dartfordians 36 - 24 at Waterhall, maintaining their near-perfect record at the top of London Three South East.

The club were runners-up last time around and have enjoyed a remarkable turn in fortunes since Watkins, a former Triple Crown winner with Wales, took over as coach at the start of last season. They can now prepare to test themselves in a new look division three, which will feature many of the second division outfits including Lewes.

Watkins admitted: "It was a curious performance. We played some magnificent rugby at times and school boy stuff at others. But it has been a good season and we've proved we are the best".

"The players have worked extremely hard for their success and deserve everything" This is the hardest division to get out of, but we've picked off results every week while other sides have slipped up. It certainly hasn't come easy. We haven't got a big squad but we have done well with injuries and some of the sides cannot hold a candle to us in terms of pace and skill". He added "What makes this special for me is that I've always been the nearly man as a coach, I've come second and third and fourth so I'm delighted to get a title".

Watkins is targeting a handful of signings in the summer in readiness for next season but warned any newcomers "If you don't want to put the work in then forget it"

Giant lock Danie Venter set things rolling in the second minute when he rumbled through some weak tackling for the opening score. Left wing Geraint Jones scorched away for a try in each half and Micky Poole, his colleague out on the right, matched that with two clever finishes.

Mark Gibb was driven over as the Brighton eight started to push their weight around after the break. Jones kicked three conversions, but there was also some slipshod defence which saw Dartfordians score three second half tries.

London and SE Division

London 3 South East	P	W	D	L	PF	PA	PD	Pts	-
Brighton	16	15	1	0	488	142	346	31	
Cranbrook	15	12	1	2	384	185	199	25	
Worthing	15	12	0	3	427	157	270	24	
Crawley	15	11	0	4	401	225	176	22	
Tunbridge Wells	14	9	0	5	386	229	157	18	
Sidcup	15	9	0	6	378	221	157	18	
East Grinstead	15	9	0	6	322	210	112	18	
Eastbourne	14	8	0	6	306	206	100	16	
Chichester	15	8	0	7	249	252	-3	16	
Dartfordians	15	7	0	8	354	293	61	14	
Heathfield & Wald'n	15	6	1	8	220	224	-4	13	
Folkestone	15	6	0	9	261	321	-60	12	
Hove	15	5	1	9	210	320	-110	11	
Park House	15	5	0	10	269	418	-149	10	
Beccehamian	15	2	0	13	161	463	-302	4	
Medway	15	1	0	14	117	632	-515	2	
Horsham	15	0	0	15	148	583	-435	0	

** denotes points deducted in right hand column*

Andy Rice earning his 'Wings'

BRIGHTON GRATEFUL FOR A HALPIN HAND
Former Irish International an inspiration to players

Gary Halpin could not have asked for a warmer welcome as he made the transition from Test rugby to London South East.

The former Irish International prop strode on for Brighton at half-time with his new Club already 27-3 up on visitors Dunstonians. They eventually won 44-3 and coach Bert Merritt was full of praise for the influence his star signing is having at Waterhall.

Merritt said ; "Gary was a major influence on the game. His presence made players on both sides want to lift their standards and there were no attempts at foul play.

"Apparently, Gary was feeling his way in for the first couple of scrums, but at the third there was a really good shunt. I was pleased with the rest of the team. I wanted them to do the job without Gary in the first half, not rely on him coming on to lift them".

Teenage scrum half Paul Pride scored two tries and earned high marks. Andy Pinnock, James Lewis, Rob Ross and Simon Peters also crossed with James adding three conversions and a penalty.

Unfortunately, the only photo I could find of Gary wearing a Brighton Shirt

The Argus, Tuesday, December 10, 2002

BRIGHTON PAY FOR THEIR PANIC ATTACK

Brighton skipper Mark Jenkins admitted a few moment of panic cost his side a precious away win at leaders Sidcup.

The Waterhall outfit went down 20-17 in London Three South East but remain in contention for at least the play-off spot. Julian Hutchens' try helped them lead 10-3 at the break and Andy Light got over in the second half, with Mark Gibb converting both and adding a penalty.

A late converted try saw off the Sussex side but Jenkins said: "We lost the game because we panicked.""I am not prepared to talk about refereeing but we conceded more penalties that we had done in our entire league campaign to date. We played really well but we have got to learn to take our chances.

We changed our fixture card to a Handbook, which was a major success.

Evening Argus, October 2004.

NEW LOOK BRIGHTON ARE OVER THE BLUES

Andy Pinnock admits he would probably have quit if his Brighton team had not done so badly last season. Instead he is giving it another crack after that horrendous winless campaign and looking to help his side restore some pride in London Three South East.

Brighton have won their last two home games, including a spectacular 53-20 rout of Cobham last Saturday in which Simon Peters and James Lewis each scored three tries.

It is a far cry from last Winter when they were docked two points and only managed a home draw against Bognor, leaving them rock bottom on a points tally of minus one.

Pinnock admits it will be a long road back from that sort of season, but said, "We have got a lot of young players starting to find their feet. "We won't win the league this year, but we can make Waterhall a difficult place to play at and hopefully we can pick up the odd away win. If we can finish in mid table this season the foundations will be there.

"The Sunday mornings after games are getting harder and I was going to finish last season, but we had such a shocking year, I thought I couldn't go out on that. "Credit to the coaches. They stuck by the style they wanted to play and the people were saying last week that it was the best rugby they had seen at Brighton for years.

Peters was in superb form at No 8 and he was ably supported in the back row by a pair of players known as Raddish and Robocop. Robocop is Adrian Murray, named as the Man of the Match at Cobham, while Raddish is James Wall. Long serving Mark Gibb is back at Lock. Paul Pride continues to progress at scrum-half and 19st second XV prop Matt Sellens has decided he wants a first team place, and has been training all Summer to be in with a chance.

Pinnock said "Last week was our best performance for four years and we had been building up to it".

Coach Gary Henderson admitted he was encouraged to see his patient approach pay dividends having avoided what he deemed as "a quick fix"

Brighton go to Charlton Park next Saturday looking for the first away win of the season.

BRIGHTON BLUES

It was during the middle part of the 2000's that it was decided to introduce our nickname the Brighton Blues. The original "Brighton Crest" with the two dolphins, the Blue Shirt and Red socks, were taken out of our constitution. The 'Brighton Blues' logo was added to our shirts, memorabilia, paraphernalia etc.. To me, as the Club Historian, it amounted to throwing 140 years of history away.

The name of "Football Club" with the omission of rugby is a great honour that can only be given to Clubs formed before the formation of the RFU (1871). I came to realise this importance when working in "World of Rugby" reference library and met other scholars who were in awe when I told them of our Club\s formation date.

I am the Club's Historian and I have tried for years to reintroduce our name with a certain amount of success and I hope I have got on peoples nerves by harping on about it.

Now, whether my constant moaning has been taken into account or the fact that 'Brighton Football Club' is 150 years old, has galvanised the committee to reintroduce the 'Brighton Football Club' crest on the shirts this year, as well as red socks.

If what I hear is true, which I hope it is, we are going through a club rebranding, commencing with the loss of the Brighton Blues Logo.

I hope this book so far has given you a greater insight into the amazing history of this famous Club, and give members a sense of renewed pride.

THE OFFICIAL OPENING OF THE ARTIFICIAL TRAINING PITCH

Gary Henderson with his knowledge and foresight put together a business proposal which he then presented to the Brighton Rugby Club committee... to create a Artificial Training Pitch at Waterhall.

It was never going to be plain sailing. Gary ably assisted by James "T" Ward, spent many months negotiating grants with both the Rugby Football Union and Football Association. Eventually with money in place, planning permission granted the 'Community' A.T.P was built and official opened by Sir Clive Woodward.

It is a massive asset to Brighton Rugby Club, as an 'All weather Pitch' which is being used to play league games not only by us but also other rugby clubs when their pitches are deemed unplayable.

There is of course the financial gain from letting the ATP to other rugby and football clubs.

Sir Clive doing the honours

Sir Clive Woodward, Sally Gunnell and friends

Colin Salter, Mike Buckingham, Johnny Taylor

I have no idea what passing comment Sir Clive made that amused us.

Chapter XVI

Mark Gibb, who has now been with the Club approx twenty years, and has already gained a "stalwart", even a "Alacado" status, in the nicest possible sense, and when Mark offered to write a piece encompassing the Twickenham Finals, I was delighted. So, in his own words.

THE TWICKENHAM YEARS

By Mark Gibb

"It was a depressing drive home from Waterhall, my kids were 18 months old and getting to games and training was the equivalent to a NATO manoeuvres exercise in the mid Atlantic. We had just lost to Seaford at home 15-10 and Brighton were consigned to mid table mediocrity in Sussex 1. Our neighbours Hove were riding the crest of the wave and going to get promoted and be 2 divisions above us in the RFU set up. We had many different coaches over the last 10 years. Some with enough time and resource to do well, and others with limited resource and made the most of what they could. We were in desperate need of fresh ideas and fresh input from someone outside the club.

It was with surprise at the start of the 2008/09 season that the club had appointed a fresh faced player/coach in Neil McGovern. He was a reformed centre with a suspect knee having played at a higher level out wide on the wings. Lloyd Jenkins was Captain and there was Tudor Ellis and myself left of the old guard who had experienced some tough loses to local sides. Neil had the ability to attract players and knew many around the Sussex circuit who had played at Brighton. Players such as Sam Hutton, James Trevis and Nik Hannay returned, Alex Finch joined who had played under Neil at Sussex University. Brighton also started a much more active chase for sponsorship within the community.

Our first game under Neil was an away day at Hove against their second team. This was a high pressure game for a first team as the amount of verbal abuse from Hove about losing to their second team was building as match-day got closer. Training had gone well as Neil had introduced his systems for defence and attack. Mark Jenkins had helped with the forwards coaching and the game arrived. After a rusty start and going 7 points down, we won the game by fifty plus points.

Alex Finch had shown that he was to be a star in the making with tries, penalties, and conversions in a stellar performance. Neil as usual for a good coach kept us grounded and talked about commitment to training and improving ourselves. It was a nice start to the season, and a special mention to Tudor Ellis who after many years of service for the club scored his first competitive try.

This was our 140th season and it soon became evident that Uckfield were our main rivals in the league as they had had several big wins. We were due to meet at Waterhall on our 140th Club lunch. As usual with these games lots of people watching and a stir of something special was just starting to be whispered. For some of the younger players such as Adam Salvage and Stavros Economou it was a case of telling them to focus on the job in hand. We played in quite a dour contest as the weather was atrocious and we had white shirts on that celebrated our 140th year anniversaries. By the end they must have weighed twice as much as when we started. The win was dominated by our forwards who were proving quite a close unit as friends as well.

After this win we had our National Cup commitments against Shoreham and Ellingham and Ringwood RFC. It's odd playing games like this as you don't ever expect to target these competitions as priority and players take these weekends off. This year everyone remained available and we put plus fifty points on two quite good sides. The draw gave us Old Walcountians in the next round in December 2008.

Our league form continued, however our naivety as a young side showed through at our nemesis Seaford in which we played in atrocious conditions to gain a 7-7 draw. The conditions were some of the worst I had ever played in and it was certainly put down as a marker of how to play in bad conditions. Wins over Burgess Hill and Holbrook took us into December. This year the weather was particularly bad and having the ATP to play games was fantastic.

The cup tie against Old Walcountians was inspired as they had sounded off on their website. They came across as an over confident and somewhat arrogant side who did not live up to their billing. In awful conditions we scored thirty plus points and limited them to a single score. The game changing moment in the 5th minute when Tom Aitken pile drives their No8 into the fence 1 yard from our line whilst celebrating what he thought was a score. We were safely in to the next round with Medway away.

Our fixtures were getting backed up due to the severe weather. However the team all agreed to train over Christmas and NY, new kit arrived and a team was gelling together nicely. We were lucky with injuries and the Physio was not troubled too much. Our first fixture was away at Medway in the cup, they were unbeaten and top of Kent 1 and had put a real focus on beating Brighton which was reflected in their website and pre match media. They had just completed two successive promotions and were very confident. Lloyd Jenkins scored the only try and Brighton won by a single score. At one stage we were down to 13 men and playing uphill against the wind and rain. It was a great result and special mention to Nik Hannay and Sam Hutton who provided massive contributions to the cause.

Our Saturday fixture list was filling up through January and February 2009 with non playing league weekends being filled with the backlog of fixtures. Sussex RFU after careful talks allowed us to play our league games and push back the County Shield cup games to later in the season. Our league results included a 120-0 league win against Hellingly, 70 plus win against Burgess Hill, and then a second game against Hellingly which was 60 plus point win. Our next tie in the cup was away again against Old Blues.

Further bad weather meant the Old Blues cup game was pushed back and from the RFU the hierarchy of games to be played due to fixture clashes was National Cup, League, County Shield. Sussex were getting annoyed that the Shield games were not getting played. We were asked to play Saturday and Sunday which was ridiculous, and after going back to them they agreed to make our league and cup games as double headers counting for both games. The Old Blues game was put back to the end of the February and wins over Hellingly (60-3) and Burgess Hill again.

Uckfield at this stage were still matching Brighton game for game but luckily slipped up against Hove away which gave us breathing space. At this stage it was still 2 points for a win.

The Old Blues game came round quickly and whilst it was a close first twenty minutes it turned in to a substantial and comfortable win. It was a good Saturday as Uckfield lost again giving us a 6 point cushion in the league and due to fixture congestion we had the Sussex County Shield Final which was to be the Uckfield game away in April. Brighton did not play many league games as the RFU Cup which was now at National 1/4 final stage included a trip to Gloucestershire and to Brockworth. They had a reputation of a hard big uncompromising pack and they had knocked Tewkesbury out who were finalists the year before in the competition. In promoting the hard pack Brockworth gave us our team speech and a quiet bus journey to Gloucestershire reflected our mood. The team had just hit its straps and had started playing some good rugby and the pack was becoming more dominant the longer the season went on. The first scrum started as a punch up as their tight head gouged Sam Hutton's eyes and he not only was given 'appropriate reception by the other seven forwards, he was sin binned for his troubles. The first 20 minutes was close as the home side had stuck us on a postage stamp of a pitch. We were fitter, faster, and stronger and the score reflected a handsome 42-8 win.

Onwards to the semi-final which we learnt was to be Hullensians who knocked out the semi pro club Leeds Metropolitan at Waterhall on the 21st March 2009.

March 2009 included with wins over Rye (87-3), Lewes (117-0), and Hove 28-10. This left Brighton in the position of one more league win to secure promotion. After the Lewes game we played Hullensians for a place at Twickenham. The 'T' word was not to be used and a £10 fine was in place for any discussion. The Hull lads turned up and were expected to be big with a rugby league background. They did not disappoint and it was a brutal game in which it was keenly contested. The Hull fly-half started impressively kicking us back in to our own 22 with pin point accuracy regularly. The game was to be turned on two outstanding pieces of individual skill by Nik Hannay in the 2nd half. He pounced on an error at the base of the Hull scrum then offloaded one handed in the tackle to send our winger over in the corner. The second half we dominated and they did not cross the halfway line. We won 21-3 and Waterhall with a crowd of about 1500 people was one big party. Credit to the Hullensians team as they stayed on in the clubhouse until after 8pm and were gracious in defeat.

Respect

Back to league duty and we had Crawley at home who we beat 75-5 in which we secured the league. It was a bit of pressure off as we faced our rivals Uckfield in the league and cup double header. We seemed a little hung over and we won the game and the cup 15-12 in the last five minutes with a length of the field try set up by an audacious dummy in our own 22 by Neil McGovern.

The league campaign went on for two more weeks with wins over Holbrook away and Haywards Heath. This proved vital in keeping in match mode for the National Cup Final at Twickenham on the 9th May 2009. We were playing the Cornish side Liskeard Looe. The build up was incredible and if ever playing club rugby was good this was like being a professional. The realisation hit when we got our stash or Twickenham kit and had a captain's run before going up to stay overnight in Heathrow hotel. I roomed with Tudor Ellis and it was a pleasure to get a good nights sleep as with us both having young kids sleep was on short supply. We undertook a tour of the stadium on Friday so to get a feel for the place and had a walk through the museum.

The morning arrived and it was bitter disappointment to Stavrous who was injured in the captain's run and could not play. His honesty was a big part of why our team culture was so successful. A bitter blow personally but handled like a true hero. Paul Giunti was called up from Brighton having celebrated his Birthday the day before. Plenty of coffee and breakfast.

Always difficult the morning before big games, it's the not knowing what to eat or how much but our time came to leave. It was unbelievable the bus journey driving in to the stadium. Family, friends, and people you knew were all cheering and shouting as we arrived. We got changed and had the team photo outside the stadium and warmed up on the school field. The changing rooms were enormous and there was a nervous tension. The day just whizzes by and in hindsight a photographer in the inner sanctum of the changing rooms would have been good. A big point that came across was that it was not a day out and that we were here to win a rugby match. Looking at the opposition in the tunnel before walking out you could tell the game was going to be competitive.

Adam Salvage and Mark Gibb

It is with great pride and excitement to walk out at your National stadium to play rugby and believe me it does not disappoint, the supporters all draped in the team colours screaming and shouting certainly put hairs on end. After the pre match handshakes the game got underway. It was a bruising affair and Liskeard Looe were a typical Cornish side and very forwards orientated. They had a good driving maul and scrum which was difficult to get parity. The problem with playing in such a venue is you found yourself staring at the stadium and then returning to the game. We were a little star struck the first half and the score was a tight 8-7 to Liskeard with our score from a piece of individual brilliance by Nick Bhouy.

The second half turned with the introduction of Tom Aitken at Fly Half and our running game opened up, two tries from Neil McGovern, one from Ash Hallett and penalties and conversions from Alex Finch secured a 32-20 win. The final whistle went and I immediately turned to Tudor Ellis and stood hugging him, the relief was immense and the night was even more historic with a reception at the Smugglers Pub in central Brighton.

2009-2010

After the rigours of the previous season everyone was keen to get back to training and start again in London South East 3. The league had been restructured and the format was home and away with 12 teams in the league. Some of the younger players such as Jess Thompsett and James Kinsella had come through the youth teams and were now pushing for 1st XV positions. We lost players such as John Fordham and Richard Burns and Tom Aitken, and Alex Finch was to return from Australia. The big loss was Tudor Ellis who was apparently numb from a disk in his back squashing his spinal cord and this left the tight prop position vacant. Our first game was away against our old foes Medway who were hyping the game up as revenge for their cup defeat. A tight game with one try and a win 13-9. Second up was Horsham and a second win 25-17, this again was a laboured performance and a Twickenham hangover was evident.

Our next 3 games were against Charlton Park, East Grinstead, and Heathfield. This resulted in 3 loses as injuries and bedding in of new players such as Ed Court resulted in the team needing a good long hard look at itself. We had Park House away and the fixture apparently had been going on since the 1900's. It was never an easy place to go and a convincing 38-22 win with Harry Leonard playing his first senior game. Harry would later represent Edinburgh in the European Cup.

We had a fixture cancelled at Hastings in November due to the pitch being unplayable which was unfortunate as we had a new recruit in Matt Morgan who was the army No 8 and played for Havant previously. His debut was against Old Gravesendians in which a much better performance resulted in a 69-15 win. Matt was fantastic and played a star performance. We continued to win and beat Folkestone away, Whitstable at home. In the background we had three walk overs for the National Cup and were at home vs. Ellingham and Ringwood where we won 53-12 in an easy game. Our next opponents were Old Alleynians away.

The weather again meant very little was played over December and our rearranged trip back to Hastings was on January 2nd 2010. We won 33-10 after having a torrid first half going in 10-3 down. This was a turning point as we had bigger games to come

The crux to the season was upon us as we had Charlton Park, East Grinstead , and Heathfield all to play in the reverse fixtures. The East Grinstead game was first played on the astro turf at Brighton due to RFU ruling that if an alternative to the home side pitch was available it had to be played. We were 9-3 down when the referee made an error under the new rules and the scrums went uncompetitive. We then won 33-9 in which we ran riot against a very good East Grinstead side. At this point we picked up a tight head prop called Richard Keen who had played many levels higher. Next was Heathfield and this was a tight affair but two tries by Mark Gibb ensured a 15-5 win. Our best win to date was against Crowborough who were 18-0 up with 20 minutes to play. We won the game 22-18 and this was with many players out injured. Matt Bellinie having his say with the winning try.

The Old Alleynians cup fixture was upon us and on a postage stamp of a pitch we won comfortably. With further wins against Park House and Hastings we had the crunch game against Charlton Park in the league, and the first Basildon away in the cup.

The Basildon game was tight and two James Trevis tries won the game as we lost Alex Finch to a broken cheek bone. The significance for me was that I took over kicking duties. Charlton Park came to Waterhall and the team at full strength (the first time in the season), including our new prop Richard Keene dispatched a very good side 32-10.

The league had become a 3 way tussle between East Grinstead, Heathfield and ourselves. Charlton Park in the defeat to us had been eliminated and it was clear that points difference would probably be vital. Further wins against Old Gravesendians (83-0), Folkestone (59-10), and Whitstable (37-100 put us into April with 2 games left. The key game in the pursuit of promotion was that Heathfield and East Grinstead had to play each other in the scheduled last game of the season. Whoever lost was likely to be in 3rd place.

We played Gosport and Fareham in the national 1/4 final in the cup at Waterhall. It was a big game and we played well and restricted them to a single score. It was one of the good days at Waterhall in which big crowd and good performance allowed everyone to enjoy the day. Ed Court and Nick Cherry scored the important tries and I kicked 4 out of 5 from the tee. We were drawn against Cirencester in the semi-final, away at the end of April

Our remaining league games against Medway could have been 80 points but all the tries were scored in the corners and yours truly managed only 11 points from the boot but we still won 61-5. Our last game was away to Horsham and Harry Leonard and Ollie Richards returned to strengthen the side more. It was the end of April and a boiling hot day, we had to win first and points second. With that in mind we played a brilliant fast running game which gave us 55-3 win. We then had to wait until the following week to see if Heathfield would beat Folkestone as they lost the vital game against East Grinstead. However due to our vastly superior points difference Heathfield needed to win by 116 clear points. They did not achieve this and we were promoted

'Twickenham Final 2010'
Mark Gibb, Tudor Ellis and Mark Jenkins

The two weeks up to the Cirencester Cup match went quickly and hype was starting to build. The Cirencester coach had fuelled this by saying his side would beat a soft south east side and that his players unbeaten at home would with a large home crowd dispatch Brighton and their soft posh boys back where they came from. An interesting point of view and as we took the field in front of 1500 home supporters and a single bus of Brighton supporters it was in to the fire pit. We won the game 13-12 with what is probably the club's best away win in its history. It was lung bursting but in the back of our mind we won the game when their entire front five were substituted at 60 minutes. A moral victory for those in the know. The home side were gutted and whether we were the better team or not it was a win at all costs and a second consecutive Twickenham Final.

Unlike the year before I looked across in the tunnel and knew we would win the game. We were fitter, leaner and more focused. Dunlop Coventry had turned up for the day out and not to win the match. After a tight first half in which we led 5-3 through an Ed Court try, we turned the screw and won 32-5 in which we flattened their pack. A satisfying win and probably one of the best Brighton packs put together with its strength and power.

2010 onwards

The season following was somewhat a finding our feet in the league above. The teams much more settled and London 2 south east a much more difficult proposition. An early exit away to Trojans in the cup and difficult games away in the league combined with injuries and a young side made the season very difficult. A mid table finish meant that as a season for learning in experience plus the requirement to recruit was established.

The following season new players came in such as Steve Cruddas and Richard Neil who had all played at higher levels helped bolster the squad and an air of expectancy began to grow. It took a season to bed in and also look at getting promotion. Several sides in the league had gone semi pro and Brighton were not at that level.

The 2012-13 Season was a good year in which the league was won impressively at Lewes with a 22-36 win. It was a mighty fine day to win the league at your neighbours. The second team also pushed very hard and finished 3rd in Sussex 1 as places for the Intermediate Cup final at Twickenham became very competitive. The cup final resulted in a win at Twickenham against Bridlington. The game highlighted by a 70m try by Alex Finch. Brighton now stand with Hartpury College as the only team who have won all 3 national cups for Junior rugby. A proud achievement.

2016 Annual Ball, Mark Jenkins and Mark Gibb

'Old Farts' in Blazers, and Alex

ROLL OF HONOUR

It occurred to me during my research into this book, that Brighton Football Club did not have a memorial to Club members that gave the ultimate sacrifice during the two World Wars.

This needed rectifying, so without further delay a email was sent out to all members asking for a subscription towards the "Roll of Honour" memorial plaque. Within 24 hours all monies for the project was raised.

I am not usually in a position to embarrass my friends, however, Mark Jenkins donated a substantial sum to this project for which I am very grateful.

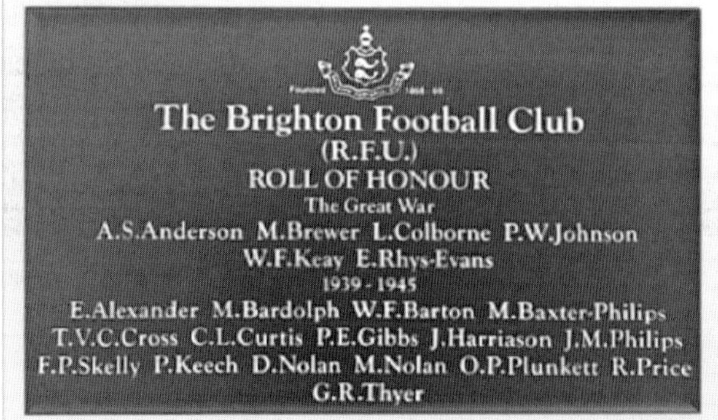

The Mayor of Brighton & Hove, Brian Fitch and his wife Norah were invited to unveil the plaque at a League luncheon, followed by a match against our local rivals, Hove, which we conveniently won.

The list of names on the 'Roll of Honour' was taken from our Handbook, and it wasn't until I actually came across the 1949 A.G.M. minutes, and after the memorial was made, that 'Harriason' is indeed 'Harrison'. Hopefully, one day my mistake will be rectified.

Steve Russell, Jo Russell, Mayor Brian Fitch, Norah Fitch, John Honeysett

And, Steve Morris (Chairman)

In attendance at the 'Roll of Honour' unveiling
From L to R ; Jeremy Smith (Capt 1990), David Lowrie (Vice President)
Alan McCarthy (President 1995-97), Bob Avery (Captain 1985-86 & 1988-90),
Dick Thoms (Captain 1986-87), Steve Russell (President 2004 to present),
John Honeysett (Vice President & Hon. Sec.)

In recent years, I, along with either the President or Chairman, have laid a wreath at the memorial service at the Steine, in honour of the members of Brighton Football Club (RFU) who paid the ultimate sacrifice

Lloyd Jenkins, Nick Cherry, Alex Finch, Neil McGovern, James Travis, Steve Morris

My collection of fixture Cards and Handbooks, 1899 - 2013, other than the War years, I am missing four...

I have seen many a programme during my research. The programmes produced in the 1930's were very special. But I must say the programmes produced in recent years by Sharon Finch are fantastic.
And long may they continue.

Marcus Smith and Jon Searle, England v Scotland U18.
Both Marcus and Jon have been through the Brighton Youth set up, and Marcus is verging on a senior England cap.
Jeremy Smith (Dad) was the Club captain in 1990.
And I predict, he will not be the last of the Smiths to wear the Red Rose..!

Sam Morley, 16th April, Brighton F.C v Dover RFU

Sam is another product of the Brighton F.C. youth system and the above game is the only 1st XV game Sam has played in (One day maybe!). Paul Morley (Dad) was another 1st XV captain in 1991-93.

Sam, who joined Exeter Academy from Exeter University, has now signed on professional terms with Exeter and has impressed for the Club this season both in the Anglo-Welsh Cup and "A" League competitions. In May 2018 Sam was called up for the England U20's.

IT'S A BITTER - SWEET WELCOME TO 2018 AS WE SAY GOODBYE TO OUR HEAD COACH OF A DECADE, NEIL McGOVERN.

During his time with the Club, Neil has led a fantastic passage in our history and has left a legacy to be proud of. He was responsible for leading the team in quick succession from Sussex One right through to London 1 South. In addition, during his watch, Brighton made three visits to Twickenham winning on each occasion bringing in the Junior Vase [2008/9], the Senior Vase [2009/10] and the Intermediate Cup [2012/3].

Brighton Rugby will always be grateful to Neil for his efforts and we wish him every success in his next chapter.

The sweet part is that we welcome Frank Taggart back to the fold. Frank was a Brighton boy growing up at the club and has been away earning international honours with Ireland, a professional contract at Ulster and more recently with Rosslyn Park in National 1. Although young he already has a wealth of experience and the enthusiasm to take Brighton on to the next phase of our development.

We are looking forward to an exciting home fixture against Cobham tomorrow, so come and support the teams!

Steve Morris
Chairman

Neil McGovern

"OLD FARTS" LUNCHEON, APRIL 14TH 2018

Ann Holt collecting 'Old Fart Lunch Fees' ;
David "Has she gone yet" Laing, Derek "I'm not looking" Pickering and Peter "I'm sure I had my wallet" Harbidge.

Mike Buckingham and Alex Pincus

Ian Barnard, and Barry Hughes holding court, (Welsh.!)

The 'Gentlemen' of Brighton Football Club (RFU)

Dave Lowrie, Frank Samson, Alex Pincus

Ray Dunk, David Athill
Ann Holt, Jackie Harbidge, Derek Pickering and Deedee Pickering

Eleanor Bradfield, Elizabeth Dunk, Nikola Browne, Claire Jarmain

Over the years I've met many Bar Staff and once and a while you get a group like these girls who just gel, work well together, laugh and smile all the time. An absolute pleasure.

Chapter XV1I

THE MODERN ERA

In this our 150th season we are privileged to have Frank Taggart as our Head Coach. Frank's foray into Brighton Football Club did not just start in 2017-18 as he was a protégé of our mini and youth. In fact, Frank even at his young age, has had a busy life in the world of rugby. I will let Frank explained in his own words ;

"It's always funny when I tell people I preferred playing football when I was younger, coming from a background that was passionate about football, I had no intention of picking up a rugby ball whatsoever! However, that soon changed in 2006 after crossing paths with the legend, Chris Jones AKA "Jonesy" and Wesley Horscroft, on my first day at Cardinal Newman School. Despite trying to avoid every possible route where I might happen to bump into "Jonesy" in

the corridors, he always managed to appear and shout in his thick Welsh accent, "Tagzy, get your arse in gear, your boots tied and out on to that rugby pitch!"

After a few weeks of refusing to play rugby for the school, I finally gave in – and thank God I did! It's fair to say that from the very first session out on the back fields of Newman, I had found another sport that I was strongly passionate about. Due to my natural build and athleticism as a youngster – I picked the game up pretty fast. However, Mr Horscroft, who I can proudly call a close friend of mine, had a massive part to play in my development as a young rugby player.

It was soon after my first season of school rugby, that I was introduced to Brighton Football Club (RFU) by my older brother, Jack, who was without a doubt the most natural all-round athlete I knew at the time. When I was younger, I would go to watch my brother play on the first team pitch at Waterhall. He was part of an extremely strong age group at Brighton F.C., playing alongside the likes of Harry Leonard, Craig Holland and other talented players. I knew from watching him that I wanted to be part of the Brighton Blues family. A week or so later, I was introduced to Neil Thomas & Karl Newell who took my age group at the time; and then that was it, the start of my Brighton Rugby career began! On the same week I turned up for my first session for the u13's, the majority of players were from either Dorothy Stringer or Brighton College, who happened to be Newman's two rivals at the time - which needless to say made me pretty nervous! But I can honestly say, despite being the only one from Newman and turning up in full Newman kit, the boys were all very welcoming and made me feel part of the team straight away.

Up until 2009 I was playing Rugby on a Saturday and Football on a Sunday pretty much every weekend, but as my rugby became intensified, I had to sacrifice one or the other. However, as my love for rugby grew stronger and the bonds I had made with other players increased, there was no way I could leave my Brighton Blues family! Throughout the years 2007-2013, I was fortunate enough to be involved in the Sussex Rugby & Harlequins EPDG set ups.

Despite the majority of my peers at school playing for Hove, I remained a "Blue" right the way through to Colts level. In 2011, I was offered a sports scholarship to Whitgift School in South Croydon. It was an offer I couldn't refuse and an opportunity I had to take, however, this meant sacrificing my availability for Brighton F.C. The season of 2011-12 is one that made a significant difference to the direction I was going in my rugby career - as it was the start of my journey in Irish Rugby.

My Irish heritage comes from my mother's side, which enabled me to go down the Irish route. As much as I enjoyed my experience at Harlequins from SOR to EPDG level, I knew I wanted to get out of the English system; it was something that was personally, the right choice for me as a player. In the seasons 2011-12 & 12-13 I joined the Irish Exiles set-up which put me on the radar of the IRFU, at the age of 17 I was selected to play for Ireland u18's and then u19s the season after, which then led to a contractual negotiation with the IRFU and Ulster ahead of the 2013-14 season.

The 2013-14 season was without doubt one of the most intense seasons I've had to date, but one that will remain my favourite. I arrived into Belfast the summer of 2013 and was pretty much straight into training camp with Ulster U20s in preparation for the U20s inter-provincial campaign. After a successful training camp, I was privileged to captain the side throughout the campaign and shortly after the tournament, saw the offering of a 3 year contract at Ulster, as well as being named in the Ireland U20s training squad for the U20s Six Nations tournament.

After missing out on the first game due to injury from an Ulster A game in the British & Irish Cup, I was involved in the remaining 4 games – this campaign saw a mixture of results for us. However, after a couple of days off to recover, it was back into full-time training with Ulster as the Junior World Cup Championship (JWC) was just around the corner and I knew I had to go through the selection process again – which was not going to be easy with the 2014 JWC being held in Auckland, New Zealand.

When I got the email to say I had been selected to represent Ireland U20s in the JWC, I was over the moon. I was one of two Ulstermen to be selected in the 28-man squad heading to Auckland. It was a proud moment for my family and me, I had messages from everyone, friends and family and old team mates from my previous clubs, particularly Brighton RFC. It had made me more determined to do well as I have always been and always will be, a representative of Brighton RFC and so there was no time to celebrate as the hard work and physical preparation had already begun. It was a tough training camp that involved 2-3 training sessions a day, but thanks to Ulster's support team, I was more than ready. The last session before heading off to Dublin for Ireland camp came round pretty fast, it was without a doubt the toughest one of them all, unfortunately my fellow Ulster teammate, David Busby, suffered a serious injury during the session – I was gutted for him because we had both worked so hard, 5:30am wake-ups for gym sessions, running in the torrential rain and gale force winds and more – which sounds dramatic, but remember we are talking about Northern Ireland here!

Overall – the experience at the JWC is one I will be forever grateful for; we placed 4th which was the highest Ireland had placed in the tournament before, I made some great memories in Auckland both on and off the pitch. I got to share the pitch with some of the World's most talented young rugby players at the time - even to this day some have become superstars in the world of rugby! But one thing that without a doubt has to be one of my greatest rugby moments is facing the Haka against New Zealand U20s aka The Baby Blacks in Eden Park, the home of New Zealand Rugby – but after 5 International games in 18 days, I was ready to get back to Brighton to enjoy some time off with friends and family.

After some strong performances in the season of 2014-15, with both Ulster A and Belfast Harlequins, I still wasn't having much luck with Ulster 1st XV and it didn't look like I was going to get my debut anytime soon – which was extremely frustrating at the time, especially after the positive feedback I had from the IRFU Senior Coaching team – Joe Schmidt & Les Kiss. However, in May 2015, I was named in the 27-man Emerging Ireland Squad for the 2015 World Rugby Tbilisi Cup in Georgia, which if I'm honest, was a real shock to me considering I hadn't even had my 1st cap for the first team at Ulster yet! But at the age of 20, it was an opportunity I was grateful for and an experience I was going to make the most of. We managed to win 3 games out of 3 and won the overall tournament. Being involved in 2 of them was a great experience, to be both training and playing with some of the most senior players within Irish Rugby. I think it's fair to say us younger guys in the squad learnt a lot from the senior players – both on and off the pitch!

Coming into the final year of my initial 3 year contract, it would seem that my development in the first 2 years had put me in a strong position to earn my first senior cap for Ulster.

However – this was not the case. To this day, it was most definitely the most challenging season I've had in my rugby career. I had suffered a couple of injuries early on in the season which put me back down the pecking order. Eventually, I got myself back on track and had a couple of strong performances for Belfast Harlequins and Ulster A. But there was still no sign of opportunity for the 1st team. It became very frustrating as I was training hard and playing well week in, week out for my club. A lot of people won't realise the extent of the psychological battles you face as a professional athlete, the constant doubts, the set-backs, weekly selections – it was tough, especially at the age of 21. In the early days of December 2015, I suffered an injury to my right foot during training. Thankfully, I had some time off back in Brighton over Christmas for rest and recovery, but unbeknown to me, the injury was proving more serious than I had first anticipated. Feeling confident and ready to prove that I deserved my shot, I had my first running session back after Christmas, but my right foot had reacted badly, so Ulster decided to send me for an MRI Scan – the results came back a couple days later and turns out I had fractured my 5th metatarsal which put me out for a minimum of 4-6. Which was the last thing I wanted to hear considering it was coming close to decision time for Ulster regarding my contract. Still, I was so determined to get my head down and come back fitter and stronger than before – which I did, after 2-3 sessions a day, 5-6 days a week for a total of 8-9 weeks.

Despite being back on the pitch a much more determined player, Ulster had already made the decision to release me from my contract at the end of the season which affected me massively. After my first two years being so successful with the IRFU, it wasn't something I was expecting to hear, even after some time out from injury – but the decision was final and I had to think to myself, what next?

I didn't realise how much the last 6-8 months at Ulster had affected me until I met with my agent, Ryan Constable. He had a couple of offers for me, however, nothing that was attractive enough to jump on. So I decided to take some time out from rugby and focus on something that no-one could take away from me, my Sports Coaching degree. I had enrolled at the University of Ulster back in 2013 when I first arrived in Belfast, I passed my first 2 years by the skin of my teeth but had fallen behind in my third year, so I decided to slow-track my final year over a course of two years and made sure I gave it the attention it needed.

*In 2016, I left Belfast and moved back to Brighton. I had a lot of frustration towards Ulster and what had happened – I was in a constant psychological battle with myself and asking questions – the "what ifs" and the "whys"? But thankfully, I had my close friends and family nearby. I was so focussed on finishing my degree that 8 months came around and I hadn't picked up a rugby ball. I went to watch a few games at Brighton Rugby Club, as I always loved going back there and watching the talent the club consistently produces. It was always nice to go back and relive some pleasant memories from my youth, picturing Neil, Dom, and Karl shouting at a bunch of 13 year olds "Run faster you lazy b*stard" up the steep hill down by the bottom pitch is one that I'll always remember!*

In the summer of 2016, I received my Bachelor of Science with Honours in Sports Coaching, and in the same week, started up my own Personal Training & Coaching Business. Because I've always had a passion for fitness, coaching and helping others achieve their goals, it was nice to be able to transform this into a profession. By this time, I was ready to get back onto the rugby pitch, a good friend of mine and ex-Brightonian, Harry Leonard, got in touch with me in the latter part of the 2016-17 season about playing for Rosslyn Park who are in the National League Division One; and before you know it, I'm back on the pitch.

I extended my stay at Rosslyn Park for the season 2017-18, however, just before the Christmas break, Neil McGovern got in touch with me about a player & coach job opportunity that had come up at Brighton F.C. Neil McGovern is someone that I will always have respect for, he plays a huge role in the history of Brighton Football Club (RFU), he was responsible for leading the team in their success from Sussex One right through to London 1 South – whilst also making three visits to Twickenham and winning on all three occasions.

Neil explained the role I would play within the squad, which after a few days of weighing up my options; I become more and more attracted to the opportunity at Brighton F.C. so I took on the role as Player & Coach mid December 2017. Soon after, I stepped in as Head Coach after Neil's departure in the latter part of the season 2017-18.

I've always wanted to come back and be part of the Brighton Blues set-up, it was just a matter of when; it is a club that produces some extremely talented players, the youth and mini's section is one of the biggest in the County and thanks to the volunteers, it has become an enjoyable environment for young rugby players to come and learn and developing in the sport.

I have always seen potential in Brighton Rugby as a club, so it's a privilege to be in the position I am today as Head Coach for the Seniors; I will pass on the knowledge and experience I have gained from previous years to the players coming through Brighton's system, I believe we have the talent within the club to push for promotion and take us to the next level – and what better year to try and achieve this goal than our 150th Anniversary.

I would like to personally thank the continuous support I have received from Brighton Football Club (RFU) throughout my rugby career, from the coaches and players I have been involved with, to the support staff that helps out on a weekly basis. But more importantly, thank you to everyone that is part of the Brighton Blues Family that makes the club what it is today'.

Brighton Football Club (RFU) now have a fantastic opportunity, with the likes of Tudor Ellis as Director of Rugby, Frank Taggart, head coach and Joel Forward as Captain. Joel has been captain since 2015. His story ;

From the beginning of my sporting career I have always felt a sports club to be far more than a pitch and changing room. Whether you want friendship, advice, employment or a reasonably priced pint, the English rugby club has all bases covered. Brighton FC (RFU) is no exception to this. It is my adopted club, but I am extremely proud to put on the blue shirt and I am certain I will spend my later years stood on the balcony, talking about the good old days!

In 2013, after 10 years along the A26 with my home club Uckfield RFC, I had sat out a season with a heart condition that required surgery and I realised I needed a new challenge to get me back on the mend so got in touch with Neil McGovern. I had a great deal of respect for Neil prior to joining the club having played against Brighton (and scoring!) and following the incredible cup runs, so was keen to pick his brains and learn his short cuts!

My first season with the club was a mixed one on the pitch, with several niggly injuries and a few average performances. But when things were tough I always felt part of the club thanks to the likes of Phil Salvage, Ian Dean and Jason Tams who would always have their own "unique" ways to inspire me and to keep pushing. Towards the end of that season I had found my feet and was playing more regular rugby in the 1st XV. I had caught the bug once again and wanted to work hard to keep my place and push the team on. The following season I went on to start every game and the club finished in a steady 6th position, a particular highlight being a 47-7 away win at Hove.

One of my proudest personal moments arrived in the form of a phone call from Neil early in November of the 2015/16 season. I had led the boys out against Charlton Park the week before, when captain Will Smith, was forced to step aside after some pretty serious concussions. He had philosophically and literally, left a giant pair of boots which I had been asked to fill. Will was one of the most professional players I had ever played alongside and it was a daunting task to follow in his footsteps. Nevertheless I was completely honoured to have been made captain of the historic Brighton Football Club.

Seasons have been a mixed bag since I became captain, while we had the "what ifs" of the 2015/16 season we failed to find any form until February in the proceeding campaign, before putting an exciting giant killing run of results together to perform the miracle of surviving relegation from 12 points under. While results have been mixed we have always been determined to have fun. Rugby is our hobby and while success is more easily measured by results, I have always felt that if we are enjoying ourselves as a squad then we are successful, whatever the league table says.I have loved captaining this rugby club over the past few years, its been a tough task at times and I have learnt how important it is to share our responsibilities amongst the clubs best blokes. I'm incredibly fortunate to have fantastic support from a generation of true clubmen both in the squad and within the clubhouse. The dedication and passion of guys like

Maxx Morris, James Trevis, Ben Herbe, Sam Callaghan, Ross James, Adam Salvage, Andrew Rowlandson and Rob Fogerty will carry the club into a bright future. The hard work of Alex Finch, Tom Taylor, Phil Salvage, Ian Dean and all of the off field staff has been instrumental in ensuring the lads are able to focus on their rugby.

Looking ahead, we now move into a new era under on and off the pitch. Neil McGovern's departure earlier in the year has paved the way for Frank Taggart to take the reins. Frank has had an immediate impact on the squad bringing a new style of aggressive attacking rugby, which has allowed our talented squad to express themselves more on the pitch. From the preview of preseason training the next 9 months looks hugely exciting.

Two of the clubs best men, Phil Salvage and Ian Dean have decided to take a well-earned sabbatical from their roles this season. It is important that their names are etched in the clubs modern history as their tireless work over the past 10 years has helped elevate the club to new levels. Most people will not have seen their incredible dedication and hard work, but their commitment to Brighton FC will always be remembered by anyone who has worn the blue shirt.

At Brighton Rugby Club, whatever a person's background, situation or natural ability, there will always be a place for them and their family. Whether a player or not, this is a club for all, where rugby is a hobby not a job, where feeling part of a team is at our core. It is a place where whatever is going on in your life you can find happiness and friendship for at least a few hours each week, it's a place full of great people who are always willing to lend a hand or an ear, a hub for the community and a true reflection of the values of rugby. If we can say this about this club in 25 or 50 years' time then we are still doing it right.

I owe a great deal to rugby and particularly to Brighton Rugby Club and I am excited to see where the next 50 years take us both.

Joel Forward.

My newest acquisition was recently discovered at a local auction house. Originally from Brighton Railway Station it was incorporated into the structural roof supports. I'm sure a good clean, sand, prime and painted with the club colours would bring it back to life.

I can already envisage a place for it in the Club.

THE END OF THE BEGINNING

It has been a manic undertaking to produce this written account of the Rugby Club history in time for our 150th anniversary celebration.

After numerous years of collecting, collating and unpicking 1000s of pieces of information on the history of Brighton Football Club (RFU) I find myself with mixed emotions as I get to the last pages. On one hand I will be glad that the days of sifting thought old musty newspapers, micro fiche, rolls or microfilm are over despite the thrill and emotion of finding a gem, such as the early A.G.M minutes in a 1870's Brighton Newspaper, but on the other a little sad that the journey has come to an end.

But perhaps it is not the end! As the British Newspaper Library continues to grow its digital database I am certain that more facts and figures will come to light, some of which may correct any errors I may have made, and some which may enhance this journey of history further.

My hope for this book is that it becomes a stepping stone to a more comprehensive account of the history of Brighton Football Club (RFU). I am of the belief that Brighton F.C was formed pre 1865 and the 'Brighton Club' has been overlooked even by the astute Brighton historians. Why did the 'Brighton School Board' use 'Rugby Football Rules' for the 'Brighton Schools'? This is just one of many unanswered questions that only time may uncover.

So as we head into our 150th season I would like to say how I have been blown away by the passion of current players which undoubtedly will take the our rugby club onwards and upwards and the future is looking rosy.

I hope you enjoy the book and I am more than happy to answer any questions, if I can, so feel free to get in touch.

honeysettdowley@ntlworld.com

Brighton Football Club Presidents

1868 - 1871, C. G. Boxhall
1871 - 1872, W. Anderson, Esq
1872 - 1882. J.E. Raven, Esq
1882 - 1893, Colonel R. W. Tamplin, VD
1893 - 1894, Captain F. C. Parsons
1894 - 1895, Brigadier-General Richards
1895 - 1898, E. A. Smithers
1898 - 1903, A. C. Borlase
1903 - 1910, Major L. Holmes
1910 - 1925, A. A. Coster
1925 - 1928, G. S. Godfree
1928 - 1929, W. Graham-Hooper
1929 -1930, Sir Harry J. Preston
1930 - 1932, C. Griffin
1932 - 1946, W. F. Moir
1946 - 1948, P. F. Friend-James OBE
1948 - 1950, W. A. Gibbs
1950 - 1954, R. R. Turner
1954 - 1956, H. D. S. Stiles JP
1956 - 1957, E. Hamilton Pope
1957 - 1961, R. C. Malby
1961 - 1965, R. H. Braybon MBE. JP.
1965 - 1968, D. E. Benjamin
1968 - 1981, W. R. B. Holt JP
1981 - 1983, D. J. Nolan
1983 - 1995, P. Ward-Lee
1995 - 1997, A. McCarthy
1997 - 2001, A. Pincus
2001 - 2004, M. Holt
2004 - S. Russell

Vice Presidents

P.H. Albrecht
G. Appleton
Mrs P. Appleton
G. Ashby
D. Atkins
R. Avery
R.E. Bashford
A. Biggs
A.J. Bradley
D.A. Browne
K. Brown
M. Buckingham
G. Bunker
G.C. Burt
John Burt
Justin Burt
A. Chapman
A. Coe
E. D'arcy
A. Davall
C. Day
R.F. Dunk
S. Dunnill
M. Ede
T. Ellis
J. Farr
S. Finch
D . Fowler
A. Fox (Gliddon)
M. Gibb
P. Harbidge
N. Hart
G. Henderson
G. Hindle

J. Hurst
J. Honeysett
Dr R. James
M. Jenkins
L. Jenkins
M. Kinsella
A. Knight
J. Laidlaw
D. Laing
P. Leonard
A. McKechnie
D.T. Malby
J. Mitchell
S. Mogridge
M. Morley
P. Morley
S. Morris
G. Nicholas
P. Noble
J.I. O'Mahony
J. Orrell
J. Philips
D. Pickering
A. Pinnock
M. Pocock
Mrs D. Poupard
J. Prytherch
J. Randle
D. Rees
J. Reeve
A. Rice
S. Russell
C. Salter
P. Salvage
F. Sansom
P. Small
H. Smith
D. Smith

D.T. Smith
P. Smith
W. Smith
B. Sutherland
Ms M. Stepney
R. Tasker
D. Taylor
N. Thomas
R. Thoms
G. Thompson
R. Thompson
Ms G. Thompson
J. Tolhurst
S. Trotter
D. Trower
Ms C. Vivian
Mrs S. Ward-Lee
P.J. Wheeler
M. Whitlock
G. Wicks
C. Wilson
N.F.K. Wilson
E. Womersley

Honorary Life Members

Mrs A Holt JP
R J McLowrie
D H A Malby
J Wallace
P Ward-Lee
J Woodley
R Greenwood
D Benjamin
A McCarthy
A Pincus
M Holt

Brighton Football Club Captains

1868-69, C.G. Boxhall,
1869 - 1870, W Stuckey
1870-1871, M.G.C. Dill
1871-1872 W.R. Lee
1872- 1873, H. K. Cook
1873 - 1875, J. E. Raven
1882 - 1885, C. Somers-Clark
1885 - 1886, J.S. S. Hamilton
1886 - 1889, E. A. Smithers
1889 - 1891, W. P. Gormall
1891 - 1893, M. F. Voules
1893 -1894, M. H. Beves / R D Budworth
1894 -1897, M. H. Beves
1897 - 1898, L. F. Duckworth
1898 - 1900, P. G. A. Broadbent
1900 - 1901, G. S. Godfree
1901 -1903, A. S. Anderson
1903 - 1904, H. T. Oliver / A S Anderson
1904 - 1906, T. O. Ruthen
1906 - 1907, J. J . Gardner
1907 - 1908, L. A. Godfree
1908 - 1909, W. J. Wormald
1909 - 1910, H. S. Moore
1910 - 1912, F. Sage
1912 - 1913, P. W. Johnson
World War 1
1919 - 1920, C. Fawsett
1920 - 1921, W. A. Gibb
1921- 1925, G. W. H. Bentley
1925 - 1926, C. A. Osborne
1926 - 1929, J. G. S. Lee
1929 -1930, A. C. N. Williams
1930 - 1932, R. R. Turner
1932 - 1933, J. F. Hampton
1933 - 1934, K. H. Tilbury

1934 -1935, A. G. G. Mitchell
1935 - 1936, F. Hyam
1936 - 1938, C. A. Styer
1938 - 1939, W. W. Sayers
World War 2
1945 - 1946, K. Oldham
1946 - 1948, R. H. Braybon
1948 -1949, J. A. Harrison
1949 - 1950, F. Thomas
1950 - 1952, R. C. Malby
1952 - 1953, R. O. Pratt
1953 - 1954, C. McDonald
1954 - 1957, J .G. Hale
1957 - 1958, D. T. Smith
1958 - 1959, J. G. Hale
1959 - 1960, G. Ashby
1960 - 1961, D. T. Smith
1961 - 1962, R. Hewson
1962 - 1965, D. J. Pickering
1965 - 1967, R. Bashford
1967 - 1970, P. Harbidge
1970 - 1971, I . Barnard
1971 - 1975, M. Brownhill
1975 - 1976, G. Nicholas
1976 - 1977, G. Hindle
1977 - 1978, I . Robinson
1978 - 1979, K. Hopkins
1979 - 1980, P. Harbidge
1980 - 1982, G. Hindle
1982 - 1983, D. Taylor / C Day
1983 - 1985, C. Day
1985 - 1986, R. Avery
1986 - 1987, R. Thoms
1987 - 1988, N. Thomas
1988 - 1989, M. Avery / R. Avery
1989 - 1990, R. Avery
1990 -1991, J. Smith / P. Morley
1991-1993, P. Morley

1993-1994, K. Considine
1994-1996, M. Sutton
1996-1997, G. Russell
1997-1998, C. Cleary
1998-1999, M. Gibb
1999-2000, M.Gibb / C. Burke
2000-2001, G. Henderson
2001-2003, M.P. Jenkins
2003-2004, A.J. Pinnock / M. Gibb
2004-2006, D.W. Groombridge / P.J. Pride
2006-2011, L.D. Jenkins
2012-2014 , W. Smith
2015-   J. Forward

Honours Caps

1885 - 86 P S Beve, J S S Hamilton
1886 - 87 M H Beves, W C Lippscombe
1887 - 88 A W Hogg, W B Stamp
1888 - 89 E A Smithers, F J Turnbull, C H Waugh
1889 - 90 E W Jomes, H Rotherham
1890 - 91 H Bremner, S Matthews
1891 - 92 *F Mitchell, ^B C O'Dowda
1892 - 93 H H Perry, *E G H North
1893 - 94 R P Wood, L F Duckworth
1894 - 95 B F O'Dowda, H N Waugh
1895 - 96 G S Godfree, T O Ruthven
1896 - 97 *B C Hartley
1897 - 98 D J Rowe, P G A Broadbent
1898 - 99 E V Jenkins, G C Morphett
1899 - 00 C P Rooke, W A Newcombe
1900 - 01 A Ffoulkes, W G Hooper
1901 - 02 A S Anderson, H C Brow, A E Y Tretsall
1902 - 03 H T Oliver, C C Roff, W A B Wray
1903 - 04 T Smith, H E Ward
1904 - 05 H G Lyell, *J G G Birkett
1905 - 06 L A Godfree, E W Izard, F W King

1906 - 07 J Nathan, J C Medhurst
1907 - 08 H S Moore, W J Wormald
1908 - 09 F Sage
1909 - 10 H Sloman, W M Wormald
1910 - 11 W K Jameson, E M Taylor
1912 - 13 P W Johnson
1919 - 20 C Fawsett, W A Gibbs
1920 - 21 J G S Lee, E H Pope, H F Taylor
1921 - 22 A Gibson, G W H Bentley
1922 - 23 T S Gracie, R L Thompson
1923 - 24 J H Densham, L Fairburne, B Richards,
A C N Williams
1924 - 25 C D Frenshaw, C A Osborne
1925 - 26 R Lee, A G W Penny, F S Reid
1926 - 27 A J Taylor, A Robinson, N MacFarlane
1927 - 28 J F Hampton, V S Hedges, W L Tiffin
1928 - 29 E G Shrubbs, R R Turner, C Lawrence
1929 - 30 N F Edwards, E I Hunter, D A R Mackay
1930 - 31 C H Baxter, B J Hogg, W H Stapley
1931 - 32 E O Plunkett, J Plunkett, K H Tilbury
1932 - 33 A N Bardolph, W P Shewell
1933 - 34 F Hyam, C A Styer, AG Mitchell
1934 - 35 J E Atkins, W W Sayers
1935 - 36 J W Cook, D Johnson, H W Sayers
1936 - 37 R J Allen
1937 - 38 T E H Gwyer, A Wilson
1938 - 39 J C Lord, R J McNair
1946 - 47 R H Braybon, R C Malby
1947 - 48 J G Hale, A Harrison, C Halamandres
1948 - 49 D Benjamin, F Thomas, P Toye
1949 - 50 G C Burt, R O Pratt, R F Weedall
1950 - 51 M Anthony, E H Barnett, D F Brown, J French
1951 - 52 E Womersley, B G Davis
1952 - 53 P Maurice, C R Wilkinson
1953 - 54 W R B Holt, P Ross, C McDonald
1954 - 55 Rev J Grogan, D Smith
1955 - 56 P Burt R Davis, L Dilley
1956 - 57 J Payne, B Swain, M Buckingham

1957 - 58 J Porter
1958 - 59 I Heath
1959 - 60 R Hewson
1960 - 61 G Ashby, D Pickering
1961 - 62 D Watkins, J Wilson
1962 - 63 P Ward-Lee, R James
1963 - 64 A Casserley, D Sherwood
1964 - 65 R Bashford, R Bodenham, D Watts
1965 - 66 A Nicholls, D Terrett
1966 - 67 P Harbidge
1967 - 68 D T C Malby
1968 - 69 I Barnard, K Nind, A Walker
1969 - 70 R Greenaway
1970 - 71 M Brownhill, G Nicholas
1971 - 72 J Jennings, T McGuinness
1972 - 73 G Rhodes
1973 - 74 C Kerrin, D Tattum
1974 - 75 G Hindle, M McNeill
1975 - 76 R Lowrie
1976 - 77 K Hopkins, D Redman
1977 - 78 I Robinson, I Barratt, S Fry
1978 - 79 J Phillips, N Tetlow, R Trafford
1979 - 80 C Day, A Holmes
1980 - 81 N Allen, A McCarthy
1981 - 82 M Holt, B McMenamin
1982 - 83 J Pope
1983 - 84 G Twynam, R Thoms
1984 - 85 A Smith
1985 - 86 R Avery
1986 - 87 P Noble
1987 - 88 M Avery
1988 - 89 D Craze, S Dunnill
1990 - 91 J Smith
1991 - 92 B Spring, M Watts
1992 - 93 M Humphries, P Morley, N Thomas
1993 - 94 K Considine, G Heath
1994 - 95 M Sutton, C Henderson
1995 - 96 C Cleary, R Parry

1996 - 97 G Russell, J Burt
1997 - 98 S Fitzpatrick
1998 - 99 M Gibb, M Jenkins, S Peters
1999 - 00 S Trotter
2000 - 01 G Henderson, J Jeffries
2001 - 02 T Ellis
2002 - 03 J Hutchings, G Jones
2003 - 04 A Pinnock
2005 - 06 J Lewis
2006 - 07 L Jenkins, T Schofield
2007 - 08
2008 - 09
2009 - 10
2010 - 11
2011 - 12
2012 - 13
2013 - 14
2014 - 15
2015 - 16
2016 - 17 Joel Forward
2017 - 18

INTERNATIONAL HONOURS

England
(Senior)

James Alfred Body........................ 1872
Richard Thomas Budworth......... 1890 -1891
Eustace Herbert Guest North...... 1891
Cyril Wells 1893
Frank Mitchell............................... 1895
Bernard Charles Hartley............. 1901
John Guy Giberne Birkett............ 1906
Ernest Dye Galbraith Hammett .. 1920-1922
W. Falcon
Mike Brownhill (5xTrialist) deserves a mention

(Junior)

Brian Davis... England U19
Jon Searle
Dino Lam Cona
Ollie Davis Smith
Marcus Smith
Ollie Richards
James Hadfield
Jack Thomas
Sam Morley

Ireland

(Senior)

A C McDonnell, 1889
Dr E F Frazer, 1891
H.J.M Sayers 1937
Jonathan Moffat 1961
Gary Halpin, 1990
(Junior)
Frank Taggart
Sam Arnold

Scotland

(Senior)

Charles McDonald...........1947
Alec Richard Valentine.....1953
(Junior)
Harry Leonard
Jon Searle

New Zealand

(Senior)

Bernard O'Dowda.............1901
Paul William Henderson 1989-95
South Africa
Clifford Atherton Riordan.........1910

Philippines
(Senior)
Matt Bellinie 2015-
Ash Heward

Cyprus
(Senior)
Stavros Kostas Economou 2013 -

Slovakia
(Senior)
Martin Majovsky 2015

Bahrain
(Senior)
Malcolm Holt

During my research, I came across this article by Mr P Shortell, written in 2010, which I found extremely interesting, and, with his kind permission has allowed me to included the article.

"NEVER LET THE TRUTH SPOIL A GOOD STORY"
Did William Webb Ellis Invent Rugby?

"There is little evidence to support the popular belief that William Webb Ellis created a new form of football. The point is that the rules of the game as it was played at the school at that time were made by the boys themselves and those rules were constantly revised. If you look at the notes of the Bigside Levees - notes made by the boys themselves - you will see that the rules were discussed almost every time the boys went out to play and that adjustments were frequently made."

Malcolm Lee, master in charge of Rugby football in 1978, talking to John Reason and Carwyn James in "The World of Rugby" ."There are so many conflicting reports of how the game of rugby came into being that the only thing that is for certain is that Rugby

School's William Webb Ellis did not spontaneously invent the game when he picked up the ball and ran with it, 'Showing a fine disregard for the rules of football as played in his time', the time in question being 1823. Not only did a schoolboy contemporary of Webb Ellis refute the notion a few years later, but there is also the fact that rugby was by no means the first code to involve running and handling. In fact, before Webb Ellis did his party trick in 1823, all codes of football involved running and handling."

The ultimate Encyclopaedia of Rugby, edited by Richard Bat

Introducing
Matthew Holbeche Bloxam
1805-1888

Matthew Bloxam was, an enthusiast that nobody but his friends had ever heard of - with the one exception that he is the sole source of the William Webb Ellis myth. We therefore need to know something about who he was, and how he came to know about WWE.

He was himself a pupil at Rugby School , where his father was a master. Born in 1805, he entered the school in 1813 and left in 1820. He qualified as a solicitor and lived the rest of his life in the town. He acquired a reputation as a diligent antiquarian, and wrote a very successful work on Gothic architecture.

He remained a lifelong enthusiast for all things Rugbeian, and maintained close links with the school. In his day there was no school magazine, but when the "Meteor " was started, he contributed articles reminiscing about the old days, his days.

What do we know about W.W. Ellis?

James Ellis was in the Dragoon Guards, and married Miss Ann Webb in Exeter in 1804. He was killed in the battle of Albuera in 1812 leaving his widow with two small sons. Thomas was 8, and William, who was born on 24 November 1806 in Salford, Lancashire, was then aged 6. Mrs Ellis decided to move to Rugby because she hoped to get the children a good education at the school at no cost as local foundationers.

William entered the school in 1816 and was a good scholar as well as a good cricketer. In 1825 he won the Second Exhibition of his year to Oxford , where he represented his university at cricket against Cambridge . He entered Holy Orders, first as minister of St George's, Albemarle Street, London, and then as Rector of St Clement Danes in the Strand. The only known picture of him appeared in the Illustrated London Post at this time, as a consequence of a stirring sermon he gave concerning the Crimean War. In 1855 he became rector of Laver Magdalen in Essex .

He died in the South of France on 24 January 1872, probably quite unaware of his supposed connection to the RFU that had been founded the year before. His grave at Menton was rediscovered by Ross McWhirter in 1959 and has since been renovated.

None of the rather small amount of further information that has been gathered about his life sheds any light at all on the claim that his action in running with the ball changed the nature of Rugby football.

How the story arose

The first article by Bloxam in the "Meteor" simply gave his reminiscences on the game of rugby football as played in his day. To quote Jennifer Macrory's excellent book, "Running with the ball", "Bloxam had originally responded that running with the ball had been introduced sometime after Dr Arnold became Headmaster in 1828. However he had made further enquiries and then he '... ascertained that this change originated with a Town boy or foundationer of the name of Ellis, William Webb Ellis. [...] It must, I think, have been in the second half-year of 1823 that this change from the former system, in which the football was not allowed to be taken up and run with, commenced.' " This was written in October 1876.

A more detailed version of this, again by Bloxam, appeared in the 12 December 1880 edition of the *"Meteor"*

"In the latter half of 1823, some fifty-seven years ago, originated though without premeditation, that change in one of the rules, which more than any other has since distinguished the Rugby School game from the Association Rules.

"A boy of the name Ellis - William Webb Ellis - a town boy and a foundationer, ... whilst playing Bigside at football in that half-year, caught the ball in his arms. This being so, according to the then rules, he ought to have retired back as far as he pleased, without parting with the ball, for the combatants on the opposite side could only advance to the spot where he had caught the ball, and were unable to rush forward till he had either punted it or had placed it for some one else to kick, for it was by means of these placed kicks that most of the goals were in those days kicked, but the moment the ball touched the ground the opposite side might rush on. Ellis, for the first time, disregarded this rule, and on catching the ball, instead of retiring backwards, rushed forwards with the ball in his hands towards the opposite goal, with what result as to the game I know not, neither do I know how this infringement of a well-known rule was followed up, or when it became, as it is now, a standing rule."

It is perhaps unsurprising that after 57 years the actual details were a little hazy. Bloxam himself writes:

"After the games of the day were concluded, however vigorously they may have been contended, all further remembrance of the game was consigned to the limbo of oblivion, our tasks to be learned that night were sufficiently onerous to allow little leisure for discussion, and there was no Meteor in which the incidents of each game could be recorded."

It is sheer chance that this snippet of memory has survived, shorn of all context. It is disappointing that Bloxam did not say whose memory he was relying on - clearly it was not his own. One strong possibility is that he had been talking to his brother John, who had been an exact contemporary of WWE at school. If so, it is noteworthy that the subject had apparently never arisen before.

These articles, written 53 and 57 years after the event and based on someone else's memories, are the sole source for the WWE story.

The original game

History abounds in references to ball games, such as harpastum, camp-ball, or hurling to goals, which had features now recognised as belonging to soccer or to rugby. Most games combined handling and kicking, and in some, such as the game at Scone , kicking was actually forbidden. In general, we should not be asking when carrying the ball was first allowed, but when it was first banned.

However the boys at Rugby School in 1820 would not have been aware of any historical precedents for their game, so we should look a little closer at the version they were playing. Hcrc wc can safely start with Matthew Bloxam's own memories:

"When all had assembled in the Close, two of the best players in the school commenced choosing in, one for each side. [...] After choosing in about a score on each side, a somewhat rude division was made of the remaining fags, half of whom were sent to keep goal on the one side, the other half to the opposite goal for the same purpose. Any fag, though not chosen in, might follow up on that side to the goal of which he was attached. Some of these were ready enough to mingle in the fray; others judiciously kept half-back, watching their opportunity for a casual kick, which was not unfrequently awarded them. Few and simple were the rules of the game; touch on the sides of the ground was marked out and no one was allowed to run with the ball in his grasp towards the opposite goal. It was football and not handball, plenty of hacking but little struggling. As to costume, there were neither flannels or caps, the players simply doffed their hats, and coats, or jackets, which were heaped together on either side near the goals till the game was over."

In those early days the game was controlled entirely by the boys themselves, and it was governed by custom rather than written rules. As the Rev. Thomas Harris (of whom more later) wrote of the late 1820s: *"Our Laws in those days were unwritten and traditionary, so that I can give no authority beyond custom."*

There are some exercise books extant that record discussions of Bigside Levees, at which such matters were argued, but the first known written rules date from 1845. Until then the game was handed down from one generation to the next, and, like the children's games you can observe in primary schools today, each generation felt free to modify the rules as they thought fit, careless of what previous generations had decided or what future generations might think.

Most of the other descriptions of the early game come from after the time of WWE, and will be considered later. One thing at least is crystal clear: running with the ball was not permitted in 1820, whatever the historical precedents elsewhere.

"The Distinctive Feature"?

Much is made of the claim that running with the ball is THE distinctive feature of rugby as distinct from soccer, but in 1820, when there were no inter-school games, each school developed its own version of football, all with their own distinctive features. Most such games have been dropped in favour of modern standardised sports (though the Eton Wall Game still survives, for example).

We must also remember that soccer and rugby were not distinct games at that time. Everybody considered that they were playing "football" and merely accepted that there were different versions. Even as late as 1871, (the FA was founded in 1863) when the first rugby international took place, it was seen as being the third match in a series between England and Scotland - the first two of which happened to be played under Association rules.

And, of course, even within each school the game could change from one generation of players to the next. However each school did tend to have a distinctive basic style of its own as the following synopsis (for about 1850) shows.

		handling			tackling		
|	scrum	stop	catch	carry	collar	hack	goal
Eton	-	8	-	-	-	8	between posts
Cambridge	-	8	-	-	-	-	between posts
Shrewsbury	-	8	-	-	-	8	between posts
Harrow	-	8	8	-	-	-	between posts
Charterhouse	-	8	8	-	-	-	under bar
Winchester	8	8	8	8	-	-	over line
Rugby	8	8	8	8	8	8	over bar

As can be seen, all games allowed the use of hands, if only to stop the ball. What would a contemporary of Bloxam's, transferring perhaps from another school, have regarded as distinctive about the Rugby game?

Before the game even started, he would have noticed the unique H-shaped goal posts, and would have learned that..... "it won't do just to kick the ball through these posts, it must go over the cross bar; any height'll do, so long as it's between the posts", as East described it to Tom Brown, eponymous hero of Thomas Hughes' well-known book.

When the game started, he would have seen scrummages and mauls, involving much pushing and heaving, kicking and hacking, the ball being somewhere in the middle.

If the ball rolled out of such a press of boys, it was kicked, and if it was caught in the air, the catcher could "make his mark". He would then retire a little way, and the opposition could come up to that mark, but not charge him until he started to kick. A player with the ball could be obstructed in some way, though what we would now call tackling was apparently not permitted.

If the mark were near enough to goal, he would attempt a place-kick or drop-kick. For the former, the player would hold the ball just above the ground for another to kick, and the opposition could only charge when the ball was actually touched to the ground - at the last possible second. For the latter, the player would let the ball drop so that it bounced on the ground before he kicked it. A goal could also be scored in what the visitor might regard as a more conventional way - by kicking it off the ground and over the bar. However this was relatively unusual.

If a player catching the ball had run forward with it instead of retiring, it might have been too subtle a breach of the rules for a new-comer, though obvious enough to an experienced Rugbeian. The rules were complex, and as the estimable East tells us *"you'll be a month learning them"*.

For us, soccer is the kicking code, and rugby the handling code; and this was probably true in the 1890s when the famous plaque was researched and written. It is not unreasonable for us to ask how this came about, but we should be wary of assuming that any such distinction was particularly noteworthy at the time of William Webb Ellis.

The Original Investigation

In 1895, the Old Rugbeian Society set up a sub-committee to investigate the origin of Rugby football. They published a report in 1897 which contained in full the most significant letters they received, but did not give details of the questions that were asked. It is however fairly clear that they specifically quoted Bloxam about William Webb Ellis: Gibbs refers to an unspecified quote from Bloxam, and Hughes writes:

"The 'Webb Ellis tradition' had not survived to my day."

The following table summarises the various points made to the sub-committee, and for convenience, I have also included Ellis and Bloxam in their chronological positions. Items in brackets represent an inference rather than a direct statement.

Name	arrived*	left	WWE	pick-up	carry	passing	mark	hacking	collaring	try
Matthew Holbeche Bloxam	1813	1820								
William Webb Ellis	1816	1825								
Thomas Harris (& John)	1819	1828	yes	no	no		yes		no	
Henry Homer	1828	?			probably					
H G Allen	<1830	1833			unclear	(no)				
John R Lyon (& Edward)	1830	1834		yes	yes			yes	yes	yes
Francis Hugh Dean	1830	1839			probably		yes			
George Charles Benn	1830	1840		no	yes	no				
H R Nevill	1830	1840		no	yes					
John Coke Fowler	1830	?			yes	(no)				
Peregrine Birch	1831	?		no	yes					
Samuel	1831	?			yes			yes		

Garratt									
Henry H Gibbs	1832	1836 (no)		yes			yes		
Sir Alexander Arbuthnot	1832	<<1850		yes					
Thomas Hughes	1834	1842	no	see below	no			(yes)	yes
F Lushington	?	1839		probably			yes		
J W Cunningham	?	?		yes					

Although correspondents are listed by their year of entering Rugby School , it would have been better to list them by their leaving year, if that were available, since in general, only the senior boys played Bigside. That implies that the information given refers to their final three years or so.

It is notable that most of the writers were somewhat vague about the rules in their time. In part this was due to their age, and the time that had elapsed since their days at Rugby ; moreover subsequent developments may have confused the issue. However the lack of formality over rules in those early days was undoubtedly a significant factor.

The oldest of all, the Reverend Thomas Harris, was surprisingly confident:-

"Picking up and running with the ball in hand was distinctly forbidden. If a player caught the ball on a rebound from the ground, or from a stroke of the hand, he was allowed to take a few steps so as to give effect to a 'Drop-kick', but no more; subject of course to interruption from adverse players."

He was also the only one to have known WWE:-

"I remember Mr William Webb Ellis perfectly. He was an admirable cricketer, but was generally regarded as inclined to take unfair advantages at Football. I should not quote him in any way as an authority."

(Perhaps he was under the impression that WWE himself was claiming to have invented carrying the ball.)

In a second letter he says:-

"As to Mr W Webb Ellis and his practices, you must observe that I was several years his junior, and had not either reasons or opportunities for closely observing his manner of play."

Harris also comments that his brother, John, who left in 1832, agrees with what he has written.

At the other end of the scale, Hughes made an interesting point which illustrates that rules were not as hard and fast as we see them today:-

"In my first year, 1834, running with the ball to get a try by touching down within goal was not absolutely forbidden, but a jury of Rugby boys of that day would almost certainly have found a verdict of 'justifiable homicide' if a boy had been killed in running in."

The famous plaque that the Society put up in 1900 is perhaps best regarded as an early example of spin-doctoring. The actual report is much more circumspect in the conclusions it drew:-

"It may, we think, be fairly considered to be proved from the foregoing statements, that in 1820 the form of football in vogue at Rugby was something approximating more closely to Association than to what is known as Rugby football to-day, that at some date between 1820 and 1830 the innovation was introduced of running with the ball, that this was in all probability done in the latter half of 1823 by Mr W Webb Ellis, who is credited by Mr Bloxam with the invention and whose 'unfair practices' were (according to Mr Harris) the subject of general remark at the time. To this we would add that the innovation was regarded as of doubtful legality for some time, and only gradually became accepted as part of the game, but obtained a customary status between 1830 and 1840, and was duly legalized first by Bigside Levee in 1841-42 (as stated by Judge Hughes) and finally by the rules of 1846."

The last part of this, regarding the 1830s, seems unexceptionable. It is however somewhat curious that, despite quoting Mr Harris on WWE's practices, they ignore his clear statement that in his day, running with the ball was forbidden - which means that the practice had not been accepted in 1828. William Webb Ellis left the school in 1825.

Conclusions

The historical evidence that William Webb Ellis

"With a fine disregard for the rules of football as played in his time, first took the ball in his arms and ran with it thus originating the distinctive feature of the Rugby game AD1823"

is unsatisfactory, since the story is anonymous and incomplete. The historical evidence that 3 years after he had left the school, the practice was *"distinctly forbidden"* is pretty strong, being a firm personal recollection from two individuals with first-hand experience.

The necessary connection between what William Webb Ellis might have done and the development of the carrying game, is not just missing, but apparently cannot exist. He therefore cannot be presented as the father of the modern game.

P Shortell